man, but for the lawless and disobedient, for the ungodly and for sinners, for unholy and profane, for murderers of fathers and murderers of mothers, for manslayers,' the reverend was preaching.

I felt the air stir behind me as I stared at a sluggish, depressed sea. Then Sparkes was next to me, our arms barely touching. His gaze was straight ahead, his jaw strong and resolute as he stood so straight in his dark suit. He turned to me and offered eyes of great sympathy. I nodded slightly.

'Our friend wanted peace and goodness.' Reverend Lloyd had turned to another book. 'He wanted the harmony the victims he championed never had. He wanted to be free of outrage and sorrow, unfettered by anger and his dreamless nights of dread.'

I heard the blades in the distance, the thudding that would forever be the noise of my niece. I looked up, and the sun barely shone behind clouds that danced the dance of veils, sliding endlessly, never fully exposing what we longed to see. Blue shown through, fragmented and brilliant like stained glass over the horizon to the west of us, and the dune at our backs was lit up as the troops of bad weather began to mutiny. The sound of the helicopter got louder, and I looked back over palms and pines, spotting it with nose slightly down as it flew lower.

'I will therefore ask that people pray everywhere, lifting up holy hands, without wrath and doubting,' the reverend went on.

Benton's ashes were in the small brass urn I held in my hands.

'Let us pray.'

Lucy began her glide slope over trees, the chop-chop hard air against the ear. Sparkes leaned close to speak to me, and I could not hear, but the closeness of his face was kind.

Reverend Lloyd continued to pray, but all of us were no longer capable of or interested in a petition to the Almighty. Lucy held the JetRanger in a low hover beyond the shore, and spray flew up from her wind on the water.

I could see her eyes fixed on me through the chin bubble, and I gathered my splintered spirit into a core. I walked forward into her storm of turbulent air as the reverend held on to his barely present hair. I waded out into the water.

'God bless you, Benton. Rest your soul. I miss you, Benton,' I said words no one else could hear.

I opened the urn and looked up at my niece who was there to create the energy he had wanted when it was his time to move on. I nodded at Lucy and she gave me a thumbs-up that rent my heart and let loose more tears. Ashes were like silk, and I felt his bits of chalky bone as I dug in and held him in my hand. I flung him into the wind. I gave him back to the higher order he would have made, had it been possible.

WHEN THE GLOVES CAME OFF

WHEN THE GLOVES CAME OFF

THE POWERFUL AUTOBIOGRAPHY OF BRITAIN'S PLAYBOY BOXER

BILLY WALKER

With Robin McGibbon

**ROBSON
BOOKS**

First published in the United Kingdom in 2007 by
Robson Books
10 Southcombe Street
London
W14 0RA

An imprint of Anova Books Company Ltd

ISBN 10: 1 86105 970 1
ISBN 13: 9781861059703

A CIP catalogue record for this book is available from the British Library.

10 9 8 7 6 5 4 3 2 1

Typeset by SX Composing DTP, Rayleigh, Essex
Printed by Creative Print and Design, Wales

This book can be ordered direct from the publisher.
Contact the marketing department, but try your bookshop first.

www.anovabooks.com

CONTENTS

I dedicate this book to my dear friends Tommy and Ann McCarthy. They have been with me through the good and bad times, never wavering in their loyalty, affection and loving support – even when sometimes, I deserved less.

With love.

ACKNOWLEDGEMENTS

Trying to remember what happened to me over six decades was not easy and I'm indebted to many people who went out of their way to help, jogging my memory on events I barely remembered and filling in the gaps on those I'd forgotten altogether.

Firstly, I must offer huge thanks to Harry Doherty, President of the Kent ex-Boxers' Association, not only for providing crucially-important details of my amateur and professional careers, but also for trawling hundreds of personal copies of Boxing News, over many months, for stories he felt I might want to mention. Where we would have been without him, I don't know. Many thanks, too, to Harry's daughter, Petra, for all that priceless photo-copying: it must have taken hours! I'm also grateful to boxing historian Harold Alderman for those laborious long-hand notes on all my fights, and fight fan Mike Hinton for his meticulous home-made book of Boxing News reports on all my pro fights.

Sincere thanks to Gary Thompson, Senior Associate Editor of the *News of the World*, for authorising Library assistants Steve, Lee, Tony and Lucy to provide invaluable newspaper clippings, covering forty years. And to my collaborator's dear friend, Mike Harris, for spending so many uncomplaining weeks, hunting for information in old newspapers at the British Library.

Others who played lesser, but, nevertheless, important roles, and who deserve thanks, are: Simon Block, secretary of the British Boxing Board of Control, Nigel Lutt (Bedfordshire Country Records Office), Liz O'Reilly (*Bedfordshire on Sunday* newspaper), Paul Fairclough (*Time Out*), Jeff Walden (BBC Written Archives Centre), Neville de Souza (National Statistics), Tom Crone, News International legal adviser, John Soloman, Chris Kempson, Ralph Oates, Jim Dawson, Terry Murphy – and DJ David Hamilton for plugging my book on radio. And to my pals, Tommy McCarthy, Melvyn Barnett, Kenny Bailey and Jean Keadell for their own memories, which, at times, were far clearer than mine!

Special thanks must go to two good pals – Colin Hart, doyen of British boxing writers, for contacting me about my autobiography in the first place, and the late, much-missed, Ron Olver, of *Boxing News*, who made my task much easier by telling readers about the book long before it was under way.

Sue McGibbon deserves my gratitude, for the tremendous effort transcribing my taped interviews and typing various versions of the manuscript over many months, and for her determination to ensure that the finished product was the best I could do.

To the people at Robson Books I offer heartfelt thanks. Jeremy Robson, publisher, for his belief in the book; his reassurance and guidance were invaluable. My editor's unfailing good humour, professionalism and sheer hard work have helped this book to come to fruition.

My biggest thanks, however, must go to my wife, Susan, for her unwavering support over several difficult months: she has been there every step of the way, giving me the benefit of her patience, tolerance and unfailing loyalty and love. Without her input, this book would never have been completed.

Billy Walker

PROLOGUE

I never wanted to fight.

Not after I saw George's face, and the pain and disappointment in his eyes. I was barely fourteen, but George was my big brother, my hero, and seeing him so bashed up broke my heart. If that's what boxing did to you, they could stuff it. I didn't want to know.

But here I am, just eight years on, the best amateur heavyweight in the country, in the ring at Wembley's famous arena. Fighting for Great Britain against the United States. It's Thursday night, second of November, 1961. And it's a night that might – if I get lucky – make my dreams come true. Make me a name and get me big money to turn professional. That's what I'm in the fight game for. To be paid for punching. I'm not one of those kids who put the gloves on at seven or eight years old and dream of winning cups or medals, or other soppy prizes they give to amateurs. I didn't have a competitive fight until I was nearly nineteen. After that – after George told me I had what it takes – fighting had been only a means to an end. And that end was money. I want lots of it. Enough to do what I want – and that's, have fun. I don't want stress or problems, never have. I don't want to be told by anyone what to do; never liked that, either. Do what I like, when I like. And be answerable to no one. That's the life money can buy. And that's why, after tonight, I'm only interested in fighting if I get paid.

I could have turned pro last April. I'd won the national ABA (Amateur Boxing Association) title and the big promoters wanted to sign me up. Or I could stay amateur and try to win a gold medal at the Commonwealth Games in 1962. Everything was open to me. The prestige of winning a medal was all very well, but you can't buy the finer things in life with a medal, can you? So, I'd been all for turning pro right then. George wanted that for me, too. But then he heard the Americans were coming to town for a big contest – their top amateurs against ours – and he felt it best to hold off. If I could beat the American champion, I'd get a better deal, he said; I'd be bargaining from strength. Better to wait.

So, I *had* waited. Of course, I had. I always listened to George. He's the only one I've ever taken any notice of. He's my brother, but he's my mentor, too. What he said went, always had, ever since we were kids in Ilford. I loved him, worshipped him, would walk through fire, swim through a river crawling with crocodiles, if he told me it would be all right. He's the reason I'm in this ring tonight. Yeah, it's my fists that do the punching, but it's George's know-how, his experience, that made me good. Good enough to win that ABA title. I wouldn't have done it without him. He's the one who picked me up when I lost badly and cried and wanted to chuck it in. He's the one who convinced me to leave the fish market and give up the late nights and dedicate myself. He's the one who said I was good enough, and strong and brave enough, to earn good money. And he's the one who's in my corner now, as I wait for the bell for the first round.

I want to win tonight for myself. But I want to win for George, too. And my dad and oldest brother, John, who're at ringside. And all the mates I know from Ilford Palais. But, really, who am I trying to kid? The guy I'm fighting, the hulking great black guy in the other corner, is three inches taller and four stone heavier. And the people who know about the amateur fight game all say I haven't got a chance. George didn't say it, but I don't think he gives me much of a chance, either. When I'd asked him what I should do, he'd shaken his head. 'There's no way you can box this guy, Bill,' he said. 'Just go out there and throw lots of leather. You never know, you might catch him.'

Mmm. Or he might catch me, I thought.

I'm not scared. My bottle's never gone before and it isn't going to now. But I *am* apprehensive. This is the biggest, heaviest, bloke I've faced in all my thirty-four fights. By far, the most experienced. And, if I believed what people said, the most gifted. If I was going to cop it, I was probably going to cop it big. And not just in front of the Wembley crowd, either. The contest was being televised live by the BBC, so my humiliation, if that's what it was going to be, would be witnessed by millions throughout the country, not just a few thousand in the Empire Pool.

So. What am I going to do? Only what I've always done. Try my best. No one minds a loser, as long as he tries. And I've always tried, always given value for money. That's what made me popular on the amateur circuit. People knew they'd see fireworks when I was on the bill. Right from that first novice fight in 1958 when my opponent was counted out before they'd had time to switch the house lights off. A few more quick knockouts and I was the First-Round KO King, the new kid on the block who had a big punch and didn't hang about throwing it. I wasn't skilful. Not stylish. But I was powerful and brave, and smashed and crashed my way to the ABA title in just three years. And I came to think I was invincible.

Not tonight, though. Not unless I get lucky. Anyway, it won't matter that much if I lose. I'll still go pro. And George will be my manager. I won't get the big bucks, but I'll get fights that'll make money, George will make sure of that. Who knows, I might make enough to have a big house. I'm not thinking of that now, though. I'm only twenty-two and have a lot of living to do. But that's what I want when I settle down, when I've met the girl of my dreams, like my dad and John and George. And not just a house of my own, either. A long and happy marriage, too. For life. Just like them.

They're all out of the ring now. It's nearly time. But I'm not looking at Goliath. I'm just thinking of what George told me. Throw lots of leather. Yeah, I'll do that, all right. Better watch out for those huge hands, though. Walk into one early on and it could be Goodnight. But I've got big hands, too. What if I could land one before the big fella got going. What if I get lucky and plonk one right on the money. What then?

Yeah, what then?

Maybe it could be my night. With those millions watching on television, maybe I could become a celebrity – a household name overnight.

THE GUY WHO BEAT THE BIG YANK.

There's the bell.

Let's get on with it.

1

As far back as I can remember, George was more than just a brother to me. He was like a father: older, wiser, always telling me what to do, always looking out for me. I had another brother, John, who was four years older than George, but he went away to war when I was barely five and I never got the chance to get close to him. It was George I looked up to, who had the biggest influence on me as a kid. He was everything a little boy could want in a big brother. I adored him and did everything to please him. If he'd told me to run through fire, I would have.

We were all born in Duckett Street, in Stepney, but in 1941, when I was two, Hitler started bombing the East End and an aunt, Lizzie Quinlan, suggested the family moved up to live with her and her family, in Bedford, about fifty miles north of London. Their house, in Worcester Road, in the nearby village of Shortstown, proved too small for all of us and, apparently, Lizzie arranged for us to stay in another one, round the corner, in Winchester Road. Less than a year later, however, Lizzie's husband Joe, who was an RAF warrant officer, was transferred to Blackpool and she and their two children, Betty and Dennis, went with him, making it possible for us to move into their home. It was only a three-bedroomed terraced house, but somehow we all crammed in – mum, George, our two grandmothers and grandfathers, and, for some reason never explained to me, a boy named Kelly who was another evacuee.

My grandparents could hardly have been more different. On my dad's side, Granny Walker was a warm-hearted, generous lady, who got on with most people. But Granny Page was a real hard cow, very tight with money, and difficult to warm to. She was always telling me off and I couldn't stand her. She was a miserable woman, who, later in life, I never enjoyed visiting. Instead of 'Hello, son, how lovely to see you,' it was always, 'About bloody time, you never come to see me.' It was a shame, really, because I ended up thinking: 'Why did I bother?'

Going to see Granny Walker, on the other hand, was a joy. And not because of her generosity, either. Even if I hadn't seen her for months, she'd open the door with a smile and immediately insist on making me something to eat. She'd always want to give me money, too, even though I kept saying I was all right and didn't need any. She was a lovely, hugely likeable old girl, Granny Walker. I'm bound to say that I get my personality from her easy-going, generous side of the family, but it's true; as much as it's true that George gets his mean streak from the Pages'. He's hard as nails and as tough as old boots, as anyone who knows him will tell you.

I remember more about Grandad Walker than Grandad Page. He'd been a brewery drayman and, not surprisingly, liked a drink. He was a drunk, no doubt about it, and suffered from DT's. He was a skinny bloke, who didn't speak much, just sat in an armchair all day and most of the night, drinking beer. At three or four years old, I wasn't aware of what drink did to people, but I do know I never saw him able to get out of that chair without someone helping him. He hardly ever said a word to me, just looked at me. I would blow raspberries at him and dash out of the door. Too drunk to do anything else, he would just clap his hands at me. I suppose if it wasn't so tragic, it would be funny. Grandad Walker drank himself to death while we were in Bedford. He was only in his sixties, but looked ancient.

Grandad Page was a bit of a drinker, too, but preferred to go to the pub, The Bull, a four- or five-minute walk from the house. He and Grandma Page did not get on and had split up before war broke out, but when things got lively in the East End he'd got scared and followed her to Bedford. Where mum put him I don't know; probably on a bunk bed in the lounge, because Grandma Page slept on a small bed in the room where I slept with mum.

When I was four and had to go to school for the first time, I cried like a baby, not wanting to go. Mum, who worked as a typist at the

RAF camp in nearby Cardington, could not afford time off to take me, so she walked me to the shops at the top of the road and waited for an older child to come along.

'Are you going to school?' she asked. When the boy said he was, mum told him to take me as well, then crossed the road to catch a bus to work, which was in the opposite direction. I sobbed my heart out, watching her go, but the other boy started talking to me to make me feel better and, by the time we reached the school and I saw lots of boys my own age, I was okay. I can't remember being picked up in the afternoon, but it wasn't long before I was walking to and from that school, with my new-found friends. It must have been a mile, past The Bull, across a field, then over a little stream, then along a footpath to the school, but we never felt in any danger. At four years old, after just a couple of years away from London, I was a country boy, and revelling in it.

I knew there was a war on because everyone in the house talked about it, and mum told me that the men we saw walking in Bedford town centre with yellow rings on the back of their jackets were Italian prisoners. But I saw no evidence of conflict: no fighter pilots firing at each other and certainly no bombs. My only clear memory of that time is being woken in the dead of night and seeing Granny Page buttoning up her stays and mum calling to her to hurry up, as she carried me downstairs and out to the air-raid shelter in the road.

I didn't see much of John: he was out most of the time with a girl he'd met, and then, in June 1944, he was called up, to serve with the Irish Guards. But George was always around and, with mum at work, he looked after me when we came home from school. Being that much older, he didn't play with me very often, but he was always looking out for me and I do remember lots of fun times, particularly splashing about in a pond by the stream. For me, those wartime years were, well . . . happy days. Blissfully happy days when the sun always seemed to be shining and I played happily with my mates, without a care in the world.

And then, two months after my sixth birthday, the war ended.

And everything in my safe and contented little world crumbled.

✳ ✳ ✳

It started when mum answered a ring on the front door bell. A stranger was standing there in air force uniform, someone I didn't recognise.

Mum kissed him, then told me to kiss him, too. 'This is your daddy,' she said. 'He's come home to us because he doesn't have to fight those horrible Germans any more.'

I was confused. My daddy? I didn't think I had a daddy. I'd heard mum and my brothers talking about him with my grandparents, and I'd seen a photograph of him standing next to me in his uniform. But, suddenly, there was this bloke there, and I didn't know what to make of it.

At bedtime, I was even more confused when mum told me I would not be sleeping in her bed; I had to sleep with George in his room. She tried to explain that little boys should not sleep with their mum and dad, but I'd been sleeping in her bed for as long as I could remember, and I couldn't understand why I couldn't any more. I cried and cried and begged to go in her bed but, of course, she didn't want me there. I lay sobbing in the dark and when George came to bed I went on and on to him about why mum wouldn't let me sleep with her.

'Don't be silly,' he said, giving me a gentle clump on the head. 'Go to sleep.'

But I was too upset to, and the moment I knew George was asleep, I got up quietly and crept out into mum's room. She heard me and whispered: 'Come on', and I quickly climbed in and cuddled up to her. Dad wasn't very impressed, particularly when it happened the next night. And the next. Snuggling in close to mum, I'd hear him cursing in the darkness. 'That bloody boy's in here again.' But I didn't care: he meant nothing to me and I was where I wanted to be. It was like being back in the womb, I suppose.

Out of all those happy, happy days, the fear I felt at sleeping on my own is the one experience I remember most vividly, because it made me terrified of the dark – a fear I could not shake off, no matter how hard I tried. It was a fear that got even worse the following year when we left Bedford and moved back to London – to a house with a haunted kitchen, where a married woman had an affair with a young lodger that ended in them both being hanged for the murder of the woman's husband.

✳✳✳

The house was in Kensington Gardens, a quiet street in a well-kept, suburban area of Ilford, on the Essex border. Mum and dad took out a mortgage to buy it because our first home had been obliterated. Number 41, it was – a lovely, double-fronted semi-detached property, with three bedrooms and gardens, back and front. And no sooner had mum and dad and George and me moved in, that summer of 1946, than the neighbours could not wait to tell us the notorious history behind it.

One October night, in 1922, Percy Thompson was attacked and stabbed to death, in nearby Belgrave Road, as he returned to the house, with his wife, Edith, after a night out in London. The killer, it turned out, was their lodger, Freddy Bywaters, a handsome twenty-year-old sailor, who was having an affair with Edith, who, at 29, was four years younger than her husband. He was found guilty of the murder and hanged, three months later. Edith was, too, for supposedly conspiring with him to bump off her husband. The case made headlines, not only locally, but in the national Press, too, because of the feeling throughout the country that Edith had not put Bywaters up to the murder and did not deserve to die.

Obviously, at barely seven, I knew nothing about the rights and wrongs of something that happened before I was born, but merely listening to everyone talking about it, and knowing the words 'murder' and 'hanging' were connected to our home, was frightening. And my fear was not helped when mum told us that the kitchen, in a part of the house upstairs that she had rented to a young couple with a baby, was haunted. I believed her, because when George and I were alone in the house one day, he said he could hear noises coming from the kitchen, but when we went up to have a look, there was no one there. As I was already terrified of the dark, you can imagine what this did to me when I had to go to bed.

George and I slept in a downstairs room at the front of the house, him in a double bed, me in a single. But I always had to go to bed on my own, because George was always out, gallivanting with his mates or his latest girlfriend. I remember, laying there, scared out of my wits, unable to sleep until he was home. He knew what I'd been going through, all right, because he'd breeze in and say, 'It's okay now, I'm home – go to sleep.' And I would. I always felt safe when George was there.

No doubt I'd have grown out of my fear of the dark had an even more frightening demon not come along to fuel my imagination – the sinister voice of Valentine Dyall, who narrated tales of terror for a BBC radio horror programme, *Appointment With Fear*. He was the menacing Man in Black and his chilling tones were heard at nine o'clock on Thursday or Saturday nights throughout the forties. The Man in Black seemed to have one purpose in life: to scare the wits out of people. He certainly succeeded with me: he scared me so much that mum and dad stopped me listening to him – even though they were in the room with me. I was told to go to bed, which, of course, terrified me even more.

My fear stayed with me and I can remember, even at eight, still waiting for George to come home before feeling safe enough to close my eyes. Now eighteen, and putting it about a bit, he'd come in the room, as late as two in the morning, tell me to go to sleep, then carry blankets from his bed into the front room. I'd fall asleep, only to be woken by George putting the blankets back on his bed, then driving off in his car. I'd lay there in the dark, wondering what he was doing: it would never have occurred to me that he had brought a girl home for some games on the sofa in the front room. Knowing George, he probably slipped dad a few quid to keep his mouth shut and not hear a thing, because neither mum, nor dad, came downstairs once.

George was obsessed with money and, even at eighteen, was never short of it. He'd always been a grafter and told me that when he was a kid, of eight or nine, he did newspaper, grocery and butcher's rounds and often did a couple of hours' work before dashing off to school. He was earning so much that when he got his first job, as an apprentice carpenter, he took a drop in wages! While other kids dreamed of being able to buy a car, George actually bought one – a huge, black American Packard that looked like something out of a gangster movie.

George craved money more than anything else in life, because it gave him the power to have anything he fancied. And, in those early childhood years in Ilford, it was a drive he instilled in me. I hated being told what to do by anyone other than George; I always wanted to do what pleased me, and that meant doing nothing but have fun.

Wouldn't it be great, I'd think, if one day I had enough money to have all the fun I wanted. *When* I wanted.

✳✳✳

Dad was about 5ft 9in, slim – never more than 11 stone – and worked as a drayman, like his father; mum was tiny – only 5ft 1in – but buxom and very pretty. She worked as a typist in the City. Neither earned much. But we weren't poor. To me, poor means going hungry, and we never did, although mum did have to make food go a long way. If we had roast chicken on Sunday, we'd have more of it, cold, the next day and chicken soup on Tuesday. And mum would always have to buy the cheapest cuts of meat.

The house had a toilet, but that was part of the flat upstairs, so we had to use one in the garden. It was bog basic and, for years, didn't even have a light until George got fed up one day and put one in. The bathroom was upstairs, too, so we'd wash in a tin tub that mum kept under a long wooden board in the kitchenette, off the scullery. During the week, she used it as a work surface, but every Friday night she lifted the board off and filled the tub with boiling water from a kettle for our weekly bath. We'd take it in turns to wash – me first, then mum, then dad. By then, George was washing at Ilford Baths, on his way home from work at Billingsgate fish market in the City of London.

I feared I was going to miss George when he was called up for National Service and joined the RAF in the summer of 1947. But the sporting rivalry between the three armed forces helped give him a cushy life and, to be honest, he seemed to be at home, as much as he was away. That summer was unbelievably hot and George was sweating it out, square-bashing on the parade ground, when an announcement was made, asking for boxing volunteers. George had never used his fists, except in self-defence, but he put his hand up straight away, because all those selected would be let off square-bashing! George *did* get picked and won his first three fights by knockouts. As something of a boxing hero, he was allowed home so much before and after fights I can hardly remember missing him. And anyway, by then, my other brother was staying with us, after getting married to his childhood sweetheart, Irene, following his demob in October.

John said he was lucky to have come back from the war. As one of the last to enlist, shortly before D-Day, the war was virtually over by the time he caught up with it. He served in France, Belgium and Norway, but was involved in rounding up German prisoners of war, and never saw any action. He might well have gone on the Normandy invasion, had he not put his name down for a tank-driving course. He'd come home in January 1946, but was kept on as one of the guardsmen outside Buckingham Palace. One day, mum took me there to see him, but, for some reason, didn't explain why he couldn't talk to me. I kept on and on, chatting to him, until, in the end, John whispered out of the corner of his mouth: 'Take him away, for God's sake mum, or I'll be on a charge!'

✳✳✳

During my brief time in Bedford, I'd revelled in having fun. And nothing changed in Ilford. Far from crying at the prospect of going to school again, I couldn't wait. It was Highland Primary School, an old blue-brick building, a ten-minute walk from home, and, once there, I quickly made friends. My best mates were David Marshall, Brian Gibbs and Brian Richardson and our playgrounds, the moment we got out of school, were bomb-sites – the remains of buildings destroyed in the war. They were the scene for many carefree adventure games, but they could be dangerous, too. When I was eight, me and Brian Richardson were mucking about, wrestling or something, on what had been the upstairs of a house when the floor gave way and we fell down into a coal hole. Brian managed to scramble up and get away, only slightly injuring a leg, but I banged my head on a brick and was too dazed to move. Fortunately, a passer-by pulled me out and I was taken to nearby St. George's Hospital, blood pouring from a huge wound that needed twenty-eight stitches. To think, if I hadn't slipped and hit my nut I could have been Einstein!

I should have been in hospital just a couple of days, but caught chicken pox and ended up staying in there a week. A few months later, a brick gave me another headache, but this time I can honestly say it wasn't my fault. I was playing with David Marshall, and we decided we wanted some pears on a tree in what remained of a garden. We climbed up a little way and got some, but couldn't reach the others. We got down and started throwing stones and small rocks at one of the branches, trying to dislodge some of the pears. I wasn't having much success, so I picked up half a brick and hurled it at the biggest branch, which I thought would dislodge loads of pears. To my horror, the brick ricocheted off the branch and landed on David's head. He started bawling and said he wanted to go home. I went with him, but as soon as he saw his mum, he shouted: 'He hit me on the head . . . he hit me on the head,' as though I'd deliberately chucked the brick at him. I tried to explain what had happened, but Mrs Marshall was having none of it. 'Yeah, I know,' she said. 'I believe you.' And then, bosh, she clumped me several times round the ear.

It wasn't the pain that hurt, it was the injustice – like the time I got hold of a piece of chalk and scrawled my name on the school wall. A teacher spotted me and took me to the headmaster, who ordered me to stand before the school at assembly the next morning. I tried to explain that I'd just written my name, not everything else on the wall, but he didn't want to know. As far as he was concerned, I was responsible for *all* the graffiti and deserved to be punished. I was caned three times on each hand, then handed a bucket and brush and told to scrub the whole wall. I kept saying, 'I didn't do it all,' but nobody gave a toss: they'd caught me bang to rights and obviously felt justified getting me to clean off every bit of scrawl, not just my own. It wasn't the pain of the cane, or the hours I spent cleaning that wall, that bothered me – it was the humiliation of being told off so publicly. I've never forgotten how ashamed I felt.

That experience was a one-off, though. Generally, I was happy at school; I thought it was great – although, like most kids, I couldn't wait to get out and have fun, out of sight of my mum and dad. Another wonderful playground was the huge Gaumont cinema, opposite the railway station, that had been empty since the end of the war. This had been bombed, too, and had no roof, but all the debris had been cleared away and made an ideal site for our make-believe games. After school, me and my mates would let ourselves in through a small hole in the outer wall and enjoy ourselves, sitting in the old seats and playing cops and robbers and cowboys and Indians among the various hideaways we found in the offices around the projection room. It was eerie, the building having no roof, and we loved it. No doubt we'd have been in trouble if the police had caught us, but the hole we got in was so small I don't think anyone knew we were there. And, anyway, we weren't doing any harm.

One cinema the Germans had not demolished was the Odeon, at Gant's Hill, and it was there that I first marvelled at the magic of 'the pictures'. The cinema was a fair old trek from Kensington Gardens – at least half an hour if you caught the bus on time – and whether I went depended on dad's mood when he arrived home from work.

I didn't appreciate it then, of course, but he put in a long, hard day. He'd leave home at 6 a.m., catch two trolley buses, to Manor Crossman and Paulin Brewery, at Whitechapel to start at 7 a.m., and often not get back until six in the evening. If he'd had a few pints he'd come in, having walked a mile from the bus stop, and go straight to the toilet in the backyard. Then he'd plonk himself in front of the fire and, within minutes, was snoring, while mum got on with cooking his dinner. She only had to look at him when he walked through the door to know whether he would be in the mood to want to go out again. If he wasn't, we'd spend the evening listening to the radio and, nine times out of ten, go the following night when dad wasn't tired. I was not that disappointed because that meant I could listen at 6.45 p.m. to Dick Barton, Special Agent – the favourite serial with most kids back then.

On Sunday afternoons, dad would encourage me to go to the pictures on my own, after I'd been to Sunday School, at St. Andrew's Church, about half a mile away. He'd come back from the pub about two, then, after lunch, hand me a shilling and I'd think 'What a great dad', because it was only ninepence to get in, and twopence there and back on the bus, which meant I'd have a penny to spend on sweets. What I didn't realise was that after a few pints and a good lunch, dad wanted me out of the way so that he could give mum a seeing-to, then have a nap.

I never needed encouragement to go to Sunday School. My regular mates didn't go, but I didn't mind: I was part of a group of between ten and twenty kids and we were enthralled by the stories of Jesus, which a grown-up read from the Bible. Sunday School went on for about an hour and afterwards I would dash out and run down the hill to Cranbrook Road and catch a bus to the Odeon. If the film was a 'U' category, meaning anyone was allowed to see it, I'd go in on my own. But if it was an 'A', and children had to be accompanied by an adult, I would go up to someone, show them my ninepence, and ask them to take me in. I didn't care what was showing: films then were so magical to a young kid it didn't matter. Of course, going into a darkened cinema with a stranger would never happen today, but in those distant days people were more naive and innocent and trusting and there didn't seem to be any child molesters around. Certainly nobody ever made any improper advances or suggestions to me.

Some of the films I saw were frightening, but an experience with the Boys in Blue scared me even more than the sinister Man in Black. A mate and I were stupid enough to nick things from Woolworth's, in Ilford High Street, and one day we helped ourselves to a set of darts and some playing cards. We thought we were so clever and that nobody had spotted us, but two coppers had and were waiting for us outside. They took the stolen items, asked for our names and addresses, then said they would be coming round to tell our parents. No one ever did, but I was shitting myself for days, dreading what my dad would do when they turned up. Which was obviously the point.

All my mates and I enjoyed a bit of rough and tumble and a wrestle, but, one weekend, I did get into a proper fist fight with a boy visiting Ilford from a different area. I can't remember what the fight was about, but it all went off in my front garden. The boy was taller than me, with a long reach, and he kept jabbing his left hand in my face. I kept going in at him, even though he'd cut my lip and eye and kept knocking me down. My brother, John, was watching from a window and, after I was knocked down for about the tenth time, he came out and stopped the fight. 'I think you've had enough, Billy,' he said, helping me to my feet. 'No, no,' I pleaded. 'Let me go. I'll get him in a minute.' But John was having none of it and told the boy to clear off, before taking me inside.

✳ ✳ ✳

No one was surprised when I failed my Eleven Plus exam. I loved school, because of all my mates, but the idea of settling down to read when there was so much to do outside held no appeal for me. David Marshall was excited to be going to grammar school, but I was looking forward more to the summer holidays when I would be packed off to Blackpool, where Aunt Lizzie now had a guest house. I spent most of the time playing on the beach with my cousins and always returned to Ilford with a Lancashire accent – much to the amusement of my pals.

That September, I started at Danes Secondary Modern School, in nearby Wellesley Road. Academically, I was useless: my reading was awful and spelling even worse. The only thing I was good at was scripture, thanks to those Sunday School Bible classes. There was a bit of 'them' and 'us' at the school – scruffy Cockney immigrants, like me, from the East End, and kids who had grown up in the area. Danes wasn't a rough and tough school, but we formed little gangs, and there was always someone who wanted to start a fight with someone else. I was a big boy at eleven, but I wasn't aggressive and certainly never started fights. No one picked on me because I was bigger and stronger than everyone else – everyone, that is, except Neville Hammond. He was a big lump, who seemed a foot taller than us, and he used his size and weight to push us around and steal our pencils and pens and rubbers – even our lunch! He was the self-appointed guv'nor and we were all in awe of him. But, sadly for him, he stopped growing while the rest of us didn't, and a couple of years later we'd caught him up and were able to wreak our revenge. I happily gave him a whack because I can't stand bullies. Most of the scuffles at school were just wrestling matches, really, with boys grabbing each other round the neck and scrabbling around on the floor, gouging and squeezing and nutting, until one started to cry and it was all over.

✳ ✳ ✳

After George finished National Service, he went back to Billingsgate as a porter. But he'd done well in the boxing ring and started dedicating himself to becoming British amateur champion, so that he could turn professional and earn more money. It was an aim he achieved at the first attempt and, immediately after winning the ABA Championship in 1951, he turned pro, earning five hundred pounds for his first fight, at Earl's Court arena, later that year. He quickly treated himself to a black Humber Supersnipe car and slipped me five bob every Saturday to wash it and clean his shoes for when he went out on the town with his mate, Tommy McCarthy. Tommy lived in The Highway, within walking distance of Billingsgate and had met George there before they did their National Service. When Tommy came to the house, he always had time for me. I liked him on sight.

Thanks to George's influence, I had more than enough money for a twelve-year-old. I'd got myself not one, but two, jobs for 15 shillings a week – a morning paper round for 7s 6d and a butcher's round for the same amount on Saturday afternoon. I may not have had much up top where school work was concerned, but it didn't take me long to spot a way to increase my butcher's pay at the expense of unsuspecting customers. I delivered their orders by bike, with a basket on the handlebars, and somewhere en route I'd stop and carefully doctor their bill. I always made sure I had the same colour pen as the butcher and if a bill was, say, £1. 9s. 1d, I'd add a stroke to the 1d, making it 7d, or if I was feeling particularly daring, turn it into 11d by adding a 1. Naturally, I'd pocket the difference and no one was the wiser. With the occasional tip, I'd often end up with half a crown on top of my wages, giving me ten bob for the afternoon. So, one way and the other, I'd end up with 17s 6d or more in my pocket every Saturday night. Believe me, that was a lot of money and meant I could easily afford to go to the open-air baths in Valentine's Park, where I virtually lived during the summer. Most of my mates went there straight from school, but I had a job to do at home before I was allowed out to play. With mum and dad and George all working, I had to let myself into the empty house and peel the potatoes to save mum the trouble when she got home. I'd do them as quickly as I could, then dash out and join my pals for a couple of hours before going home for tea.

Even then, I was showing an interest in girls and was thrilled when I discovered an easy and exciting way of watching them undress without being detected. The female changing area was on the sunny side of the pool, so me and my friends would go round there and stretch out beside the cubicles as though we were sunbathing. Anyone looking down at us would not have guessed we could see under the cubicle doors, but we could, and caught many a glimpse of young ladies taking their knickers off.

Around this time, I joined the Scouts and was so enthusiastic and dedicated I was appointed a patrol leader – a role I took very seriously, particularly when we went to summer camp at Gillwell Park, in Essex, and a pennant was awarded to the tidiest group. We had to roll up our tents, lay out all our bedding neatly, and clean our respective kitchens, where we cooked on open fires. I was so determined my group would win the pennant that once we had everything neat and tidy I banned everyone under my control from going into the camp area until morning inspection was over. Anyone who went in and messed things up would get a bashing, I said. One day I got told off by the Scoutmaster after one of the kids went to him, crying, saying he needed something from his rucksack, but was too frightened to go in and get it. Very gently, the Scoutmaster told me he admired my keenness, but it was wrong to stop boys going in for something they needed. I was furious with those little sods, messing up everything we'd taken ages to make neat. For a twelve-year-old, I was a little tyrant!

A lot of the boys in the troop were very sporty, but not me. I wasn't any good at football or cricket and, consequently, had no interest in either. I liked swimming and wasn't bad at it, although I never entered any competitions, either at school, or in the Scouts. The only activity I showed any flair for was running, especially over long distances.

By now, 1951, George's boxing was going well. After that first fight at Earl's Court, he'd had another four and won them all. In July, he'd had another glorious victory at Mile End Arena – a former bomb-site behind Mile End station – and I was thrilled to be taken to his next fight there, the following month. George won that one, too, out-pointing Johnny Barton, over eight rounds, but I remember being very upset at the vicious punishment he took, and distressed when I saw his horribly disfigured face afterwards.

George had told me he was only in the fight game for the money and, what with his Billingsgate job, he certainly seemed to have plenty of it. But the hours of training he had to do, and the pain he suffered in the ring, didn't seem worth it to me. George was my hero and, quite honestly, the sight of his battered face that August night frightened me. I'd given no thought to what I was going to do with my life, but what I did know, even at twelve, was that I never wanted to be a fighter. I'd had little interest in it before. And after seeing my brother so badly cut and bruised after winning, I had none now.

If poor George's face had shocked me then, it was nothing to what confronted me when I came downstairs for breakfast one Friday morning in March, 1953, just after my fourteenth birthday. I barely recognised him: both his eyes were half-closed, the left one by the biggest, purple-black bruise I'd ever seen, and his lips were so lacerated and swollen he couldn't speak. He looked as if he'd been in a terrible road accident, but the injuries had been inflicted in the ring, at Liverpool stadium, the previous night when he'd fought Dennis Powell for the British light heavyweight title. Without exception, newspaper journalists who reported the fight, described it as the most savage and brutal contest they had ever seen. The *Daily Mirror* said that no adjectives could describe the punishment each man took and, Peter Wilson, of the *Daily Express*, said that 'contest' was too polite a word: it was a battle 'that took one back 200 years and more when men fought with bare fists for scores of rounds, bleeding and blinded.' It was the most bitter, bruising and gory fight he had ever seen 'in any ring in the world'. And George 'appeared to have aged ten years in the thirty minutes of fighting'.

George lost the fight because his left eyebrow swelled 'to the size of a cucumber' in the seventh round and burst in the tenth. After battling through the next round, able to see only with one eye, his second (trainer) told the referee it was all over. Looking at George now, I didn't know what to say. What was there to say? He couldn't speak much anyway.

Mum and dad had to go to work, so mum said to me: 'You're not going to school today, Billy. You'll stay home and look after your brother. George needs to bathe his eye, so get him hot water every hour.'

So that's what I did. I also gave George soup and tea and cold drinks and he had to drink them through a straw because his lips were so swollen. I loved not having to go to school, but I didn't like George's face. My feelings must have been written all over mine, because George put his arm round me and said: 'It's not the end of the world, Billy. You win some and lose some. You can't win 'em all. I wanted to win, but I didn't, and moaning and feeling sorry for myself isn't going to change a thing.'

That was typical George: so brave. But now, looking at the bruises and cuts, and seeing the pain and disappointment in his eyes, I felt the same as I had that night in Mile End: the fight game, and all the money it offered, was okay for George. But it wasn't for me, never in a thousand years. And I told him so.

'Good,' George said, through those bashed-up lips. 'Do well at school and get a good profession behind you that pays good money. I had to fight to make real money. But you don't have to.'

I could see George's point, but knew I wasn't brainy enough for a profession. I had no idea then what I wanted to do, but felt sure that whatever I did, I'd be using my hands.

2

That June, 1953, was the Queen's coronation, and I was thrilled and proud to be chosen, with Scouts from other areas, to sell programmes for the historic event. There was not an official price on the programmes: people were simply expected to make a donation of not less than two shillings. It didn't work that way with me, however: when people came to me and asked how much the programmes were, I realised I had a chance of a scam. We'd all been told to give change, but who was to know if I did? And, with people being asked to donate what they wished, who was to know how much I collected? So, when someone asked me how much they had to pay, I said two shillings. If they had the right money, they dropped it in my tin, but if they needed change, I made sure I put only a shilling in the tin and the other shilling in my pocket. Looking back, I feel terrible. I was put in a position of trust and I abused it. But I thought nothing of it at the time: I was an East End boy and a scam that copped me a few extra shillings was a lovely pay day.

I loved being a Scout. And, that memorable year, I was in love with a girl, too. Her name was Joan Lock and I met her one Friday night at a youth club, held in my old primary school. She was a pretty blonde, a few months older than me, and I thought she was gorgeous. Joan didn't know I was in the Scouts. To her, I was a big boy, in long trousers, who was always being Jack the Lad at the youth club. Well, one evening I was walking up the hill to St Andrew's Church, in my Scout uniform, when I saw Joan and some of her friends coming down the other side. I was so besotted with her, I thought: 'Oh, God, if she doesn't smile at me, I'm going to die.' Joan did not smile at me. Neither did her mates. They stopped and stared at me, as though they could not believe their eyes. And then they pointed at my short trousers and started laughing. Loudly. All of them. At nearly six feet, I suppose I did look daft in short trousers, but it had never occurred to me until that moment. I didn't know what to say. And I didn't know where to look. I just looked down, feeling my face burning with embarrassment, then hurried back down the hill. I went straight home, took off my woggle and shorts and threw them away. And I never went back to the Scouts again. It was a shame, really, because I'd loved everything about scouting, and all it stood for, and for the next few months I missed it dreadfully. Joan Lock was my first love, but she never knew it, and certainly was never aware of how she changed what could have been an important course of my life.

I had no time to dwell on my lost love, however, because, the following summer, 1954, I was about to leave school and needed to consider what I was going to do to earn a living. Dad had little money and was expecting me to, at least, pay mum enough for my keep and buy my own clothes. Going on the dole wasn't an option: that would be shameful. But, with no qualifications, it was going to be hard finding a job that paid well.

I was open to any ideas and I talked to my uncle, Joe, who was a printer on a national newspaper. He was a real dapper character; a chubby, short man, who loved the company of women, and was often to be found propping up the bar at his favourite watering hole, The Albion, at Ludgate Circus. He seemed to have a great life and when he told me the printing trade paid good money, I agreed to take an examination to be a compositor, a person who sets and corrects type. Unfortunately, one needed to be able to spell, and I couldn't. I did my best, but failed spectacularly. I'm told the examiners had never experienced anyone who spelt so badly. A few weeks later someone told dad about an electrician looking for a young lad to work as an apprentice to one of four senior electricians on his payroll. I wasn't mad about electrical work, but at least it was something, so I went to see the man and got the job.

I didn't have to start until September, which gave me the best part of the summer to have some fun. And I did. In fact, I went with some mates to a Warner Holiday Camp, at Puckpool, on the Isle of Wight, and was thrilled to lose my virginity! I can't remember the young lady's name, but I'd call her a bit of a lump today, and she was not the best-looking holidaymaker there. She was about six years older than me and must have fancied some young stuff because she made all the running. We ended up in her chalet one night and, well, she had her way with me. Not that she got much out of it: I was so excited that it was all over in a matter of seconds, and I couldn't wait to get out of the chalet and tell my mates: 'Guess what!'

✳✳✳

My boss at work, was a big, fat bloke, in his late-thirties, named Jack Bryant. And he made it clear very quickly that he liked another apprentice more than me. I couldn't understand why, but it became clear that it was less to do with me than George, who had begun to get a bad reputation in and around the East End after giving up boxing.

He was a tough nut, George, no doubt about it, and he renewed a friendship with a ruthless villain, named Billy Hill, who he'd met at Jack Solomons' gym when he was fighting. Hill, who ran an organised crime racket in London's West End, had made many enemies, notably a flamboyant, but vicious, Polish Jew, named Jack 'Spot' Comer, who ran illegal gambling clubs, in the city, and felt he needed a fearsome and respected 'minder'. George fitted the bill perfectly. The country's crime reporters picked up on Hill's activities and, that summer of 1954, George found himself in a Sunday paper, photographed with Hill and his cronies, sunning themselves on board the gangster's yacht, The Flamingo, off the coast of Tangiers.

George returned to London and, on the first Sunday in August, got involved in a violent street fight in Hackney, apparently watched by a crowd of some 200 people. I remember him coming home, his head bleeding, saying someone had hit him over the head with an axe. The next day, he appeared at North London Magistrates' Court with four other guys and was conditionally discharged after admitting to using insulting behaviour. Bryant had read about George in the papers and kept goading me about what a despicable gangster my brother was. I wonder if he would have had the guts to say it to George's face!

✳✳✳

Starting a full-time job was a huge step for me. But I'm sure it hit mum hard, too. Although I was a six-foot teenager, I was still her little boy and, much as she wanted me to get out into the big, wide world and enjoy myself, there was part of her that wanted to hold on to me. She demonstrated this, to my excruciating embarrassment, one evening, shortly after I'd started working.

I'd got in with a group of interesting guys at the youth club, who wore duffle coats, black trousers and checked shirts. Some had beards and looked and sounded more intelligent than me. One Friday night we all went to a party at someone's house, near Kensington Gardens, and I was sitting there, a girl on my lap, a glass of beer in my hand, and holding a cigarette, when there was a knock at the door and I heard a woman's voice, asking, angrily: 'Is my son here?' I recognised it as mum's. And cringed. She strode into the room where we were all gathered, took the beer out of my hand, and slapped me hard round the face. 'Come home with me,' she said, sharply, pulling me out of the chair.

Head down so that I didn't see the looks on my friends' faces, I followed her, meekly, to the door, my face burning with shame and, once away from the house, called her all the names under the sun for making me look small. I was fifteen years old, I fumed. And if I was old enough to work for a living, I should be able to go out on my own and enjoy myself. It was only eleven o'clock, I yelled and I was hardly out of my head at a drunken orgy.

When we got home I told dad what mum had done. He told her she was out of order for hitting me in front of my friends but, unfortunately, it wasn't one of those times when he cared enough to put his foot down. He was an easy-going guy, who usually went with the flow, only getting out of his pram when pushed. For a long time, I thought mum was the dominant one, but she wasn't, not when it came down to it. Dad would let her have her way ninety per cent of the time, but if something mattered to him he would make his point. They had their code and mum knew when to shut up.

I was upset that dad didn't put mum in her place that night. But he must have said something to her later, because she left me alone after that, much as it was tough for her, accepting her little boy was flexing his muscles.

And flex them I did. With Bryant's arse-licking favourite. He was a bit of a wally and it was only a matter of time before we clashed. Although he was only a couple of years older than me, he delighted in telling me what to do and generally making me feel useless. I still hated authority of any kind and, one day, I refused to do something and he snapped: 'Do as you're told,' and tried to give me a cuff. I grabbed hold of him and wrestled him to the ground then smashed him a couple of times in the face. He started to cry and Bryant came and pulled me off, accusing me of being a bully. After that, the boy was far more respectful towards me and we got along okay.

I was never going to be long in that job. It wasn't only that Bryant was so horrible to me, it was the job itself. And the pittance I was paid. In the main, the company worked on new houses, but it took on other jobs, too, and one we were assigned to was a Dr Barnardo's Home, in East London, five miles from Ilford. The quickest way to get there was obviously by bus or tram, but I went by bike and claimed travelling expenses. My wage was about three quid and, after tax and contribution to the housekeeping, I was left with less than I earned at twelve. So I needed to make money where I could. I didn't mind cycling to Stepney in the cold early mornings, but I didn't like working in the draughty Barnardo's building.

With Christmas coming up, I would have stomached it if Bryant had not asked me to do something dangerous one day and caused me to lose my cool. We were working high up in the building when he pulled a couple of floorboards up and handed me a wire. Then he pointed at a vast amount of darkness and ordered me to climb down into it and look for a place to attach the wire. I looked down into what must have been a fifteen-foot drop. That, and the fact the building was about one hundred years old, scared me. 'You must be out of your mind,' I said. 'I'm not going down there.'

'Get down there,' he said, and clumped the side of my head.

I said: 'Bollocks', or something to that effect and went to have a go back at him. I was only a kid, though, and no match for such a big old bruiser. So I swallowed it and just said: 'That's it – I'm off.' I had a meeting with the company boss who said that if I wasn't prepared to take orders, I'd better leave. So I did.

✳✳✳

I may have been out of work and not flushed financially, but that didn't stop me going out with my mates. One Saturday night just before Christmas, I was getting myself all dolled up when George, who was getting ready to go out himself, took a long look at me and said: 'Why are you wearing that crap?' It was the start of the Teddy Boy era of velvet collar suits, 'drainpipe' trousers and 'bootlace' ties. I had not gone that far, but I *was* wearing a black and white dog-tooth jacket and thin 'Slim Jim' tie and tapered, narrow-bottomed trousers – a fashion on the edge of the unruly Teddy Boy image. I thought I looked okay, but George didn't.

'If you go out in that gear, where are you going to get in?' he said. 'The decent places will think you're going there to cause trouble.'

It didn't cross my mind to argue: George was so worldly he obviously knew what he was talking about. He went to his wardrobe and took out one of his suits – an expensive dark blue mohair – and handed it to me. 'Put this on,' he said. 'You're coming with me.' As I took off my jacket and trousers, he sorted out a lovely, pale blue shirt and maroon tie. The trousers were a bit short, and the jacket a little big for me, but not much, and I felt great getting into George's Humber. 'Where we going?' I asked, quietly excited.

'The Hay Field,' he said. 'It's about time you started mixing with men, not boys who're going to be a bad influence.'

The Hay Field was a huge, popular pub, in the Mile End Road, at Stepney Green. I was only fifteen, but big for my age, and nobody batted an eyelid. I didn't have much to drink there, but when we went on to a party, I was introduced to a promising East End boxer, named Terry Murphy, who persuaded me to join him in 'a drop of gin'. After that, I got carried away and started dancing with the pretty girls – including the wives of some of the chaps there. I got away with it, not just because I was a young kid on his first 'outing'. but because anyone who took offence would have been too shit-scared of George to say anything! Finally the gin got to me and I rushed to the toilet to be sick. Poor George! He had to get me in the car and drive me home. He knocked on the door and said: 'Mum, he's been sick – take him in,' then raced back to the party.

It was my first experience of throwing up from drinking too much and I vowed never to let it happen again. But some good did come out that drunken evening: I took George's advice about what to wear, and elbowed all the gear that made me look like a Teddy Boy. I wanted so much to be like George, that from that day on I started saving up for my own suits – quiet, conservative ones that would make me acceptable at any establishment and in any company. Teddy Boys were synonymous with trouble, and I didn't want that label. Even at fifteen, I wanted to be a sophisticated man-about-town and, thanks to George, I was aware that, like manners, dress maketh the man and that first impressions can be crucial.

George was so, so important in my life then: whenever I was in a spot, he was the one I turned to. I met and fell in love with a girl named Darlene Bryant and, being Jack the Gent, offered to take her home to Chadwell St. Mary, near Grays, a bus and train journey from Ilford. It was a long way, but I wasn't bothered because I fancied her like mad and knew there was a late train back to Ilford. What a wally I was! Darlene didn't invite me in, just stood on the doorstep, allowing me a kiss and a cuddle. Having gone all that way, I did my best to make it worthwhile by trying to have a fondle inside her blouse, but Darlene was having none of it. I persevered, but, in the end, gave up, said I had to go, and rushed to the station, only to discover I had missed the last train by ten minutes. I had no option but to ring George and beg to be picked up. My hero didn't let me down.

✳✳✳

Coming up to my sixteenth birthday, I hadn't found a job that suited me and dad started nagging me about lazing around at home. I could understand him worrying, but work had always been a nasty, four-letter word to me and, quite honestly, I hadn't been looking too hard. But when mum showed me an ad by a local print firm, Dray's, of Barking, asking for apprentices, I got mildly excited. Remembering what uncle Joe had said about workers in the print trade earning big money, I cycled down to the firm's offices, by the docks, and got taken on, no problem.

The company printed colour magazines and all I had to do was stand by one of the machines, making sure that the rolls of paper being printed landed in the right place. It was a vitally important job, because if the paper was in the wrong place the colour registration would be wrong, too, which would obviously be a disaster. But it was boring, standing there for hours on end, just staring at a printing machine. Sometimes I'd lose concentration and the minder who checked that the print was all right, would call out: 'You're not watching,' and give me a bollocking.

Yes, the job was tedious, but it did teach me something very important in life – punctuality. My hours were 8 a.m. to 6 p.m., two days a week and 8 a.m. to 5.30 p.m. the others, and I was introduced to the clocking-on system, which confirmed when we all arrived at work. If you were one minute late, you were stopped five minutes' pay; five minutes and you were stopped a quarter of an hour. I wasn't earning a lot more than I picked up as an apprentice electrician, so this certainly concentrated my mind. As with the first job, I quickly worked out that it was cheaper to go by bike to work. It was a damn sight faster, too, because I needed to take not one, but three buses to get me from Kensington Gardens to Thames Road. Travelling by bike saved me two shillings a day – ten bob a week. A fortune! Mind you, it was nearly four miles and took half an hour or so, which wasn't funny when it was pissing down. But I was a young kid, full of go, and I coped with it all right.

I must have been good at what I did, because, after a couple of months, I was given a more important job – feeding paper into machines, printing technical literature. This was more interesting and I loved the responsibility. Who knows, I may have stayed at Dray's and gone on to earn big money in Fleet Street, if it hadn't been for another dust-up with another apprentice who – like Jack Bryant – had a chip on his shoulder about George.

Charlie Long was his name. He was a Teddy Boy. And he thought he was Jack the Lad – the bee's knees. He was about a year older, and a lot taller, than me and worked in the warehouse where all the printing paper was stored. As soon as we met, he seemed to have it in for me, jibing me all the time, about how George could fight and I couldn't.

I put up with it for a few months, but one afternoon, Charlie and I found ourselves in the toilets together and he made one jibe too far. 'Right, you long, flash streak of piss,' I said, grabbing him round the neck and throwing him on the floor. I was a heavy lump and he couldn't move. I pummelled his face a few times, then got up, leaving him on the floor with a bloodied nose. When we came out, other staff saw what I'd done and someone told Mr Sanders, the boss, who called us into his office, demanding to know what had gone on.

I was severely reprimanded and warned that if I hit Charlie again I'd be in big trouble. I didn't care. By then, I was getting fed up with the long hours and low pay and would have been happy to chuck it in if another job came along.

That's when I met Jimmy Bedford.

3

I met Jimmy at Ilford Palais which was then THE place for youngsters to go in and around East London. It was built as a cinema in 1912, then transformed into a Palais de Danse in the twenties. Now, it was just plain Palais – a popular dance hall, with a live band, every night, except Monday, which, with the rock and roll craze, was Rock Night. There was no alcohol in the place, just an upstairs lounge for tea and coffee. Ilford Palais was very genteel and I loved it, particularly Monday nights when everyone jived to the records of Elvis Presley, Bill Haley and the Comets and other emerging rock stars. I was a great jiver – and still am!

I was introduced to the Palais by David Dobbs and Kenny Syrett, who worked with me at Dray's. They were four years older than me and took me here, there and everywhere, introducing me to all their friends, one of whom was a dark, stocky guy, no more than a year older than me.

He said his name was Jimmy Bedford and he worked at Billingsgate Fish Market, by the Thames near London Bridge.

'What do you do?' I asked.

'I'm a porter,' he said.

'What, just carrying fish around?'

'Yeah.'

'Do you get good money?'

'Ten pound a week,' Jimmy said, proudly.

'Ten quid! You're joking.'

'I'm not. That's what porters get.'

'Fucking hell,' I said. 'I'm in the print. I'm only on four quid. And that's with overtime on Saturdays. What do you do for ten quid?'

'Four hours a day, six days a week,' he said. 'Six in the morning, till ten. I'm nearly always back home by eleven.'

I couldn't believe it. I mean, I *could not* believe it. Nearly three times what I was getting for half the time!

Over the next few days I could think of little else, and the next time I saw Jimmy I asked him if he could get *me* a job at the market. He said he'd show me around and introduce me to a few people so, without mentioning anything to mum and dad, I took a couple of days off work and went to the market with him. It turned out Jimmy wasn't actually a porter; you had to be eighteen and he was only seventeen. He worked for a firm of seafood distributors, named Scutts, where you didn't have to be a licensed porter. He still earned ten quid a week, though.

Jimmy showed me round all the Billingsgate fish importers and I spent a few hours asking if there were any vacancies. I was despairing at all the blanks I was getting when I went into MacFisheries, at the corner of Pudding Lane, and was told that, yes, they wanted a shop boy to help load on to lorries taking fish to the firm's retail shops around the country. The man who took me on was a saucy sod, named Harry Marsden, who had the nerve to ask me if I could read. I said I could – just.

Harry explained I had to be able to read a chitty, listing what fish was required and send an appropriately-sized box, lined with grease-proof paper, down a runway to be filled up.

It sounded a doddle. 'How much do I get?' I asked.

'Eleven pounds a week,' Harry said.

Blimey, I thought, a quid more than Jimmy Bedford. I was over the moon.

'Lovely,' I said. 'I'll take it.'

'Fine. See you Monday. Five o'clock.'

'Hold up,' I said. 'Five o'clock? The market doesn't start till six.'

Harry laughed. 'Yeah, the market does. We don't. That's why you're getting a pound more than the boys down there.'

That knocked me back a bit: getting up an hour earlier that time in the morning was a big difference. But so was a pound. I reckoned it was worth it and went home happy, excited that I'd trebled my wages and wouldn't have to work such long hours.

I wasn't relishing telling mum and dad though: because George was getting into so much trouble, they associated the market with bad people, and I knew they'd hit the roof when they learned I was going to work there, too. I kept schtum all weekend, but when I said I was going to bed around 7 p.m. on Sunday night, I obviously had to explain why. Mum and dad weren't happy and they gave me a hard time, but it was too late.

Feeling very excited, I got my head down and set the alarm for 3.45 a.m., giving me enough time to catch a train from Ilford, which got to Liverpool Street at 4.45 a.m. I then had to run down Pudding Lane and be changed and ready for work by the time the start bell rang on the stroke of 5 a.m.

For the first few weeks, I arrived on time, but one morning I missed the train and had to thumb a lift. As we reached Pudding Lane I jumped out and dashed down the hill, thankful that I'd made up some time was only ten minutes late. But I was shocked to see Harry outside the shop, waving his hands at me and shaking his head. 'Come back tomorrer,' he was shouting. 'Come back tomorrer.'

I continued down the hill and ran up to him. 'I'm sorry, Harry,' I said breathlessly. 'I missed my train. I'll be ready in two minutes.'

It cut no ice. He just said: 'Come back tomorrer.' I called him all the names under the sun, but he kept repeating, coldly: 'Come back tomorrer.'

The next day I was on time and had a right go at him. 'You rotten bastard, Harry' I said. 'You lost me a day's pay.'

'I know,' he said, smiling. 'You won't ever be late again, will you?'

He was right. If I hadn't learned my lesson at Dray's, I had now. And I never forgot it.

✳✳✳

At sixteen, me and the group I went to the Palais with were all a bit silly. Some would say we were tearaways, villains, who, because we were big and could handle ourselves, were always looking for trouble. I don't see it that way now and I didn't then. It's true that if someone in another group took what we thought was a liberty and upset us, we'd say: 'We'll have that little mob,' and then steam in and sort them out. But it would be only a quick punch-up and a few kicks, and then it would be all over. I like to think it was done in fun, rather than like today with kids being tooled up with knives and even guns.

One of my pals, Bobby Powell, was good-looking and pulled all the birds. But he loved starting fights, too. His technique was to amble over to an unsuspecting mob and stand with his back to them, casually smoking a cigarette. He would gradually inch backwards until he nudged one of them. Nine times out of ten, the guy would say something like, 'Oi, what you doing?' and Bobby would turn round, stub out his cigarette on the floor, then swing a right hook on the guy's chin. That would be our signal to dive in and throw as many punches as we could at the rest of the mob before the bouncers moved in. Those caught fighting would be chucked out, so, in time, we learned to throw just three or four quick punches then fade into the crowd before we were spotted. As I say, we all found it good fun. Nobody got seriously hurt. Certainly I didn't. I can't remember ever being hit.

The manager of the Palais was a friendly Yorkshireman, Jimmy Savile – who became a famous disc jockey. He was a real character. He was nobody's fool and once barred me for a week for fighting. But he always had time to chat to our little group and told us he kept in shape by working out with weights in his office. Jimmy Bedford came up with the idea that we should go to Wag Bennett's gym, in East Ham, which was popular among local body-builders. I was all for it: I wanted to be like Charles Atlas, muscular, but with more body definition, and more attractive to the ladies.

With more money in my pocket than most kids, I indulged myself in my passion – having fun with my mates, not only at The Palais, but in pubs in and around Ilford. My closest pal was Lee Hicks. He had done well at school and worked in an office, but when he learned how much I was earning at Billingsgate, he asked me to fix him up with a job there. His family were furious that he was chucking away a good job, with prospects, to work in a fish market, but Lee was young and wanted to have as much fun as he could. And that meant having as much money as possible. Money really was the be-all-and-end-all then. If you didn't have it, you couldn't go anywhere. And, for a sixteen-year-old, where was the fun in that?

George, more than most of his pals, was desperate to be rich and, five days before my seventeenth birthday, he got involved in something nasty that could have destroyed him. All mum and dad told me was that George was in trouble with the police and had to appear in court with another man. It was all over some nylon stockings, they said, which had been stolen from the docks with some boxes of woollen goods. What they failed to mention was that there were more than 500 pairs of nylons, which, with the other goods, were worth £1,754 – enough to buy a house, a car and have a lot left over! They also failed to mention that there had been a pitched battle between three robbers and the police, in which one officer was savagely beaten over the head with his own truncheon as he tried to stop a getaway van. The driver escaped, but George and the other man were arrested and appeared at the Old Bailey two months later, accused of theft. On 13 April, the day before his twenty-seventh birthday, George was jailed for two years.

A couple of months later, Jimmy told me he'd turned eighteen and got his licence to be a Billingsgate porter. 'Shoot down and see Bert and Geoff,' he said. 'You'll get my job.' I didn't need to be asked twice, because I knew he was now earning more than me. The next morning I applied for the job and was told I could start at the end of the month. I handed in my notice to Harry and enjoyed a fabulous weekend, made up that I'd now be getting not only more money, but an extra hour in bed!

✳✳✳

Lee and I had been putting a few quid away for a holiday, but, what we really wanted was a car. Not a small, boring Ford or Austin – something bigger, flashier, that would impress the ladies. And something spacious enough to get hold of them in the back if we got lucky. That summer, we heard that Jimmy Bedford's brother, Billy, was selling a huge black Chevrolet, just nine years old, with eye-catching chrome bumpers, and we fell in love with it. Billy wanted £300 and we gave him £100, agreeing to pay the balance over two years through a finance company. It was the time of the Suez crisis and, with petrol difficult to come by, that was probably why Billy decided to get rid of the car. But Lee and I were all right; I'd go and see George's girlfriend, Jean, whose father owned a petrol station, and she let me buy enough petrol to keep us on the road. At only seventeen, Lee and I had to drive on Provisional licences until we passed our driving tests.

The striking, highly-polished American motor did make us feel the bee's knees, I must admit. We'd park right outside the Palais and bask in the attention and undisguised envy of other young guys who used the place. Wearing George's camel Crombie only added to my allure. He'd worn my coat on the nylons' raid and I felt it only fair I should wear his while he was away.

Mind you, he wasn't too impressed when I walked in on a prison visit wearing it. 'You bastard,' he growled. 'You've got my bloody coat.'

'Well, I can't get mine,' I said.

He thought for a moment, then remembered that clothes worn by prisoners at the time of their arrest are kept under lock and key until their release.

'Yeah, you're right,' he said. But he clearly didn't care for his kid brother turning up in such an expensive bit of gear he was unable to wear himself.

***

The Chevvy was a definite bird-puller, no doubt about it; Lee and I struck a deal to decide who drove it when. There were nights when one of us would have it on our own, but if we were out together and he got lucky, he'd drop me home first. If we both pulled, we'd toss a coin to decide who had it. One wintry night, we decided to enjoy the company of two ladies in the car together – me in the front, him in the back. We pulled on to the edge of a field, by the side of a country lane, in Hainault, Essex, and were having a kiss and a cuddle when it started to rain. We were all too pre-occupied to consider the consequences of this, but when we felt it time to drive the ladies home, the back tyres had sunk in the mud, leaving us stranded. The romantic feel of the evening now gone, the girls decided to walk home and Lee set about jacking the car up, while I looked around for something solid to lodge into the mud to grip the tyres. We were getting nowhere fast when we were bathed in the headlights of an approaching car. Thrilled at the prospect of much-needed help, Lee sprang up and dashed into the lane, brandishing the huge iron jack, yelling: 'STOP!' In a dark Crombie and Fedora, and fourteen stone, Lee looked like something out of a forties' gangster movie. And he must have cut a fearsome, terrifying sight because the Samaritan who was almost certainly going to stop to help us, changed his mind and roared away.

I glared at Lee and screamed: 'You prat. You look as though you're out to murder someone!'

'I just wanted them to see us,' he said, shame-faced.

We did finally get the car out. But it taught us a lesson: we never drove the Chevvy into muddy fields again.

✳ ✳ ✳

All my late, fun-filled, boozy nights were great but they came at a price: I started to get fat. What made it worse was the weight-lifting. So-called experts at the gym had assured me that drinking four or five pints of milk a day would build me up even more. But all it did was make me fatter. I'd ballooned to fourteen and a half stone and wasn't happy about myself. I was more muscular, but had no body definition. Then, one Saturday night at the Palais, we were having the usual laugh when a tall, good-looking and very fit-looking guy, about three years older than us, joined the group. He said his name was Nobby Eady and he'd recently come out of the Army. He seemed to know so much more than us about life and we were impressed, particularly when he said he was an Army boxing champion. The talk got round to physical fitness and he said that if we wanted to lose weight we should stop body-building and start training with him at a gym in West Ham: it would cost us only half a crown a week and there were lots of facilities to help us lose weight and get fit. The thought had never occurred to us and we agreed, there and then, to go. I mean, who were we to argue with such a fit Army champion?

Watching Nobby pummel the punchbag with powerful left and right hooks, I could appreciate why his handsome face was untouched. He had fast hands. He was skilful. And he was strong. He looked every bit the champion and I couldn't imagine anyone lasting more than a couple of minutes with him. So, you can imagine how I felt, after a few months, when I was asked to get in the ring and spar with him.

I refused, not only because it was Nobby, but I'd never forgotten George's battered face, and had no interest in boxing. I'd gone to the gym to lose weight and had done that. I'd lost about a stone and, thanks to George's mate, Tommy McCarthy, I was much fitter, too. I'd bumped into him in a pub one night and told him I was training at a boxing club, and he immediately invited me to join him running round Victoria Park in Hackney, after I finished at Scutt's. It was the start of a great friendship.

The gym could not force anyone to fight, as long as they paid their weekly dues, but the trainer – Billy Walker, ironically – clearly didn't care for kids like us, just using the gym to slim down.

'Are you scared to have a go with Nobby?' Billy said.

'Not particularly,' I said. 'But I've never boxed in my life. And Nobby's an Army champion.'

'He's what?' Billy said. 'We'll see about that. Now get the gloves on and get in there.'

It's true that I wasn't frightened. I've never been frightened of anyone in my life. Except The Man in Black, of course. But I *was* apprehensive. *Who* wouldn't be, fighting a bloke who looked so good, so experienced? Who'd won an Army championship?

For the first minute or so I kept my head down and tried to defend myself. But Nobby was so quick, I didn't see a lot of the punches coming and took a bit of a pummelling. It was all a bit one-sided and I thought: 'Yeah, you *are* good.' But his punches weren't hurting me, and I gained confidence. Suddenly, I saw an opening and swung a right hand, bosh!, on Nobby's left ear. I didn't think it was a particularly hard punch, but it seemed to hurt him because he buried his face in his gloves, like a kid would, and shied away from me, moaning. After a few seconds, he complained he'd hurt his arm and couldn't carry on, so we stopped.

Later, I said to Billy: 'I can't believe that guy. He's not much of an Army champion.'

Billy scoffed. 'Army champion? He's a punch bag champion!'

And he went on to explain that it was common in boxing that certain guys look great on the bag – because the bag can't hit back. Once they're in the ring and took a punch, their bottle went. I was chuffed I hadn't humiliated myself, but shocked to discover Nobby was just a load of wind. I couldn't take in that me and my mates had believed all his bullshit. Not surprisingly, we didn't see much of him after that. I'd burst his bubble.

4

As soon as I was eighteen, I applied for my licence to be a porter at Billingsgate and, because I was known as a good worker, I got it, no problem. The fish market was a place where muscles mattered more than brains, and it suited me down to the ground. It was a place where I could earn more money than I'd ever dreamed of – more than most blokes my age were earning, and, boy, was I going to enjoy it! I was a carefree teenager, who lived for fun. And the more money I had in my pocket, the more fun I could have. In those days, young blokes like me had suits made, and the first item on my list was to order a suit from Jimmy Lefko, an old bespectacled Jewish tailor, in the East End, who George always used.

My first morning at the market was exciting and I'll never forget it, not so much for the work I did, and money I earned, but for what happened before I'd lifted even one crate of fish. Porters were issued with a rubber apron to protect their clothes and boots to save wearing out their shoes, and what I didn't know was that every new worker was initiated in a special way. Unknown to me, someone had nailed my boots to the floor of the changing room, so that when I got up, eager to get stuck into my new job, I was rooted to the spot. I didn't get it at first, but when everyone started laughing, I saw the joke and joined in. It was all done in good spirit, just a friendly way of welcoming me into their team.

Billingsgate was all about loading barrowloads of fish on to waiting vans – as many barrows as possible, as fast as possible; where the more barrows you loaded, the more you earned. And I was perfect for the job. Fit. Strong. Fast on my feet. And a tireless worker. I couldn't fail to make a lot of money. And I didn't. Within days I was picking up more than double what I'd earned at Scutt's – and loving every minute of it. The beauty of Billingsgate was that the working day, while tough on the body, was very short: three hours, from six a.m. till nine. From the moment you started, you were on the go so much that it was time to go home before you knew it.

I was one of hundreds of licensed porters, who carried boxes of fish – each weighing eight stones – to vans, parked nearby, which took the fish to various wholesale and retail outlets all over the country. We were given a list of fish required, stacked the appropriate boxes on our barrow, then loaded them into the vans, before rushing back for another stack. It was fast, frenzied work and, not surprisingly, tempers got frayed very quickly. If someone pulled his barrow in front of yours, blocking your way, you had no time to stand and argue, or have a knuckle. You just swore and told him to get the fucking thing out the way. He wouldn't give a monkey's, of course, because he was in a rush himself, so he'd just swear back at you. The noise in the place was deafening, with porters effing and blinding all the time.

We were paid 4d for every stone we loaded. If they were stacked right, I could carry twelve boxes, giving me 384d for every barrowload. If I did ten trips, that was 3,840d, which was sixteen pounds – more than a month's wages for many people, and an absolute fortune for three hours' work, particularly for a teenager with no academic qualifications. And sometimes, I'd earn even more, if I was asked to carry foreign fish into the market. For some reason, we were paid an extra 2d a stone for that privilege.

Working as a porter was called 'going on the stone.' In theory, we had to stand in front of the foreman and he would pick who he wanted to work for him. There was no room for favouritism or the old pal's act. Just because you were a nice bloke, or a friend of the foreman's family, wouldn't guarantee you work. All he wanted was someone he knew would load as many boxes on to those vans as possible. He could be Jack the Ripper, but if he was fit and strong and tireless, he'd get the job. I rarely failed to be taken on because everyone knew I would bust a gut for three hours to earn as much as I could. Sometimes, though, there wasn't enough work to go round and I'd go to the Labour Exchange and sign on the dole for 12s 6d.

The lane to where the vans were waiting was on St Mary's Hill and it took a lot of strength to pull my loaded barrow up that slope. Around the market were numerous homeless drunks, who slept rough until the market opened for business. We called them The Meths Boys, and they stood around hoping to earn a few pennies. All us porters soon got to know who were the best workers. I'd pick out one of them to help me pull the barrow and slip him sixpence for his help. Some of them were gone before you could blink – over at The Cock buying a pint with their tip. But there were one or two strong guys who I'd use all morning and they would help load the boxes on to my head for me to slip it on to the van. It was obviously worth my while because, with their help, I'd be at the van and unloaded, then back to the foreman for another load, in double quick time. I earned more, and so did they. Suited everybody, that little arrangement.

I loved the market, I really did. Not just because I earned a lot – but because it was fun, too. Okay, we screamed and shouted and called each other all the dirty names under the sun, but none of us meant anything by it and when we were finished for the day, we were all mates together. All the insults were forgotten and we'd sit in the café, or outside, if it was warm, with cups of tea and bacon sarnies, waiting for the foreman to come to pay us out. He'd go through his big black book, telling us how many barrowloads we'd carried, and how much we were due, and we'd all have to be right on the case, because it was well known he'd do you if he could. Until then, I was as bad with figures as I was with spelling, but working in the market wised me up. I'd totted up how many barrowloads I'd carried and I always made sure the foreman knew that, too. I wasn't going to be done out of one penny that I'd worked so hard to earn.

Despite the good money we earned, a lot of nicking went on. There was so much fish about, it was easy; everyone was at it. I mean, no one was going to miss one fish from a box of fifty, were they? Throughout the morning, I'd help myself to a plaice here, or a cod there, and hide it in a little box at the bottom of my barrow. My uncle, John, was one of the van drivers, so when I saw him in the line, in front of the Custom House office block, I'd nip over and whack the fish into the van and tell him what was there, then he'd knock it out at one of the shops on his round later that morning. I never knew what he made, but he always bunged me a couple of quid. This was great bunce and it paid for the petrol the very thirsty Chevvy was guzzling.

Lee and I nearly always drove to the market. We'd leave Ilford at 5.30 and, with few traffic lights, and no cameras to clock our speed, we'd be parked up, changed, and on 'the stones' when the six o'clock bell rang and the foremen came out to pick which porters they wanted. Sometimes, if it had been my turn to have the car and I'd found myself miles away in South London, or somewhere, at three in the morning, after taking a girl home, I'd think: what's the point in going to Ilford for two hours' sleep? And I'd drive straight to Billingsgate, hang up my gear in a plastic bag to stop the smell of fish getting to it, then put on my smock and crash out on a bench until the other porters arrived at ten to six.

In the summer, one of our best bits of fun would be winding up the office girls, walking past on their way to Custom House. A couple of us would nip into a nearby poulterer's and come back with some chicken blood, which we'd conceal in our hands until we saw a group of pretty girls approaching. When they were near enough, we'd start screaming and shouting at each other, as though we were having the most almighty row, and one of us would pick up one of the irons we used to lift the boxes of fish, and pretend to lash out with it. A couple of us would fake being hit, splosh the chicken blood on our faces, then roll around on the ground in front of the girls, as though we were dying. It always had the desired effect: the girls would scream in terror. In those days coppers actually patrolled a beat and the two on duty would come running over, thinking someone was being murdered. After a while, of course, they wised up that it was all a joke and took no notice – like the girls themselves when we whistled and called out to them. We weren't low life, but we were a right mess, all covered in slime and stinking to high heaven and, not surprisingly, not one lady ever responded to our noisy overtures. To them, we must have looked and sounded like ignorant yobs.

✳✳✳

I started going out with a seventeen-year-old girl, I met at the Palais and she took me to her home, in a block of flats, in Mile End, and introduced me to her parents. They asked me what I did for a living and when I said I worked at Billingsgate the mother asked if I would get them some fish. 'No problem,' I said. 'I'll drop some round in the week.' 'Lovely,' said the mum. 'Make it Wednesday, so I know to stay in.' I took the fish round and had a cup of tea, and it was clear the woman didn't want me to go. She started talking about her husband, how he was getting old and was always tired after work, and I could see she wanted to know. I did, too: she was in her late thirties, with long dark hair and big knockers – my type, even then – and very good-looking. I decided to try my luck and, the next minute, we were all over each other and she was leading me into her bedroom. After that, I took fish to the flat every Wednesday morning after I'd finished work. I'd think: Lovely, I'll nip round for a quickie before going home. I was well up for it and the mother was, too: it was a highly charged, lusty relationship, no strings attached, that suited us both. Whether she knew I was having it off with her daughter as well, I don't know: I didn't ask and I didn't care. I was not yet twenty and interested only in what affected me.

I had to call it a day with the daughter after three months or so, however. I sensed she could hear wedding bells and I couldn't have that. But I carried on taking fish round to her mum. Eventually, though, I got fed up with it. I left one morning, saying I'd be round next week, as usual, but I didn't turn up. Not very gallant, I know, and today I'm not proud of myself. But, as I say, I was young and selfish and didn't give a monkey's. And, besides, she never did pay me for the fish!

✳ ✳ ✳

It had never occurred to me to be a bouncer until Lee got a job on the door at the Palais. He was picking up an extra £2.5s for Saturday night and two nights in the week, which wasn't a lot, but if I could chip in that as well, it would help with the hire purchase payments and running costs for the car. I applied for the job and was interviewed by the new band manager – an effeminate, but charming man, named Nat Allen, who walked around carrying a chihuahua. I'd gone to the Palais straight from Billingsgate, dressed casually in a jacket and trousers and open-necked shirt. Nat looked at me, disappointed. 'Haven't you got a suit?' he lisped. I said I had and he asked me to come back wearing it.

I went back an hour or so later and when he saw the blue mohair suit George had given me, he smiled, warmly. 'Oh, that's immaculate,' he cooed. 'I'll have you in a nice bow tie and you can play the records on Monday nights.' I couldn't believe it. I'd gone for a job, sorting out troublemakers and now I was going to be a part-time disc jockey too!

When I first started on the door, older guys, who feared they might have trouble getting in, took liberties with me. They'd look at my baby face, curly hair, and think I was too young to be able to handle myself. 'Out of the way you little idiot,' they'd snarl, and try to force their way past me. I had to bounce a few on the pavement to make them view me differently. Generally, though, I was involved in very little trouble – certainly inside the ballroom. Lee and I made sure of that. We knew all the chaps who liked a ding-dong, so, if anything was about to go off, one of them would tip us the wink. I'd say: 'Have your little punch-up when you see me go upstairs.' Their scuffles were always sorted out by the other bouncers by the time Lee and I'd had our break and come back downstairs. One bloke I always made sure I avoided was Roy Shaw, a legendary hard man, in the Essex area. He was only a middleweight when he boxed professionally, but he'd built himself up and was easily the strongest man I'd ever encountered. He was also a nutcase, who loved a fight and biting people. At eighteen, I didn't fancy taking on a nutcase, so I definitely made sure I was on a tea break when I saw him getting into what he called his 'fighting position'.

Bouncers were entrusted with pass-out tickets to give to punters wishing to leave the dance hall, then come back in – and it didn't take us long to spot that we could use this to our advantage. On our hour's break, halfway through the evening, we'd trot across the road to The Havelock pub and sell the tickets to our mates, and anyone else who wanted them, for half the normal admission price. We would probably have got the bullet if we'd been caught, but we were sure no one was going to squeal on us if they were saving money themselves. That naughty little scam bumped up our Palais earning to four pounds each.

Playing records on Monday nights was a doddle, too. All I had to do was sit at a record stand on the stage, in my lovely blue suit and red and white dickie-bow, and say who was singing what, then put a record on. I wasn't a celebrity, but I felt like one, with all the pretty teenage girls hanging around in front of the stage, making eyes at me, trying to persuade me to play this or that record. I'd joke with them: 'Play your cards right and I'll take you home in that big motor outside.' I was a king in my own castle and I revelled in the little power I had. It was great fun, lovely fun.

One of the girls who couldn't take her eyes off me was a stunning, little blonde. I fancied her on sight and when she asked me to play Elvis Presley's 'Jailhouse Rock', I was only too happy to oblige. As soon as I finished my stint, I chatted her up and she agreed to let me run her back to her home, in Barking. I tried it on in the car, of course, but she was an innocent young kid of fifteen or so and didn't want to play any games. When we got to her home, above her parents' pie and mash shop, in Liverpool Road, we sat in the car, chatting. Suddenly she spotted someone at the door of the shop and tensed.

'Oh, God, it's my dad,' she said. 'I'm in right trouble.'

Her father strode up to the car and demanded to know what was 'going on'. Thankfully, nothing was.

'Dad,' she said. 'This is Billy Walker.'

Her father broke into a smile. 'Ah,' he said, knowingly. 'Any relation of George?'

'He's my brother,' I said, proudly.

'Good to meet you,' he said, offering his hand through the window. 'How are you?'

'I'm very well thank you,' I replied. 'How about yourself?'

The young girl could not believe it. One minute she's expecting a bollocking for staying out so late and the next, her old man's treating me like an old friend. George did me a favour that night. I arranged to see the girl again and we went out a couple of times. We had some fun, but never really got on: she was a good-looker, but far too opinionated for me. She wanted to argue all the time and never backed down. She was like a man inside a beautiful body. If she'd been big enough, she'd have stood up and had a knuckle with you. Her name was Pat Booth. And she went on to do well for herself, first as a model, then as a novelist.

✳✳✳

Early in the summer of 1957, George was released from prison, having served thirteen months of his sentence, and married Jean Hatton, the petite, blonde girl he'd been courting before he was jailed. It was a good move for George because Jean's father was wealthy and owned the garage and petrol station, in Plaistow, where I filled up the Chevvy. In no time at all, he'd put George in charge of running the garage while he used a big van to build up a local removal business.

George quickly saw the financial potential and it was good for me, too: when there wasn't any work at the market, George would give me a few quid for working the pumps and, in the summer, I'd be asked to take East Enders on hop-picking trips to farms in Kent in the removal van. Once, I invited Pat Booth to join me and we had great fun with our passengers, taking in a pub crawl en-route.

Sometimes, though, Pat and I didn't have a good time when we went out. There was one time I picked her up in Barking, for a night out in the West End, and, by the time we got to East Ham we were arguing about something stupid. The row developed and by the time we got to Stepney, I had had enough.

'If you don't shut up, I'll chuck you out of the car,' I said, loudly.

'You would never do that,' she goaded.

I stopped the car and shouted: 'Get out!'

Pat, who always wanted to win a point, shouted back: 'Don't worry – I'm getting out.'

She slammed the door and I drove off. Very ungallant, I know, but Pat was such a strong character, who made out she needed nobody, it was like leaving one of my mates to find his way home. And, in my defence, I had dumped her close to Mile End Station! We didn't speak for a couple of months, but then I rang her and we laughed about that night. We were ambitious young kids, who worked as good mates but were never destined to make it as a couple.

For us lads, the great fun that summer was jibbing into Butlin's Holiday Camp, at Clacton, which was less than an hour's drive from Ilford. More often than not, there'd be four of us – me and Lee and two friends, Jack Fairbrass and Connie Farmer. They were big lumps – well over six feet and each weighing fifteen stone or more. They were dockers, but never fighters. They were pussycats, really, but to look at their huge physiques no one would have guessed. If Lee and I had had a good week at the market, we'd arrange cover for the Palais, and all pile in the Chevvy and bomb down to Clacton. Sometimes, Lee and I did a Saturday shift at the market to earn enough to cover what we'd have got on the door, so we would leave early in the afternoon. We'd park discreetly round the back of Butlin's, away from Reception, then climb over the high wall surrounding the camp. That was the easy bit. Far more difficult was beating the system they had devised to help its patrolling security guards prevent interlopers like us enjoying the amenities for nothing.

Holidaymakers slept in wooden huts, roughly 14ft by 12ft. They were called chalets and each one had its own key. Anyone suspected of not being a genuine paid-up camper would be asked to produce their key. If they couldn't, they were turfed out. If they tried to con the guard that a mate had it, they would have to prove it. No key meant instant expulsion. The aim for each of us lads was to get chatting to a girl as quickly as possible and persuade her to let us carry her key. It wouldn't matter if the girl was unattractive and you weren't going to have a game with her; you just had to kid her along to get the key. If you didn't, you'd have nowhere to sleep and would have to kip in the car. That's why we always left the car keys under one of the wheels. It says much for our charm and powers of persuasion that the car was rarely used!

I fell on my feet with one young beauty who sorted us all out for a few visits. She was the manager of the Wallis shop concession on the camp and she arranged a chalet whenever I wanted it: all I had to do was give her a few days' notice. This was great because it meant me and the gang would have a place to wash and get dressed before going out to enjoy ourselves in the camp's bars and ballroom – not just a place to sleep in. But the bad news for me was that I was stuck with the same girl every time we went there. After a while, I wanted to dump her and have fun with different girls, like my mates, but they wouldn't let me because they loved having a regular chalet. In the end, I had to call it a day. It was getting ridiculous. I was only eighteen, but I felt like I was married!

If the weather was nice, we'd jib in every other weekend. Being the size we were, we hardly faded into the background and, inevitably, there were times we got caught with no key to produce. We always left quietly, but, once through the exit door, we slipped round the back and climbed back in again, making sure not to be spotted by the same guard. Many of the guards knew we had no right to be there, but turned a blind eye – not simply because we looked too tough to confront, but because we were clearly there to spend money having a good time, not to cause trouble. Unfortunately, there were two silly guys who didn't turn a blind eye, where I was concerned. And I'm sorry to say that one of them paid a heavy price.

I was asked to show my key and produced it. But one of the guards sussed I wasn't a camper and ordered me to leave. I handed the key to the girl who'd lent it to me, then brazenly told her I'd get back in and see her later. That was a mistake, because the younger guard – a flash sod – grabbed my shirt and ripped it. 'I'm warning you – DON'T come back!' he said, threateningly. In a split-second, a red mist came over me and I lost it. I smacked him in the mouth, knocking him to the ground. Then I gave him a couple more. His mate tried to grab me, so I gave him a couple, too. I wasn't proud of myself, but I felt they were out of order, because I'd accepted that I had to leave and was going on my way, quietly. Okay, it was a mistake, making it so obvious I was going to jib back in, but I wasn't there to cause trouble.

Worried that the camp would call the law, I decided not to go back over the wall and slept in the car. That's where Lee and the others found me in the morning. They said they'd seen a guard with a black eye, busted nose and swollen lip and wondered who'd done him. I owned up it was me and told them it had been lovely while it lasted but my Butlin's jibbing days were over.

✴ ✴ ✴

At the West Ham gym, Billy Walker obviously saw something in me, for, almost as soon as we were back in training that Autumn in 1957, he said he was going to arrange for me to fight someone else. I wasn't that interested. I was getting hold of a few girls by then, and having a lot of fun. And, as boxing was never going to play any part in my life, I couldn't see the point. But Billy went on and on and, in the end, I said I'd have a word with my brother to see what he thought. George was shocked that I was even considering taking up boxing, but said that if I wanted to go ahead, he'd come to the gym and give me a few pointers.

The guy Billy chose to fight me was called Van Helsen. He sounded foreign, but was as cockney as jellied eels. He was a light-heavyweight of twelve and a half stone, but I was still down to nearly thirteen stone, so there wasn't much in it. There was a big difference in class, though: whereas I was rough and ungainly and couldn't get near him, Van Helsen was fast and skilful and, from the start, boxed my head off. But then, suddenly, I landed a right hand on the chin and it hurt him. He didn't go down, but, from then on, he was very wary, and treated me with respect. Afterwards, George told me that Billy Walker had said: 'I don't think your brother's got it. I don't think he'll make it.' But George had seen how hard I could hit and told him: 'He's got something we can work on.'

I had so much faith in George that I believed him. At the same time, if he'd said I didn't have what it takes to make a fighter, I'd have given up there and then and thought no more about it. So, when he said: 'Let's work hard together and see how far you can go', I said, 'Yes', immediately.

After all, I'd trusted him all my life. Never once had I disagreed with anything he'd said.

For most of that year, the awful spectre of National Service had been looming over me. But there was a lot of talk about it being abolished, and when the Government kept deferring it, I thought I was going to escape. Shortly after the Van Helsen fight, however, I got a letter, summoning me to go for a medical. Bloody hell, I thought, I don't need this.

I didn't have the nous to consider that two years in the RAF – which is what I'd have wanted to join – would have been a positive experience; that I could have had a cushy life, done a lot of boxing, and maybe come out good enough to win the ABA title. Apart from that, I was enjoying life as a carefree teenager and the thought of being stuck for two boring years with a bunch of wankers in some godforsaken hole miles from anywhere filled me with dread.

George wasn't thrilled, either. He saw it as two years in which he could turn me not only into an amateur champion, but a fighter good enough to go pro and start earning big money. So he devised a cunning plan to cause me to fail the medical.

I had to play an idiot, who didn't have the brains to be any use in any of the military services. He persuaded two doctors to write letters, confirming my poor mental ability and, to give the plan an air of authenticity on the day, arranged for me to be dressed as Norman Wisdom, a famous comic actor, who played the archetypal simpleton on TV and in the movies. Norman squeezed into a suit far too small for him, so George borrowed a cheap suit from someone smaller than me. Norman also wore a stupid-looking check cap, so George got me one, too.

When I looked in the mirror, I thought: Good God, Walker, you look ridiculous. But George was delighted. 'Perfect,' he said. 'You look a complete dummy.' Thanks, George, I thought.

'Are you coming with me?' I asked.

'No,' he said. 'I don't look the part. I don't look silly enough.'

Instead, he enlisted the help of a mate called Johnny Murphy, a huge, lumbering former boxer, whose battered face bore all the hallmarks of a bruising career in the ring – cauliflower ear, flat nose that went right across his face, the works. He wasn't thick, not by a long way, but, my God, he looked it.

The medical was being held in a small hall at the back of the Rialto cinema, in Wanstead, and before I left to go there from George's place, he thrust something in my hand. It was the *Beano*, a popular children's comic. 'Take that with you,' he said. 'And when you get there, start reading it. All the time. And, don't forget – you're an idiot. Act the idiot.'

When we arrived, I was asked my name by one of two men in pin-stripe suits, sitting behind a desk in the centre of the hall. I made out I didn't understand why they wanted to know, and Johnny told them. Then, just before leaving me to it, he told the men: 'Gents, if there's any problem with him, I'll be right outside.'

'What sort of problem?' one of them asked.

'No, he won't be a problem,' Johnny said. 'But, you know, if he acts up and causes you any trouble, just call me.' Then he gave me a whack round the ear. 'Now, behave yourself, Billy,' he said, and walked out.

I'd put in for the RAF and had to sit a written examination to see if I was suitable. The questions were so simple and straightforward a child could have answered them, but I gave stupid answers in babyish writing. When I finished, I sat there, seemingly engrossed in my comic, before being called to take the medical. Remembering George's words, I went on and on jabbering about how fit and strong I was, and how much I was going to enjoy flying areroplanes like my dad and brother. The doctor and his staff were most understanding and considerate and did their best to calm me down, so that they could examine me.

When it was over, I quickly started reading my comic, as though it was the most fascinating publication I'd ever seen. Twenty minutes later, I went before the two enlistment officers again. 'We're terribly sorry to have to tell you, Mr Walker,' one of them said. 'But you are not qualified to join the RAF.'

I dropped my head, feigning disappointment, and stamped my foot. 'But I WANT to,' I said loudly. 'My dad and brother were in the RAF. Why can't I be in the RAF as well?'

'We have had to pass you as Grade Four,' he said.

'What's that?' I asked, open-mouthed in childish bewilderment.

'It means you'll only be called up in an emergency, like a war.'

'Oh,' I said.

As I turned to leave, the man put a consoling arm round me. 'The best thing you can do, son, is volunteer for the Army.'

'Yeah,' I replied, quietly. 'I might do that.'

Johnny was waiting for me when I came out and I told him the good news. Then we went to the nearest pub to phone George. I couldn't wait to tell him that his plan had worked a treat.

'Grade Four,' I said, jubilantly.

'Lovely,' he said. 'Now we can get down to business.'

5

Throughout the winter, I took in everything George told me and, by the end of the year, was ready for my first competitive contest for the club, on 16 January 1958. I was the first fight on, at West Ham Baths, and George and the rest of them were anxious, wondering how I would perform. Would I go in there and throw powerful punches as I had in the gym – or would I lose my bottle and freeze? Certainly I didn't feel scared: just pumped up. Now that my big night had arrived, I was eager to get on with it and do well.

My opponent, was a guy named Terry Drudge, from the Sir Philip Game Club in Croydon, and as soon as the bell rang, I rushed towards him, just one thought on my mind: to land a right hand on his chin. I swung three hooks and missed. But Terry was obviously shocked by the speed of my onslaught because his guard dropped and he caught the next right-hander on the point of the jaw, and went down. I stood in a neutral corner, staring at him, spreadeagled on the canvas, as the referee counted him out. It was the first time I'd knocked anyone out and, frankly, I was amazed how easy it had been. The fight was scheduled for three, two-minute rounds, but I'd finished it in just twenty-eight seconds – so fast they hadn't had time to turn the house lights off!

Until that night, I wasn't sure I could fight competitively. But the knockout gave me a surge of confidence and I felt invincible. I thought:

I *can* do this. We went back to the garage and celebrated with the family. Everyone was delighted, none more so than George: he had seen the evidence of what his instinct had told him about my wicked right hand. It was, indeed, something we could work on.

The next day, everyone at Billingsgate seemed pleased for me, too – particularly my mate, Terry Warren, who'd been a good amateur boxer himself – but the reaction at the Palais that evening took my breath away. Not only my mates, but people I barely knew, came up to shake my hand, anxious to tell me how good I was and how pleased and proud they were for me. Suddenly, I sensed a respect for me that maybe hadn't been there before. I did my best to be modest, but I revelled in the praise, basked in it. Having trained so hard and succeeded in such spectacular style, I felt a terrific sense of achievement. And as someone who'd always wanted to be a lover, not a fighter, it was a bonus that the ladies seemed more interested than they had been before. Going home that night, I was walking a foot above the ground!

I was keen to get back in the ring, but didn't fight again until the third week in April when I was outpointed by Mick Gannon in the semi-final of a novice's competition, organised by the City of London Police, at Bishopsgate. The defeat was a bitter disappointment I was keen to get over, but I didn't get a chance, because West Ham couldn't find me any opponents. The following November, however, after an ad in the trade paper, *Boxing News*, I was lined up against George Newell, a promising twenty-one-year-old from Bradfield Club, in Peckham, South London.

George came into the ring, at West Ham, confident after a points win the previous month, but I was far too powerful for him and the fight was stopped in the first round. Another quick victory restored my confidence and I followed this up a month later by beating an Italian-born fighter, Sergio Parkins, in the final of a St. Pancras Club tournament, at Kentish Town. Sergio, who had sparred with the then ABA champion, Dave Thomas, had reached the final with two knockouts, and George told me not to get into a fight with him 'because he's a banger.' I took his advice and achieved a highly satisfying points victory.

That winter, the Palais announced it was closing for refurbishment. Lee and I had to find alternative employment to help run our cars, so we took on a job, looking after a little disco, above the Royal Oak, in Green Lanes, Dagenham. All we had to do for a pound each a night was stand at the door to ensure that nobody jibbed in after 10.30. It was a doddle and we'd take turns doing it on our own. If the job had interfered with my boxing, I probably would have chucked in the boxing, because I needed money more. But it didn't and I just made sure I stuck at my training at the gym and kept the fight nights free.

I was brought down to earth again at West Ham in January 1959, however, when I lost on points to Len Hobbs, a Grenadier Guardsman, but five weeks later I stopped a Frenchman, Albert Roussel, in the first round, in a team match against Ring Olympique, in Dieppe; George now considered me good enough to enter the North-East London Divisional Championship – a preliminary stage of the prestigious ABA Championships. This was an exciting prospect: if I could get through the divisional section, I'd compete in the London Championships at the Albert Hall and, if I won that, I'd go through to the national finals, which were televised live from Wembley's Empire Pool, the sporting arena a few hundred yards from the historic football stadium. *Boxing News* did not agree with George: it felt that, with only a handful of fights under my belt, not all successful, I should wait another year to gain more experience. But the paper was confident I'd walk through the divisionals, which was George's logic.

Surprisingly, there were only two entries for the divisional stage – me and a guy named John Bailey, from King's Lynn. We met at the famous York Hall, in Bethnal Green, three weeks after my twentieth birthday, and I had him down twice in the first round before the referee stopped the contest.

Before that fight, few people in the amateur boxing world knew anything about me. But they did now. Word was spreading that there was a new kid on the block: a big, strong kid, who packed a meaty punch and didn't hang about throwing it.

✳✳✳

Shortly before the London finals, on 9 April, Lee and I decided to sell the Chevvy and buy our own cars. He went for a Zephyr Zodiac, me a sporty, four-door Sunbeam Talbot, with a sliding roof. The Sunbeam was only a two-door, so I devised a way to hold the front seats forward by tying them with string attached to the sun roof. This gave me more room in the back when I got hold of a pretty girl. I was full of what a twenty-year-old boy should be full of. I was fit and strong and healthy. I had money in my pocket, and a smart car that helped me pull all the birds I wanted. And now, little more than a year after my first competitive contest, I was about to step in the ring at the famous Albert Hall, where some of Britain's most famous boxers had fought. What a stage on which to demonstrate my power, show off my potential.

That Spring, I felt that life could not get much better. It was, most definitely, Happy Days.

✳ ✳ ✳

There were four of us in the finals – Dave Ould, an eighteen-year-old from the Fisher Club, Bermondsey; a guy I'd never heard of, Billy Wells, from Wandsworth; and Dave Thomas, a dustman from the Polytechnic Club, in Regent Street, who had won the ABA national title for the past two years and had been runner-up in the Commonwealth Games. I was thrilled to have got this far and didn't care who I fought in my semi-final, but was delighted when I was drawn out of the hat to fight Wells, because he was a flash sod. When he heard he'd got me, he said, loudly to his mates: 'Great. We're in the final,' meaning I was a nobody and he couldn't lose. He was a fool to be so cocky because it made me angry and, in the second round, I thrashed him so badly the referee stopped the fight. I honestly felt it was my night and, later, in the final, I tore into Dave Thomas the moment the bell sounded. I rocked him with some juicy right-handers, but he boxed his way out of trouble over the next two rounds, and his experience finally earned him a points win.

I was disappointed, but not down-hearted. Well, not for long, anyway. As George had said, 'You can't win 'em all.' And there was bound to be another day when I'd meet Dave again, and maybe beat him. Right now, I was less concerned with feeling sorry for myself than going out with my mates and having a few bevvies and a laugh. Then there was the summer to think about. With the boxing season over, I wasn't going to give fighting or training another thought. What was the point of dreaming about winning the ABA title when there was booze to be drunk and girls to get hold of. First on the agenda was a holiday at Butlin's. Lee and I, and a couple of pals, had booked a couple of weeks at Clacton in June – paying for our chalets, for a change – and that meant fun. Lots of it. I couldn't wait.

The weekend before our holiday, I was on the door at the Royal Oak, shortly after eleven, when this big lump came up the stairs and tried to go past me. 'I'm sorry,' I said, politely. 'You know the rules – no one after 10.30.' The guy, who was about ten years older than me, sneered: 'Yeah, yeah, I know that,' then put a hand to the side of my face, pushed me aside, and walked into the disco. I went after him and touched his shoulder. I was going to ask him to leave, but he threw a punch at me. I ducked inside it and, bosh! hit him with a right hand, knocking him down. Then I bundled him outside and pushed him down the stairs.

I thought that was the end of it, but a couple of minutes later, the guy came up again and grabbed me. Somehow, we ended up grappling on the floor among all the young dancers. I got up, dragging him with me, and smacked him hard on the chin, knocking him out. Another guy who worked there helped me carry him down the stairs and into the street. By now, the idiot had come round and I stuck my face into his. 'Now fuck off,' I growled. 'I've had it with you.'

I went back upstairs, unhurt, but shaken by the experience. Jesus, I don't need this aggravation, I thought. Not for a quid. When the disco closed, I collected my money, said goodbye to the staff, and walked across the car park to my Sunbeam Talbot. Suddenly, out of nowhere, was the prat who'd attacked me. 'I'll have you now, you fucking bastard,' he said, and lunged at me. I was so pissed off, I lost it totally. I laid into him and really worked him over and, by the time I'd finished, my shirt was ripped and my suit spattered with blood.

The next morning, mum saw the state of my clothes and gave me a right bollocking. When she asked what had happened, I made light of it, sounding more concerned about my suit. I didn't dare go into details about my fight, because all mums are worriers and she wouldn't have left me alone. Actually, I *was* concerned about the suit: in those days, young guys had just one – for best – and I knew that mine would have to be professionally cleaned and wouldn't be ready by the time we left for Butlin's. I was choked that I was not going to look my best for all those beauties waiting for me. In the end, mum, bless her, saved the day: she picked up the newly-cleaned suit on the Saturday we left, and posted it to the camp. It arrived on Tuesday and, that night, I put it on, proudly. I now felt complete and ready to pull. Which I did with impunity!

Something mum asked in our morning-after *tête-à-tête* nagged at me on that holiday: why, when I was earning good money at the market, did I have to stand on doors and risk getting hurt? It was a good question. Why did I put myself on offer to morons, high on booze and bravado, who fancied themselves in a punch-up? Okay, I was unlikely to come off worst in a knuckle, but if I seriously hurt someone it could kill what hopes I had of a boxing career. Not only that: a lot of yobs were now going out, tooled up and my experience in the ring would be no match for a knife – or worse.

When I got back from Butlin's I handed in my notice at the Palais and told the Royal Oak they would have to find another doorman. My bouncing days were over.

✳✳✳

George felt I needed to take training more seriously and arranged for me to spar at the gym above the Thomas A'Beckett, a pub in the Old Kent Road, the other side of the water, which was well known by boxers and newspapermen. The gym was run by Joe Lucy, a former British lightweight champion, who had been a porter with George at Billingsgate. Sometimes, I'd spar with Tommy Gibbons, a good light heavyweight, who owned the pub, but more often than not, Joe or Tommy would ring George and tell him when useful boxers were coming to the pub and we'd go over and I'd spar with them.

It was commonplace for famous fighters of the past to drop in at the Beckett and take a look at promising newcomers and, one day, Freddie Mills turned up to watch me work out. I was thrilled: Freddie was a brave, popular fighter, who won the World light heavyweight title in 1948, and one of my heroes. After I'd finished sparring, I stretched out, face down, on the treatment table for my rub-down, listening to George telling Freddie about his plans for me. Suddenly, I felt a hand gently squeeze my left leg, then my arm, and heard Freddie say: 'Oh, yes, George. He's a really lovely boy. He's in great shape.' Without moving my head, I caught George's eye on the other side of the table and surreptitiously crooked my right forefinger. George answered with his eyes and, equally surreptitiously, put a finger to his lips, indicating I should say nothing. I lay there, shocked. I knew next to nothing about homosexuality and the thought had never crossed my mind that one of Britain's most famous fighters – a huge household name – might be what was then known as a 'queer'.

✳ ✳ ✳

I had five more fights in 1959, winning four of them, two in the first round. I beat Ken Potter – half-brother of the great British heavyweight champion Don Cockell – on points in October and in the return two months later. I knocked out Ernie Ball, from Stoke, in less than two minutes, in November, and forced a German, Hober Helfer, to retire in the first round in a North East Divisional v Middle Rhine competition at York Hall, in December. The only fight I lost was on points to my old Army adversary Len Hobbs, at the annual London v the Army contest, at Seymour Hall, in Marylebone, at the end of November. And that was a fight I feel I should have won. I had Len down for an 'eight' count in the first and felt I was on top for most of the three rounds. But he got the verdict. I had some consolation, however: at the start of that series of fights I was rated No. 6 British amateur heavyweight. By the end, I was No. 5. George and I felt it had been a good year: I'd had fourteen fights and, apart from my novice defeat, I'd only lost twice – to the ABA champion and the best heavyweight in the Army. For someone who hadn't wanted to take up boxing, that wasn't bad. Things could only get better.

Or, so I thought.

I had a chance to avenge my ABA defeat by Dave Thomas when we faced each other again at Romford Road Baths on the second Thursday in January, 1960. But, again, he kept jabbing out that long left hand and I couldn't get near him. I caught him a few times in the third and he began to tire, but the bell came too soon and I needed another round. My supporters booed the referee's decision, but it was the right one: Dave's experience had proved too much yet again. How I wished I could have a six-rounder with him!

Five weeks later, *Boxing News* rated me as the No. 2 British amateur heavyweight; and no one, it seemed, wanted to fight me. West Ham Boxing Club even wrote to the French champion, seeking a match, but never got a reply. Then, when I'd almost given up hope, Len 'Rocky' James, an experienced boxer from the Patchway Club, in Bristol, came on, saying he fancied a rumble. We fixed it for the following week, and I oozed confidence as I climbed into the ring at Romford Road Baths. Confidence? That's a laugh. I was cocky. Lairey. Having won seven fights inside the distance, six in the first round, I really did believe I was Whirlwind Walker, the Invincible Man. And when I landed my trusty right hand on Rocky's chin and he slumped to the canvas, I assumed it was going to be business as usual. But Rocky got up and came back at me. I clubbed him another vicious right hook and down he went again. I thought that must be it, but he got up and before I could do him a third time, the bell went.

I went back to my corner, deflated. 'Don't worry, I'll do him next round,' I told George, cockily. 'Be careful,' he said. 'Take it easy.' But I was too pumped up, too full of myself to listen, and when the bell went, I moved casually to the centre of the ring, arms by my side, chin jutting out arrogantly. I was sure I could pick him off how and when I liked – easily. But it didn't work out like that. While I was caught up in my stupid egomania, Rocky threw a long, loopy right hook. I saw it coming from the floor, but instead of going forward and letting the punch go round the side of my head, I went backwards and copped one right on the chin. I went down like the proverbial sack of potatoes, my thirteen stones crashing on the canvas with a sickening thump. I got to my feet slowly and staggered towards Rocky, trying to clear my head enough to throw my right hand. But I was clearly in no shape to defend myself and, after seeing me take two more whacks to the head, the referee stopped the fight. The next I knew, George was in the ring, gently guiding me to our corner.

All my mates were there, as usual, and I felt so embarrassed, not just because I'd lost, but because I'd got done by showing off, by being Jack the Lad. Afterwards, everyone tried to comfort me, saying I was the better fighter and should have won; that I'd been caught by a lucky punch. I appreciated their support, but it did little to allay the fear and doubt Rocky had instilled in me. Until that loopy right hook, I believed no one could knock me over. I really did. But now I was thinking: if *he* could, maybe other fighters could, too. And not with lucky loopy punches, either! I tried to make light of my defeat but, deep down, I was terribly hurt and ashamed for being so cocky.

And when I got home, I sat on my bed and cried.

Over the next few days, I decided I'd had enough: I was going to chuck it in. I'd never wanted to fight in the first place, so why should I continue? All the time I was knocking my opponents over quickly, all the time it was easy and fun, I'd loved it. But, now, I felt humiliated and stupid. And very vulnerable. Losing so badly had made it all very serious and I didn't like it. I wanted to go back to the life I'd been enjoying before putting on the gloves. I wanted to go out and have a good drink and a laugh without worrying about my fitness. I wanted some carefree fun back in my life.

George left me alone because he knew how devastated I was. But when I told him I was turning it in, he gave me a right bollocking. 'You'd be a fucking idiot if you do,' he said. 'You CAN fight. And if you were to win the ABA title and go pro, you could make a lot of money. *Lots* of it. You were a flash bastard with James. You went out there, leading with your chin. Anyone could have knocked you over. It was your own fucking silly fault. You had him down twice and should have beaten him easily. We'll get him again, don't worry. And you'll knock him over, I know you will.'

I wasn't convinced. But then we learned that no one had entered the North East Divisionals for the ABA Championship and George said I'd be a mug not to put my name down and go through to the London finals on a walk-over. Dave Thomas was favourite to win the national title for the fourth time and I was unlikely to beat him, he said. But I might win the semi-final and fighting Thomas a third time would be invaluable experience.

Once again, I had to agree that George was right. I did my best to put the humiliating James defeat behind me. We called off a scheduled re-match at the Round House, Dagenham, on 24 March. And I started getting myself together for whoever I was to face at the Albert Hall.

✳ ✳ ✳

My opponent in the semi-final, on 13 April, was Ken Potter, whom I'd beaten twice on points in the last six months. They'd been close encounters, and the Albert Hall crowd were expecting another bruising battle, going the distance. They didn't get it. Unfortunately for Ken, I knocked him down with a beauty of a right hand in the first minute and he didn't stand a chance. He took an 'eight' count, but was clearly in a world of his own and I was on him, before he got himself together, hurling leather from all directions. I half-punched, half-pushed him down again and he rolled halfway under the bottom rope, winding up on his back. The demolition job had taken just 2min 40sec. I was in my second London ABA final later that night – to fight Dave Thomas, who had beaten a South African, Jim Danielson, in the other semi.

My quick victory inspired me and I went into the fight confident of landing a similar heavy right early on that would stop Dave getting into his rhythm, and make him fight, not box. I did land a peach on the jaw that made his legs buckle, but he got on his bike, back-pedalling and, again, I found it hard getting past that long left hand. Although I went to my corner after the first round with a bloody nose, I felt I'd done okay and was ready for more of the same in the second. The crowd were yelling as I steamed in, throwing punches in my usual style but, unfortunately, most of them were wild and didn't hurt Dave, or missed him altogether. Then, I was floored by a left hook and had to take an 'eight' count. It cost me the round and I knew I had to go for broke in the third because I was so far behind. I gave it everything I had and we slugged it out for the final three minutes to a continuous, deafening roar. I honestly thought I'd done enough to snatch the verdict. So did George. But the judges gave it to Dave the Dustman – and he was Wembley-bound, in search of his fourth successive national ABA title. He didn't get it: he lost to Len Hobbs in the semi-final.

In the dressing room afterwards, George insisted that I'd deserved to beat Thomas and was sure Dave got the decision because he'd been selected to represent Britain in the Rome Olympics that summer. It didn't matter a damn to me *why* I hadn't been given the verdict. I had lost the fight and that was that. I didn't like it, but there was nothing I could do about it.

I just wanted to get out, put it all behind me, and have some fun.

6

A few weeks later, George asked me to go to the garage for a serious chat. He'd been doing some thinking, he said; and he could never see me beating Dave Thomas unless I had more time, or got fitter and did better in an earlier round. 'The only way you'll win the ABA is if you take boxing more seriously,' he said. 'You have to give up the late nights and booze, and train like a pro.'

That didn't sound like much fun to me. And I said so. 'I'm only twenty-one, George. Why should I stop having fun with my mates when I don't know if I can make it as a fighter anyway?'

George looked me straight in the eye. 'Trust me. You've got tremendous potential. Look at the fights you've won. Look at the guys you've knocked over. Believe me, you've got what it takes to be a good fighter. Even a great one.'

Noticing I wasn't sure, George looked at me intently for several seconds, then said: 'Do you want to be a market porter all your life, Billy? It's all right now. You're young and strong. But what about when you're forty and the muscles begin to ache? Do you still want to be pulling barrows then? In the pissing rain? Trust me. If you can win the ABA and go pro, you could make a lot of money. You could make enough to have all the fun you want. Why not give it a couple of years? If it doesn't work out, you'll still be young enough to go back to doing what you are now.'

I didn't need a lot of convincing. George knew what he was talking about. He knew the fight game because he'd won the ABA and fought for the British title as a pro. And he knew Billingsgate because he'd done that, too.

But most of all, he understood my hunger to get more of the fun things in life. That took money. And, for me, there were only two ways to get that – fighting or thieving. And George had taught me that crime did not pay: the holidays I wanted were not those at Her Majesty's pleasure. I'd had a taste of success and the respect it brought, and I wanted more of that, too. But, realistically, money was the problem. Even if I was going to knock boozing on the head, I still needed to live.

'Come and work for me at the garage,' George said. 'You can work on the pumps. I'll give you a few quid. The rest of the time, I'll train you. We'll make next year's ABA's our goal. Dedicate yourself for six months, Billy, and you'll walk it. Promise.'

I thought the world of George, admired and respected him so much, and I was carried along on his wave of enthusiasm and belief. I knew I wasn't the most skilful fighter, but if power and courage counted for anything I might stand a chance. And with George behind me, giving me the benefit of his vast experience, that chance had to be a good one. I said I'd give it a go when I came back from a holiday that me and half a dozen mates at Billingsgate had booked at a new-style holiday club, in Southern Italy. We were going to be away all of August, and George suggested I took Tommy McCarthy with me – as it was my first holiday abroad, I think he wanted someone to keep an eye on me. I didn't mind. Tommy was ten years older than me, but he didn't look or act it. Like me, he was a bit of a rascal, who liked a drink and a bird and, as the holiday club was for young people, there was certain to be lots of both.

Setting off for Paris, and the two-day train journey to Palinuro, on the western coast, I was more excited than I could remember. Not only was it my first holiday abroad, but, for the first time, I had an aim in life. Four weeks in the Italian sun, not worrying about my fitness, would be heavenly. Then, when I got back, I'd put myself in George's hands and focus only on what he showed and told me. I had so much faith and trust in him that I believed I could achieve what he said. I was so fired up, enthusiastic about what lay ahead, that I couldn't wait to get the holiday under way.

Club Mediterranean was the ideal place for a young guy or girl seeking sun, sand and sex. It was exclusively for eighteen to thirty-year-olds and everyone slept in sleeping bags, in straw huts, with sand on the floor. Our meals and wine were all-inclusive but, to distinguish us from any of the locals who might have jibbed in, we bought different coloured beads, which we used as currency in the disco and bar. We helped ourselves to wine from huge vats, and all sorts of food, in a large open-air communal eating area. Everyone could sit where they liked, which I thought was great because it was an easy way to get chatting to anyone you fancied. Not that I waited that long! My mates and I quickly discovered that the best way to beat the other guys was to go to the local railway station and watch the new arrivals get off the train. Something else I quickly learned was that the girls were mainly French – and, if they didn't speak English, it could be hard-going. I'd go up to one I fancied and ask in my best Ilford French: 'Parlez-vous Anglais?' If they did, it would be: 'Hello, darling, how you doing?' – and off we'd go. Call me arrogant, or lazy, but I didn't bother to try to chat up any girl who didn't speak English, no matter how beautiful they were, because there were so many tasty ones who did.

Most of the guys at the club were French, too, and we'd been there a week when my mates urged me to take on one of them, as a matter of national pride. If I'd had to fight in the ring, I wouldn't have been interested – I was on holiday, for God's sake – but all I had to do was sit astride a greasy pole and try to knock the other guy off with a pillow. I couldn't resist it because, the previous week, we'd seen this big, athletic-looking lump – one of the club's 'monitors' – fight off all challengers, and I was sure I could beat him. As we faced each other on the pole, I clenched the pillow tightly in my right hand, like a huge glove, and waited for him to take a swing. When he did, he missed slightly and, thanks to my boxing timing, I went, bosh!, with my right before he could recover his balance, and he fell off. He wasn't too happy: not only was he used to winning the competition every week, but he and everyone else had to sing the British national anthem, which he clearly didn't care for.

Our national pride was boosted even more a few days later when the nine of us joined a load of French guys on a boat trip. Seeing us knocking back the wine, Monsieur 'Monitor' warned Tommy: 'Be careful. It can make you very drunk.'

'Don't worry, pal,' Tommy said. 'The lads can handle their drink.'

Froggy didn't look convinced, but when we got back to the shore after an afternoon at sea, all the French guys were so drunk we had to carry them off the boat. That didn't do much for ze old entente cordiale, either!

✳✳✳

That month in Palinuro was the most enjoyable holiday I'd ever had and, having indulged myself in all the pleasures befitting a healthy, virile twenty-one-year-old, I returned home, eager to lose the half stone I'd put on, and get into shape. I hadn't been back two weeks, however, when a lie I'd told came back to haunt me.

It started with a phone call from Tommy.

'You know, that girl you had some fun with?'

There had been several, so I asked him for a bit more information.

'The Belgian,' he said.

'Brigitte?' I ventured.

'Yes,' Tommy said.

'Well?'

'She's here. She's come over to see you. To stay with you.'

'WHAT!'

'She's just phoned me,' Tommy said. 'She said you told her you loved her, and would see her after the holiday.'

Shit!

I really did like the girl and we'd had a great time – in and out of the sleeping bag. And I did tell her I loved her. And I did say I'd write and we'd meet again. But I hadn't meant it. Of course, I hadn't. It was just chat. That's why I'd given her Tommy's phone number, not mine. I thought she might ring, but – turn up, with no warning?! Fucking hell! What was I to do about that? Ask mum and dad to put her up for a few days?

One thing was certain: I wasn't going to let her get in the way of my training. What I did was: I bottled it. I didn't see the girl. I was a coward, and I ducked it and let Tommy deal with it. She stayed with him for a couple of days, then he took her to the airport and sent her home. She was in a state most of the time, apparently, saying she loved me so much and thought I loved her. I felt terrible, but I was only twenty-one, with my whole life ahead of me, and not ready to tie myself down.

That dreadful experience taught me a lesson: never tell someone you love them unless you mean it. And, after that, I never did.

***

I got up for training every morning at 5 a.m. Sometimes, I'd sleep at Ilford, and drive to the garage. If I'd been manning the pumps while George and Jean went out, I'd stay over. But always, no matter where I'd been the night before, I got out of bed at 5 a.m. and we'd be on the road as soon as possible after that. George would cycle ahead on a bike, taking me about five miles, from the garage in New Barn Street, on to the A13 and then the Beckton by-pass, and back. Most of the time I jogged steadily, but George made me sprint every so often and, by the time we got back home, and I'd done my sit-ups and press-ups, I was knackered. I'd have a shower, sleep for a few hours, have some lunch, then do a couple of hours on the pumps. At 4 p.m., George would drive us to the gym at The Black Lion and we'd spend hours in the ring, with George, a heavy pad on his right hand, coaching me on the correct way to punch. I didn't appreciate, until he told me, that to be really effective, you have to dip the hips, not rely solely on the arm.

At first, getting up so early and punishing my body so much, was a chore I dreaded. But the harder I worked and better I became, the more I enjoyed training. And having kicked the boozy late nights into touch, the more I looked forward to spending the evenings with George and Jean and sleeping over. The house had a kitchen-cum-dining room that looked out on to the forecourt, so we could see when motorists pulled in, wanting petrol. We took it in turns to go out and serve and we got so passionate about a card game, called Kaluki, that whoever had to go out took their cards with them, in case the other two cheated!

I loved those evenings, I really did. They were fun. And George was, too. I could not see anything ever changing between us, only getting better.

***

I had a fight arranged at Grange Road Baths, in Bermondsey, in October, but George withdrew me from it. I have no idea why. George organised all the fights and I never questioned his judgement. I was due to fight the ABA champion, Len Hobbs, at Forest Gate the following month, but *he* had to pull out because of an eye injury and George wouldn't accept 'Rocky' James as a substitute. We were despairing of finding a suitable opponent when Dave Thomas withdrew from the annual London ABA versus the Army tournament and I was selected to replace him – against, ironically, Len Hobbs, whose eye injury had healed. Len, who was also the Army heavyweight champion, had surrendered his Sergeant rank to Lance-Corporal to give him more time to train, so we were each at our physical best when we faced each other at Seymour Hall, in Marylebone, on 24 November 1960.

That night, I proved to myself – and George, of course – that I had, indeed, come on a lot, because I out-pointed Len, partly avenging my two previous defeats. I was thrilled to have beaten the reigning ABA champion. And my performance obviously impressed the Hobbs camp, because his trainer came up to me after the fight, eager to know how old I was.

'Twenty-one,' I said.

'Why aren't you doing National Service?' he asked.

'I'm Grade Four,' I said, dead-pan.

The trainer looked at me, disbelievingly, then patted me on the head. 'Good luck, son,' he said, smiling. He knew I'd pulled a flanker.

✳✳✳

I rounded off a satisfying year with a points win over a Birkenhead farmer, Robin Jones, at the East India Hall, in Poplar, on 9 December, and was thrilled to be chosen to represent England in a team match against Scotland early in the New Year.

My opponent, a light heavyweight named Tom Menzies, was deputising for my scheduled rival, who'd been injured. And if I needed any proof of how important George was to me, how much I relied on him, I got it in the first round, that Friday night, 5 January, in Glasgow. I'd travelled up with the team and George went separately, but when I arrived at the venue, Storemont Hall, he wasn't there. I didn't think anything of it at first because I was tenth, and last on, but, nearly two hours later, when I was called to the ring, and he still wasn't there, I began to worry. It wasn't like George: he was never late for my fights; if anything, he was early, always wanting to be in the dressing room, with plenty of time to get me warmed up and in the right frame of mind. Had he had an accident? Was he lying injured somewhere?

Maybe he'd even been . . . no, I couldn't go there! As I walked to the ring, my worry gave way to panic. In all my fights, George had always been in my corner; I admired and respected him so much, our bond was so close, that sometimes I swear I could feel his presence in the ring with me, willing me on.

And, quite honestly, I didn't think I could perform without him.

When the bell went, I was thinking more about George than Menzies and before I knew it, I'd copped a brutal right-hander in the eye and was down. I got to my feet, but was dazed and badly shaken, and an easy target – even for a guy far lighter than me, who'd already fought three rounds earlier in the evening. I tried to pull myself together, but couldn't and I took a real hiding for the rest of the round without seeming able to defend myself, let alone throw any worthwhile punches. At the bell, I trooped back to my corner, dejected, feeling a pain in my right eye – and very sorry for myself.

And there was George!

He mumbled something about missing the train, then lashed into me, viciously: 'What the hell are you doing, you fucking little idiot! You're all over the place. You're going to lose this fight. Now, get out there and start fucking punching!'

I know it sounds like something out of the movies, but it did the trick: having George there, swearing at me the way he did, brought me round, gave me the motivation I'd lacked, and I went out for the second round fired up. Poor Tom Menzies didn't know what hit him. I was a different fighter and smashed him down three times. He was a brave bloke and managed to survive, but the same happened in the third and the ref stopped the fight shortly before the final bell.

My eye injury forced me to withdraw from a bout against Ron Davies, from Manchester's Ancoats Club, the following Friday, but it healed in time for me to face Manfred Markgraf in an England v Germany match, at the Albert Hall a week later. And, with George not having trouble with trains this time, I walked it, with a second-round win. Markgraf had a good couple of minutes, but I hurt him at the end of the first and had him down twice in the second before the ref stepped in.

Four convincing victories in four months had shot me to the top of the amateur heavyweight rankings, proof that George's coaching and my focus and dedication were paying off. I was busting a gut for another fight, but had to wait a month before I was lined up against

John Bodell, whose twin brother, Jack, was also a promising amateur. And, then, it lasted just two minutes. I wasn't one to get carried away by newspaper reports, but I did think *Boxing News* was right on the money when they said my demolition job, at Coventry, 'was one of the coolest executions you could wish to watch'. I couldn't have put it better myself!

George reckoned I was now ready for 'Rocky' James. And so did I. The pain I'd felt at losing so badly the previous year had long since eased, but the hunger for revenge was as strong as ever. I had a score to settle. And the way I was feeling, I was going to wreak it unmercifully.

Our fight was at West Ham again, eight days before my twenty-second birthday, and I gained the revenge I wanted when the referee stopped the contest in the second round after Rocky had been down four times. Rocky claimed he'd been rabbit-punched – hit on the back of the neck – and vowed he'd win the decider if we met in the ABA Championships the following month. George told me to ignore that: my goal was to win the ABA National title, not worry about beating Rocky James again. If I did come up against him, fine, we'd deal with it then. But we were looking at the bigger picture, George said; one that might change my life, not a personal squabble that meant bugger all. I understood that, but deep down, I relished another chance to smash Rocky. What he'd said about the rabbit-punch had got up my nose.

I breezed into the London ABA's on the back of two swift victories in the North-East Divisional championships at York Hall, Bethnal Green – the semi-final against Brian Daltry, on 9 March, being stopped in the second round, and, the next day's final ending after just 85 seconds when my opponent, fellow East Ender Billy Hamilton was knocked down for the third time.

Not surprisingly, I found it far tougher in the semi-final of the 'London's' against the ABA champion Len Hobbs, but won a hotly-disputed points decision and went through to meet Bob Wallace, from Hampstead Boxing Club. That was barely a contest: I battered him so hard from the first bell that the ref called a halt after only 75 seconds. George and I hugged each other. It was my tenth fight since we'd started out on our mission and I'd won them all, eight inside the distance. We hadn't reached our goal, but it was in sight.

The other semi-finalists in the 'London's' that Friday night, 28 April, were Robin Jones, whom I'd beaten in December, Rocky James, and Peter James, a 30-year-old sailor, who'd represented England against Russia a few years before and was making a comeback. Naturally, I fancied either of the two I'd already fought, but I was drawn against Peter James. In the end, it didn't matter a damn: he put up a brave resistance, but I was all over him from start to finish and finally knocked him out in the third.

And so it was the sack-making factory foreman from Bristol in the final. Rocky was six years older than me and far more experienced. This was his third successive Wembley appearance and from what he was saying, you'd have thought he only had to turn up to win.

Boxing News said I was one of the outstanding boxers among the 40 on show that night, but I didn't let that go to my head. I had to keep focussed on the job in hand. George kept telling me that all the work we'd done in the past eight months would count for little if I blew it tonight. It was a daunting, almost terrifying thought, but those eight gruelling months had come down to just nine minutes. How I handled myself in those minutes would decide my future. If I held my nerve, performed at my unstoppable best, and fought the way George had shown me, I could win and turn pro; maybe even wait and enjoy a trip to the Commonwealth Games, in Perth, Western Australia, the following November, 1962. If I froze, let the importance of the occasion get to me, and got caught by one of Rocky's loopy swings, who knows, it might be Goodnight Vienna, Hello Billingsgate!

Like me, Rocky was a crowd-pleaser and the volume at the 'Pool' that night was cranked up as he came fast out of his corner, trying to get the upper hand. I bided my time, manoeuvred him into a neutral corner, and floored him with two straight lefts, then a crisp right hook. Rocky struggled to his feet at eight, but was very groggy and unable to defend himself. When the referee stopped the fight, Rocky argued that he was okay to go on. But it was the right decision. Nothing was going to stop me then. I knew victory and the ABA title was just a few punches away. And I *would* have landed them and possibly hurt him.

As the referee stepped between us, I just stood there, arms raised in victory, not sure what to do, where to go. And then, suddenly, George was in the ring, arms round me, lifting me up, telling me I'd done it, and I basked in the deafening cheers acknowledging my triumph. All I kept thinking was that this was the most thrilling, most satisfying, moment I'd ever experienced.

All the sacrifices had been worth it. I had believed in George. He had believed in me.

We had achieved what he had said we could. And we had done it together.

7

Life's funny isn't it? If I hadn't beaten Rocky that April night in 1961, there would have been little point turning pro and I'd have gone back to Billingsgate and no one would have heard any more about me. But I *did* win – and now the two biggest boxing promoters in the land (Jack Solomons and Harry Levene) were fighting over me and guaranteeing George as much as £1,000 a fight for my signature.

The money was tempting; after all, that was why I'd dedicated myself so religiously. But I'd never seriously thought I'd win the ABA title and, now I had, I didn't want to rush into anything. Apart from anything else, I was now automatically part of the Great Britain team and the prospect of representing the country in the Commonwealth Games held a certain appeal: for a kid from Ilford who'd only been abroad a few times the thought of flying to Australia and coming home with a Gold medal was the stuff of dreams.

George and I kicked it around and, in the end, money won. He could see why I fancied the Games, but saw a danger that I didn't. What if I reached the final, then some big lump from the Congo swung a lucky right hand and knocked me out? he said. I'd have lost everything I'd gained at home. I wouldn't be so much the ABA champion as the beaten Commonwealth Games finalist. Whereas now, I was the best amateur heavyweight in Britain, with a big market value. I could see it was a risk that wasn't worth taking, but, just as I was looking forward to signing on the dotted line with whichever promoter offered the most, George saw a good reason to keep them waiting.

That November, the ABA were staging a huge, prestigious tournament against the top American amateurs at Wembley, which would be televised live. We had good deals on the table now, but what if we hung on and beat the American heavyweight champion, not only in front of a packed Empire Pool, but millions of TV viewers as well. 'We'd be able to negotiate from strength,' George said. 'Maybe double, or even triple, the promoters' offers.' I was a boxer, not a businessman, and, to be honest, I didn't know what to do. But I could see a similar risk to the one I'd face in Perth. What if we did hold on and the Yank knocked me out? It wouldn't be as big a blow, losing to the top American amateur, and certainly wouldn't wreck my chances of turning pro, but it would make me less of a high-profile, saleable commodity. On the other hand, if I took on the best the United States could offer and I gave him a belting . . . what then?

As usual, I left it to George to decide – and he felt we should take the risk and wait. So, he thanked Messrs Levene and Solomons for their interest and offers, but said the new ABA heavyweight champ was off to Belgrade in June to represent Britain in the European Boxing Championships and would be staying amateur until the Americans came to town.

Before we left for the Yugoslav capital, I was among the twenty-four British contestants who met not only the Prime Minister, Harold Wilson, at No. 10 Downing Street, but also the Queen. I felt privileged on both occasions, although, to be honest, I was somewhat overawed and can remember little of what went on. I do remember that Harold went on and on about what the Government was planning to do for sport in Britain, and that Jimmy Greaves, the footballer, was among dozens of other sportsmen there. I liked Harold: he seemed a jovial sort of bloke, who made us all very welcome, and he reacted well when I told him that I always voted Conservative. 'To vote as they feel is everyone's prerogative,' he told me, puffing away on his pipe. I wasn't impressed with No. 10, though: it was a bit shabby and in need of a good make-over.

As a staunch Royalist, I was particularly honoured to meet the Queen and was amazed when she told me she'd watched me fight on television. 'You're a very exciting boxer,' she said, with a broad smile. She was such a pretty, charming lady, with lovely teeth, I was almost tempted to ask for her phone number!

My trip to Belgrade was memorable because it was the first time I received big national newspaper publicity. One of the best-known sports writers, Peter Wilson, now with the *Daily Mirror*, crowned me 'The Bull of Belgrade' for my performance against a big lump from East Germany, named Sigmund Guenter, in my second fight of the tournament.

I'd taken just a minute to knock out a twenty-one-year-old West German bricklayer, Adolf Brandenburger, in what was called the 'first series', then faced Guenter, a bronze medallist at the Rome Olympics, in the quarter final. Although he was two stone heavier than me, I thought he was going the same way as his mate when I caught him with a hard right to the head in the first round and he staggered and reeled around, not looking too clever. He recovered his senses and raised his arms to continue fighting when the Italian referee jumped in and insisted he took a standing 'eight' count. This obviously gave him time to recover. The three Western judges made me a clear winner. But the East German ones gave Guenter the verdict because of the number of points he'd mounted up. The crowd went berserk, shouting and throwing chairs into the ring, in disgust. A gorgeous little blonde number thought the East German judges had got it wrong, too, because, as I came out of the ring, she rushed through the crowd, flung her arms round me and started kissing me. 'You won! You won!' she kept saying, between kisses. I was loving it, but George was still seething about the verdict that had robbed me of a medal and only wanted to get back to the hotel. 'I don't want to know anything about any birds – let's get out of here,' he fumed, pulling me away from my admirer.

The next day, the British team and journalists covering the championship were taken on a sight-seeing tour and I'd just sat down in the coach, next to my room-mate, a bantamweight, named Peter Bennyworth, when Blondie appeared at the window, mouthing: 'Is there a spare seat in there?' Not quite believing my luck, I quickly turfed Peter out and motioned her to come aboard and sit next to me, which she did indecently swiftly. She spoke very good English and we started chatting like old mates. When I told her I was out of the championship and would be kicking my heels for another week, she said: 'Why don't we go out for dinner. I can show you a bit of Belgrade.'

As it turned out, the young lady, whose name was Yulanda, showed me a lot more than Belgrade. She had her own flat and I ended up spending more time there than in my hotel. Unfortunately, this got

George into trouble with the rest of the British team, who didn't know where I was, but were angry that I wasn't at the fights, supporting my team-mates. To keep the peace, I gave in and spent every day watching the boxing before dashing back to Yulanda.

✱✱✱

A month after I returned, I was with Tommy in The Log Cabin – a drinking club he and George had opened, next door to the famous Latin Quarter nightclub, in Wardour Street – when Tommy invited us to the twenty-first birthday party of a friend's son. The friend was Micky Barnett, who ran The Albion pub on the corner of Ludgate Circus and Fleet Street, and I'd met his son, Melvyn, a couple of times at parties, thrown by my mate Sophie, the previous year. He was a tall, good-looking boy and was so successful with the ladies, I thought: I'll have to go and knock him out in a minute – who is he? Well, I went to the party and had a great time. Melvyn loved having fun, like me, and we started a friendship that is still going strong today.

After spending a couple of weeks at Club Med again, this time in Cefalu, I got in shape for the only fight I had scheduled before the big one against the Americans. With nothing to prove, I would have welcomed a good three-round workout, but didn't get it. My opponent, in a London v South Poland match, at the Albert Hall, on 19 October 1961, was a lanky twenty-five-year-old turner, Klemens Malkiewicz, who simply did not look, or act, the part. He ruffled me with some right swings and uppercuts in the first round, but when I felled him with a right hook to the jaw in the second, I knew it was all over. He got up and bravely tried to carry on, but he was unsteady on his feet and easy to hit, and when I dumped him again, his seconds waved the towel.

✱✱✱

That November, the Americans arrived for the Anglo–US Championship at Wembley. And when I saw who I had to fight – the man I'd put my professional career on hold for – my bottle nearly went. The guy was huge, a giant. Cornelius Perry was his name. He was about my age and one big black boy, from Philadelphia: six feet, three inches and a few pounds under eighteen stones – four bloody stone heavier than me! As if that wasn't daunting enough, he held The Golden Gloves and was now telling the newspapers he was here to enjoy himself because it was his last amateur fight. After he'd won, he told them, he was going to chuck in his baker's job and turn pro and, hopefully, be fighting for the world title within a year. How was I to know then, at just twenty-two, that this was probably paper talk: boxing writers' exaggeration and hype, aimed at putting bums on Wembley seats?

When I read all this, I was scared. No, not scared: apprehensive. All I could think was that if his boxing technique matched his size, I was probably in for a pasting. George didn't think I had much of a chance, either. But he didn't want me to disgrace myself. We talked it through and he said he couldn't see me boxing the guy: I had to go out fast and throw as much leather at him as possible. If I could keep it going, the man mountain would have to be bloody good to stop me. And if he was that good, I was unlikely to get slaughtered by the Press for losing. I had everything to gain and not much to lose, George said. Even if I did get beaten, the professional route to the money would still be open.

I could see his point. But that November evening, when I got into my boxing gear in the dressing room and went into the ring with the rest of the British team for the pre-fight preliminaries, the spine-tingling apprehension came back. Standing opposite Perry, as the respective national anthems were played, I saw for the first time just how massive he was.

All my early fights, when I'd rushed off my stool and, bosh!, knocked guys out in a matter of seconds, suddenly seemed irrelevant, totally unimportant. Even with my ABA title, it dawned on me that I was really only a big fish in a small pond. Now, I was in a huge lake and, looking at Perry, I felt like a tiddler. I was going to do my best, of course. I was going to throw lots of leather, as George said, and hope for the best. But, quite honestly, I couldn't see me beating the guy. Not unless I got lucky. Very lucky.

What did nothing for my nerves that night was being the last fight of the evening and having to sit in my dressing room for nearly two hours, waiting for my turn. And what made it even worse was that all my team-mates, without exception, came back to the dressing room after their fights, announcing, triumphantly: 'I won.'

First, flyweight Alan Rudkin stopped his opponent in the third round. Then Peter Bennyworth, my Belgrade bantam mate, won on points, as did light welter, Brian Brazier. Next, middleweight John Fisher stopped his man in the third and Jim Lloyd, welter, won on points. Featherweight Frankie Taylor did it in the third, and so did light heavyweight Dennis Pollard. Then, to cap a spectacular evening, Dick McTaggart won on points, giving Britain an unbelievable 8–0 lead. I was thrilled, because trouncing the Yanks would give British boxing a big boost, but, personally, I was going through murders. I know it was wrong, but I had divided loyalties: the way it was going, it looked like I was going to be the only Briton to lose. That wouldn't be enough to stop me going pro, but how would I live it down at the Palais?

When lightweight Dick came in, victorious, I thought: Shit, that leaves only Derek Richards, the light middleweight, before me. Derek was a nice guy and a good boxer, but I have to admit I hoped he'd lose his fight. It wouldn't matter a damn, as far as the contest was concerned, but it would take the pressure off me.

I didn't have time to dwell on it, though. Just as Derek was psyching himself up to go down to the ring, an ABA official came running in, breathlessly, and looked at me: 'Walker, he said. 'You're next.'

'What about Derek?' I said. 'He's on before me.'

'No,' he said. 'The TV people say they want the heavyweights on. They're running out of time.'

I looked at George. He shrugged. We had no options.

In the corner, he said: 'Be positive. Just go out and throw punches. Don't hold back. Keep throwing punches. Lots of 'em. If he's going to knock you out, get knocked out going for it. Go out in style.'

When the bell went for the first round I moved quickly to the centre of the ring, focussed on our battle plan. I was pumped up, aggressive, all my apprehension gone. I felt I could knock a wall down. I'd always had a whirlwind style, but this time I would go for it more than ever. I had to. If I'd gone in there, thinking, 'Oh, my God, he's a big bastard, I might get hurt', I'd have been lost before I started. If I *was* going to cop it, I was going to make sure I got a few good digs in first and go down all guns blazing. I thought Goliath was a bit chubby when I'd seen him up close. Who knows, if I could stay out of trouble and make him fight, he might run out of steam.

In the end, the fight didn't last long enough for him to run out of steam. After less than a minute, he came towards me, sticking a feeble straight right towards my nose and I ducked inside and caught him with a right, then the most delicious peach of a left hook on the chin.

He crashed to the canvas, all six feet three inches and eighteen stones of him. He didn't move as the referee counted him out. And, indeed, he didn't move a muscle for the next ten minutes until the American team's physician brought him round.

I couldn't believe it. Cornelius certainly couldn't. I don't think anyone could. But the evidence was there, laid out for all to see. And Wembley was going barmy. The reporters must have been licking their lips at the story unfolding before them. It was great news anyway: little Britain thrashing mighty America 9–0. But if Derek Richards could do the business, it would be an unprecedented whitewash. What a story! What a great night for British amateur boxing! Derek, bless him, didn't let us down. He stopped his opponent in the final round to complete a night of glorious triumph for us and humiliation for the Yanks.

The annihilation was big news the next morning, and, because my victory was so unexpected and dramatic, I got my fair share of the headlines. I wallowed in the glory, although I did keep my delight under control, at lunchtime the next day, when both teams met for the presentation of prizes, and I came face to face with Cornelius again. I spotted him looking at me, perhaps wondering how it had all happened. In his suit, he looked even more imposing. Fucking hell, I thought, I wouldn't want to meet you on a dark night!

I wouldn't have minded having a chat to Cornelius; he seemed a nice enough guy. But my left hook had split his mouth along the jaw and the stitches made it hard for him to speak. I asked if he was all right and he mumbled, 'Yeah,' but he clearly wasn't in the mood for conversation. I could understand that. If I'd been odds-on to win and been dumped on my backside in a couple of minutes, I don't suppose I'd have felt like making small talk – especially with the bloke who did it! What I do know is that shock defeat scuppered all the plans Cornelius had for himself. He went back to Philly and retired, all hopes of fighting for the world heavyweight title forgotten. If he'd won, who knows what might have happened. He may well have gone on to become a great fighter, and I may never have been heard of again. I'd certainly have turned pro, but I doubt I would have made much of a name for myself. As it was, that sweet punch sent the awesome Goliath into oblivion and changed my life. Thanks to TV, many millions saw my dramatic knockout and I became a household name – literally overnight.

I'd love to say that the punch that did it was planned; that I cunningly lured Cornelius onto it. But the truth is that it was luck. And

I've got photographs to prove it. When I threw the punch, my eyes were closed. I had no idea where my fists were going to land – if they were going to land anywhere! I was simply throwing as many punches as I could, praying that some would connect. I'd had fights when I'd thrown left and right hooks from first bell to last, with not one landing where I wanted. Yet, that night I landed one right on the money.

Everyone needs luck to do well in life. And that Tuesday night, I did get lucky. Lucky enough to begin a professional boxing career that would make all my dreams come true beyond my wildest imagination.

8

If Jack Solomons and Harry Levene were keen to sign me as a pro before the Anglo–US tournament, they were busting their guts now. They saw me as a courageous crowd-pleaser, who fight fans would queue to see, and both men were on the phone almost every day trying to out-do and out-bid each other. I left all the negotiating to George: I trusted him to do the best for both of us; after all, we were 50–50 on everything. And, anyway, what did I know about the finer points of negotiating?! I was still only twenty-two and interested only in what I was going to get for going in the ring. That, and having fun outside it, of course.

One unexpected bonus from my new fame was that I was paid to model shirts for the designer John Stephen. Mind you, that was tough: I had to keep smiling for the camera – while posing with pretty girls.

Talking of birds, my mate Pat Booth had a pretty face and was now living in London, trying to break into modelling. I was now driving a light blue and cream Austin Healey 106 and, knowing she was skint, would drive to her little flat to take her out for a meal. She was also cold in the flat, so every time I went I'd take her a can of Esso Blue parafin, which we sold at the garage. Hardly a romantic gift, but it was what she needed.

George's talks were barely under way when I scored my second first-round knockout in seven days, despatching twenty-three-year-old

North Eastern Counties champion John Spenceley in just eighty seconds at Forest Gate the following Tuesday. But when I went to Dublin in the first week of December for the Four-Nations Tournament, I was staggered to hear that Levene was prepared to guarantee £4,000 for my first three fights. That was a lot of money in 1962: you could buy a house and a car for that – and have some left over for petrol, which was under five bob (25p) a gallon, and a few beers that cost just over a shilling (5p) a pint.

I was even more shocked to hear that George had turned down the offer and told Levene we were looking for three times that. I thought George was mad, but had so much faith in him that I said nothing and waited to see what would happen next. It was an exhilarating time for me. Thanks to the power of television, I was the man of the moment and, quite honestly, was flattered that the two biggest promoters in the country were fighting for my signature. George was certain that one of them would come up with what he wanted and, frankly, I didn't give a toss which one it was. After all, I wasn't getting in the ring with either of them! All I wanted was their money.

However, nothing was agreed by the time I faced Rocky James in a semi-final in Dublin. And, to be frank, I was so pumped up for my fourth fight against the whingeing Welshman, I didn't care: I was more concerned with really doing him this time, so he would have no cause to complain. And I did: I coped with his first-round rush, had him down in the second, then three times in the third before the referee stopped the fight, three seconds from the bell. Great, I thought – he won't have any excuses this time. I went back to my corner and had my back to him when George said: 'Fucking hell, he's only coming over again!' I turned round and saw James striding towards me. Thinking he wanted to carry on fighting, I tensed, ready to let him have the right hand again.

'You know the trouble with you, boyo,' he said.

'No. What?' I said, defensively.

'You're too bloody good for me, that's what,' he said. 'Let's go out and have a pint.'

And we did. He turned out to be a really great guy.

Two days later I took just 2 mins 15 secs to beat Jim Monaghan, from Derry, in the final, bringing to an end the most incredible year. I'd had sixteen fights and won fifteen inside the distance – seven of them in the first round! It would have been the most spectacular and satisfying farewell to my amateur career, but George was still holding out for more money at the end of the year and, on 11 January, I was still an amateur when I stopped Jackie Fitch in the first round at Forest Gate.

Unknown to me, George had a target of £9,000 for my signature. We'd decided from the off that we'd be partners in everything, and he was keen to buy his father-in-law's garage. Mr Hatton wanted £15,000 – £9,000 now, and the balance over an agreed period. George obviously hadn't got Solomons or Levene up to that figure by 1 February because I was in the ring again, as a special additional attraction at an England v Scotland international at the Albert Hall. Ideally, I would have faced a Jock, but Scotland could not find anyone good enough, so the ABA arranged for the Austrian champion, Emil Svaricek, to have the pleasure. He surprised me with two left hooks to the head, but failed to cash in and I hit back with right and left swings to the jaw. A left hook to the body forced him to take a standing 'eight' count, then, seconds from the end of the round, I dropped him with a meaty right, again to the body, and he failed to beat the count. I was thrilled with another first-round win, but I was lucky to get it because the bell rang while the referee was still counting. Fortunately, the ABA had introduced a new rule, stating that a boxer can only be saved by the bell in the last round.

A few days later, George told me we were going to Harry Levene's office in Soho. Solomons had increased his latest offer, but it was clearly not enough, and George had a plan to squeeze more out of Harry and, hopefully, clinch a deal. All I had to do was tell Harry I didn't want to turn pro yet and that I'd decided to go to Australia the following November and try to to win a gold medal at the Commonwealth and Empire Games.

We walked into Harry's Wardour Street office, in Soho, well-rehearsed. After the usual pleasantries, George looked Harry in the eye and said: 'I've told Billy you've made a very good offer, Harry, but he doesn't want to take it. He feels he can do better if he goes to the Commonwealth Games and comes back with a gold medal.'

George sounded so convincing, I almost believed him myself, so when Harry turned to me and asked if that was right, I nodded enthusiastically. 'It's what I want to do, Mister Levene,' I said. 'Now I've beaten the American champion, I'm sure I can win the gold medal.'

'Gold medal!' Harry scoffed. 'With the money I'm going to pay you, you'll be able to buy a sackful of gold medals.'

He then turned to George. 'I tell you what I'm going to do. I'll pay you £6,000 for Billy to turn pro, and guarantee you £1,000 for his first three fights.'

It was all George and I could do to keep the grins off our faces.

Nine thousand pounds!

It wasn't enough to set us up for life, but it was a massive amount of money. I'd read that Britain's latest sports car, the E-type Jaguar, was on the market for a whopping £2,196, yet we were being offered enough for my first three fights to buy two each – with enough left over to pay the running cost for a year!

When George told Solomons of his rival's offer, Jack was contemptuous. 'Levene will do his bollocks,' he sneered. 'He's mad guaranteeing you that sort of money.'

What Solomons didn't know – and neither did George, nor I, until later – was that Harry Levene was watching on TV as I smashed Cornelius Perry into oblivion and admitted going to bed wishing he still managed fighters, so that he could get himself a piece of what he called a 'fistic goldmine'.

Who knows, if Harry hadn't seen me that night he may not have been prompted to fork out such a colossal amount for my signature. As it was, he'd booked Wembley's Empire Pool for 27 March and was stuck for a big name to put bums on the 11,500 seats. His instinct told him I was the fighter who could do that. It was a huge gamble, but Harry was convinced I had that magical star quality and was prepared to put his money where his belief was.

With British boxing's biggest secret still under wraps, I went over the water to South London to be presented with the Toby Noble Belt, a coveted trophy, awarded each year to London's most outstanding amateur. Posing with Toby and the belt, in the Black Bull pub in the Old Kent Road, I was asked if I was going to display the belt when I took on Robin Jones, at West Ham Baths the next week. I gave my customary smile and said I probably would, but I knew the fight was now not going to take place. I was going to pull out the following Monday morning – the day after my plans to turn pro were revealed in the *News of the World*.

We hadn't told the paper's hugely-respected sports editor, Frank Butler, the money Harry Levene had guaranteed because we were asked not to, but I did say it was a record for a professional debut, and would be going into a new company, Walker Brothers Ltd, which

George had set up to control my boxing income. I told Butler I was now a 50–50 partner with George and all the money from my fights would go into building up a business empire. George had many plans, and if the Wembley roof caved in on my debut, at least I'd have done all right, moneywise, by just signing the Levene contract, without throwing a single punch. George was the boss, I stressed, and always would be: he'd been through the amateur and pro ranks and knew all the angles – the rewards and the pitfalls. Despite the money I was being paid to turn pro, I was going to carry on working at the garage and living at home. Every penny I earned from boxing would be ploughed into our new company and invested for the future – both George's and mine. I didn't intend ending up broke, with nothing to show but scars, I said.

And I meant it.

The story caused the biggest stir in British boxing history. George's phone didn't stop ringing and newspaper and TV reporters descended on the garage, desperate to know what I was being paid for my first fight. Speculation varied between £1,000 and £2,000, and it was only Frank Butler, who revealed the true figure, in the next week's *News of the World*.

By the last week of February, Levene and fight matchmaker, Mickey Duff, had not found an opponent for me, but coloured posters advertising the fight were already printed with only one name on them – mine. There was a photograph of me knocking out Cornelius Perry and, underneath, the words: *'The sensational Blond Bomber, Billy Walker, the idol of TV millions, will be making his professional debut at this tournament in an international heavyweight contest of eight, three-minute, rounds.'*

For a bloke who'd be only twenty-three a few weeks before the fight, it was a bit scary. I was a national hero, it seemed, because one lucky punch had been seen by millions on television. I didn't have time to dwell on the enormity of this however: I had to start getting into shape and make sure I was fit and strong enough for an eight-round fight. I hoped my right hand, which had served me so well as an amateur, would do the business early, but obviously, I could not rely on it. Against an experienced pro, whoever he might be, I had to be prepared to go five more rounds than I'd ever fought before.

George arranged for me to begin toughening up at his father-in-law's farm, at Pitsea, in Essex, and if I was concerned at fighting an eight-rounder, I didn't show it when I held my first Press conference there. 'I feel altogether more relaxed,' I said. 'I'll have eight rounds to do my work – winning won't depend on doing it all in three. People used to say, "That Walker takes a few punches." But what else can you do in three rounds? You daren't lose the first, in case you can't make up in the other two.' Then I endeared myself to them by holding a calf, and telling them: 'Look how lucky I am, being able to come down here whenever I like. The average boy turning pro has to do a day's work and fit in the training when he can, but I don't have to worry about those things. I work for my brother, so there's not trouble about time off.'

I don't know why I said I worked for George. We were now partners and my public appeal, if not my boxing skill, had made us rich. But old habits die hard: he'd always told me what to do and, at that time, I was happy for him to assume the role of boss. It did seem a bit odd, though, me being the one in the front line, taking the knocks.

The newspaper coverage fuelled the public's interest and when I arrived at Joe Bloom's gym, at Cambridge Circus, in London's West End, two weeks before the fight for the second, more intense, stage of my training, the place was packed. 'We didn't get such a crowd when the world champion, Floyd Patterson, came here,' Joe told the reporters, proudly. Maybe it was the big audience, I don't know, but I was in a mean mood that day: for some reason, my regular sparring partners were not there and I had a workout with Jack Fitch, who I'd fought a couple of months before. Our sparring lasted only a round and a half before Jack was withdrawn, blood cascading from his nose, following a short left hook and right-hander. After just three minutes with another sparrring partner, I proceeded to split the punchbag, before calling it a day. By the Friday before the fight, I was down to my fighting weight of 13st 8lb and ready for my first fight for money.

I now knew the name and nationality of my opponent: a Belgian called Jose Peyre; I knew little else, except that he was twenty-eight and was third choice, after two other European fighters – or Continentals, as we called them then – dropped out. He'd had thirty-seven fights, losing almost half of them, many inside the distance and, interestingly, there was a four-year gap in his career when it appeared he had not fought at all.

I didn't allow myself to be fooled by the guy's poor record. Okay, for the money I was getting, I was hardly going to be put in with someone dangerous, who could burst my bubble before I'd got started. At the same time, Peyre had been around the professional circuit and was bound to have more ring craft than me. I knew I had to be confident, not cocky. Look what had happened with Rocky James. I wanted the public to be patient, to appreciate that I was a pro novice. But would they? The Press were cynical, suggesting that Peyre was a no-hoper, who'd been chosen to provide me with no more than a gentle entree into the professional world. They questioned whether George and I had made a mistake, taking so much money when I was a novice. Had we not priced ourselves out of the small provincial halls where new pros got used to fighting extra rounds and traditionally learned their trade? George took the view that, if we could get thousands for fights, why take hundreds? And, anyway, I would learn my trade in the gym, he said.

We would soon find out how much I *had* learned. And just how good – or bad – Peyre was. Obviously, I was on a hiding to nothing: if I nailed him early, everyone would think he was a pushover, rented out to ensure a Walker win; if I won, but the fight went the distance, they'd think I looked good among the amateurs, but not so hot among the pros. And, obviously, if I lost, I'd get a mauling from all sides.

In the end, I won. And still got a mauling. I tried to put Peyre away in the first three rounds, but he kept me at arm's length, tapping me with a long left, then getting on his bike. I finally got him, 1 min. 57 secs. into the fifth, with a hard right into the kidneys. He went down, complaining it was a low punch, but it wasn't, and when he appeared unable to defend himself, the referee, Harry Gibbs, stopped the contest – if you could call it that!

The crowd weren't pleased at what had been a messy, fumbling fight and booed their displeasure. And the Press went to town on what a disappointing anti-climax it was. The *Daily Express*'s Desmond Hackett, who appeared to like me, but had a problem with the money I was getting, said it was 'a shabby fight that would not have been distinguished as a heavyweight test in the early series of a talent-spotting competition.' I could see his point, but you can only fight as well as the other person lets you and Peyre hadn't come to win, or put up a good show; he was there simply to survive, collect his money and go home. And that made for a very boring battle. Another criticism that hurt was that I looked amateurish. Well, the day before the fight, I *was* an amateur. What were they expecting: for me to look like a world champion?

I've never been one for making excuses, but there were reasons for my disappointing performance that night. Despite my picture on the posters and the front page of the programme, I was not top of the bill – yet when I entered the arena, I was bathed in the spotlight and given the full fanfare treatment, as though I was already British heavyweight champion. Quite frankly, it overwhelmed me. Yes, I'd fought at the Empire Pool before, but not in front of so many noisy fans, expecting another hard-hitting, thrilling display by Whirlwind Walker. I most certainly didn't bottle it, but all the pre-fight ballyhoo, and my worry that I might run out of steam over eight rounds, did take away much of my confidence and bravado.

And there was another, more significant, reason why I was so lacklustre. Until then, George had been in my corner, advising, cajoling, always encouraging, and bringing out the best in me. But blood relatives were not allowed in a fighter's corner in the professional game then, and, that night at Wembley, I was looked after by George's pal, Joe Lucy and my trainer, Frank Duffet, while George sat in the closest ringside seat a few feet away. Joe and Frank were experienced, knowledgeable and highly accomplished, but they weren't family. They didn't know me like George did. And much as I liked and respected them, I didn't have as much faith in them as I had in him. Apart from that first round with Tom Menzies in Glasgow, this was the only time George hadn't been in my corner when the first bell went. And it played on my mind, no doubt about it.

Boxing News, the respected trade paper, added to my disappointment by heavily criticising the use of my picture on the front cover of the programme, and the fanfare, 'which was usually reserved for champions'. The paper said it was unable to secure photos of the two top-of-the-bill fights, because every photographer left the arena after my fight and never returned. 'It was a crazy set up. We doubt the wisdom of this extravaganza. It is certainly not good for Billy Walker at this stage of his career.'

I didn't let this get me down, because all the ballyhoo had nothing to do with me: it was just Harry Levene's publicity machine making the most of the occasion, to convince everyone I was someone special. But what bothered me was that throughout my amateur career I'd always prided myself on giving value for money and I'd clearly not done that at Wembley.

I couldn't wait for a chance to put things right and it came just two months later when I went back to Wembley to face Mariano

Echevarria, a very tough, barrel-chested Spaniard who, only a month before, had taken the then undefeated Johnny Prescott, from Birmingham, the full ten rounds. I was warned that, unlike the elusive Peyre, Señor Echevarria had, most definitely, come to fight me, but I was happy with that: I was sure I could put him away and hear the crowd cheering, not jeering.

Fortunately for Levene, if not for me, the fans had forgiven me for my dismal debut: the Empire Pool was sold out again and I went into the ring, pumped up, eager to show everyone I was more than just a good amateur who'd got lucky. At the bell, I went out like a bull and landed a cracking right on the head. I expected Echevarria to go down, but he just shook his head and came at me. I caught him another right, but he didn't seem to feel it. I thought: 'God, what have we got here? This isn't good.' And it wasn't. He was a hard nut, who gave as good as he got and, in the third round, knocked me down with a left hook. I got up at seven and hung on until the end of the round, but I felt I was in for a battle that would probably go the distance. I was right: we stood toe to toe, for the rest of the fight, knocking the shit out of each other. The crowd loved it and, in a way, Mariano and I did, too. We had great respect for each other and the sporting spirit with which we fought was typified in the last round when, almost out on my feet, I missed with a punch and fell to the canvas. Mariano ran to me and helped me up and we slammed into each other for the remaining seconds. I hit him with everything I had, but couldn't put him away. At the final bell, we grabbed each other and had the customary cuddle, as relieved as each other that the battering was over. Some of the crowd booed when the referee gave a draw, but I wasn't unhappy with it. Mariano had the edge that night and I was lucky not to get beaten.

Also satisfying was the crowd's reaction when I left the ring: they'd loved seeing a British fighter who could dish it out and take it and I was cheered as I walked to the dressing room. I went home to Ilford, pleased with my night's work. I felt I'd done a lot to redeem myself – and learned a lot in the process. Things would get better, I was sure of it.

9

With my share of Levene's £6,000 I couldn't wait to splash out on a new car and, although I could afford the E-type, I plumped for a 3.5 Mark Two Jaguar. It was still a whopping £1,619 7s 9d – and an extra £48 2s 6d for wire wheels – but, as I was still living with mum and dad, I was swayed by the four doors and plush back seat!

I had more than enough to buy the car outright, but George said it made more sense to put £200 down and pay off the rest in instalments over two years, using the balance to buy out his father-in-law, so that the garage was ours. If it struck me that the agreed split of two-thirds for George and Jean and one-third for me was not entirely fair, I didn't show it, or say anything: I was far too anxious to get in my shiny, new, midnight blue Jaguar and take off on a scuba-diving holiday in Sicily with my mate, Melvyn, and Charlie Curtis, a *Daily Express* printer, I'd met in The Albion.

We decided to stop off in Cannes – and, by coincidence, bumped into Harry Levene and his girlfriend, Georgina. Harry took the three of us to lunch at the famous Carlton Hotel and allowed us to see the genial man behind the tough boxing negotiator. He was a lovable gentleman, Harry, who loved to laugh, and we had a great time before moving on to Cefalu, to team up with two guys I'd met the previous summer.

Although the point of the holiday was to scuba-dive, we all had a healthy appetite for the birds and shared a common aim: to pull as many as we could. I'd always fancied myself as a ladies' man, but Melvyn quickly showed why he was so successful. He was very laid back with an air of sophistication, a well-modulated voice, and an effortless charm that never seemed to fail. He was well-mannered, too, never failing to light a lady's cigarette or stand up when female company arrived or left our little group. I'd never given those gestures a thought in my life, and looked on in amazement at the effect they had. After watching him in action, I decided to hone my own pulling technique! Although Melvyn was a year younger than me, he was far more worldly. Nothing ever fazed him. He wore a cravat and a proper dressing gown, and when we made fun of him he took not the slightest notice. He wasn't interested in talking about boxing or, indeed, any sport and, now that I was away from London, neither was I. Birds and booze, not necessarily in that order, were Melvyn's priorities. And they were mine, too. We were the perfect match.

Even though I was on holiday, with no fight on the horizon, I kept myself in shape by running four miles or so every morning along the beach. Which was just as well because we'd been away only a fortnight when I got a call from George: 'You've got to come home. I've arranged a fight for you in three weeks.' Having just got into my stride, I wasn't mad about breaking my holiday, but I had no option. I was now a pro fighter; I went where the money was. And although this particular fight was in the less fashionable venue of Blackpool, against a German boxer few fight fans in Britain had heard of, the money was fantastic: fifteen hundred quid. I hated the thought of leaving my new Jag behind but, again, I had no choice. I drove it to the airport, then got on a plane to London, leaving Melvyn to drive back to Cefalu with Charlie, to continue their holiday.

In the second week of August, I was reunited with the beautiful Jag and George and I drove to Blackpool, experiencing, for the first time, the M1 motorway, which had opened just under three years before. My opponent, Erwin Hack, had distinguished himself by going the distance with Johnny Prescott five months earlier, but couldn't handle my punching power. I had him down three times in the first round before the referee stepped in, after just 1 min 12 secs.

The trip home the next morning was far more memorable: George and I were lucky not to be killed! We were roaring down the motorway, George at the wheel, when a lorry pulled out in front of us. There were only two lanes then and only a grass verge, about a dozen feet high, separating us from oncoming traffic. George had no option but to swing over on to the grass. Because of our speed, the car spun and we ended up on the other side of the verge, facing the opposite way, the driver's door rammed against the verge. The lorry driver obviously saw what happened in his rear-view mirror and stopped further down the road. I got out of the car and climbed to the top of the verge. Wild with rage, I ran to him, shouting: 'You bastard, you bastard.' I pulled open his door and was about to teach him a lesson about motorway manners when I heard George screaming from the Jag: 'Don't hit him, Bill. Don't hit him.'

The driver's face was a picture. For a second it was frozen in fear at this big, angry guy about to drag him out and give him a belting – then it broke into a smile as he recognised me. 'Look who it is. Billy Walker. I've seen you on the telly. I'm sorry mate, I honestly didn't see you. Don't hit me.'

Of course, I didn't. But it was a close call. Okay, George was doing nearly 100mph, but the lorry driver should have checked his mirror before pulling out. I turned to walk back to George, wondering what state my precious Jag was in, when the lorry driver took a piece of paper off his dashboard. 'Would you mind signing this for me, Billy,' he said. I reached into my pocket for a pen, signed my name, then walked back to the Jag dismayed at the damage, but thrilled that I'd been recognised and laughing at the guy's cheek.

It was further proof of the power of television. Earlier in the year, I'd had a call from George asking if I wanted to join some other famous faces judging a beauty contest. What a silly question! Of course, I would, who knows, I might be able to get hold of the winner.

'Where is it?' I asked.

'Butlin's. Clacton,' he said.

Well, there you go! After all that bunking in, I was now being invited through the front door as a celeb, no less. When I arrived, I was greeted by the holiday camp manager and, after the usual pleasantries, introduced to various members of his staff. I recognised one young man instantly.

'This is our head of security, Mr Walker,' the manager said.

I put out my hand. 'How nice to see you,' I said. 'We've met before, haven't we?'

'We have indeed,' he replied. 'I made a terrible mistake that night, didn't I?

With my father, at the age of 2, in Stepney before he went off to war in 1941. I didn't see him again until 1945.
(Author's private collection)

Mum and I were very close as Dad was away at war. This is me, aged 3, with my mother in the garden of the house in Shortstown, near Bedford.
(Author's private collection)

In the garden of the house in Kensington Gardens, Ilford, aged 7.
(Author's private collection)

This picture was taken in a gym, prior to my turning pro – not a care in the world and my whole life before me. I'm about 21.
(Author's private collection)

With Johnny Prescott at the weigh-in at the Cambridge Gymnasium in London, 12 Nov 1963.
(Author's private collection)

Fighting Joe Erskine at Wembley on 27 October 1964 – I won on points.
(Author's private collection)

Meeting Sonny Liston in September 1963 at my brother's father-in-law's Blue House Farm in Pitsea, Essex, where we set up a training camp. He came down to watch me spar. (Author's private collection)

BILLY WALKER

Recording my first record, 'A Little On The Lonely Side', and I certainly was when it came out! (Author's private collection)

Helping on the farm in 1964. I loved the outdoor life. (Author's private collection)

Staying with Tom and Ann in their spare room in 1965, deliberating which new car I wanted to buy!
(Author's private collection)

The bachelor years: in my flat in Ebury Street in 1965. What great times I had in that flat!

(Author's private collection)

A 1967 publicity shot taken with my trainer Freddie Hill. I used to spar with Joe Bugner when he was about 17 – he's standing next to me here. (Author's private collection)

British Heavyweight Championship at the Empire Pool, Wembley. 7 November 1967. (Author's private collection)

A very proud moment - meeting Her Majesty the Queen. (Author's private collection)

Celebrating my wedding to Susan Coleopy in 1968, with my good friend David Hutton. We are still friends today.
(Author's private collection)

'You certainly did.' And we both laughed.

I honestly can't remember if I got hold of any of the beauties on display, but I do know I drove home to Ilford, counting my blessings. I could only wonder at how my life would have turned out if I'd been arrested and charged with assaulting that security guard. A shameful court appearance . . . a police record . . . who knows, even prison. It didn't bear thinking about. I put my head on the pillow thinking how lucky I had been.

✷✷✷

Having seen me earn £1,500 for a few minutes' work, George was eager to get me back in the ring as fast as possible and, just three weeks later, I was in Liverpool, facing a Ghanaian, named Robert Archie Moore. The guy's colour was the only thing he had in common with the legendary American light-heavyweight champion and I had him crouching and covering up from the first bell and soon dropped him for a count of nine. After two minutes in the second, he drove me against the ropes, hammering away with both fists, but I caught him with a short right to the chin, decking him. He sat on the canvas, looking bewildered, then got up, unaware he'd missed the count. He was a no-hoper, who seemed to have gone down a little too easily, but I was delighted with the victory: it was great to have won with an early knockout, again. It boded well for when I went back to Wembley for the last of my three-fight deal with Harry Levene.

My opponent, on 13 November, was a hulking great French-Canadian lumberjack from Newfoundland, named Phonse LaSaga, who did his best to intimidate me by vaulting over the ropes into the ring. At the bell, he hurled himself towards me, head down, and threw a series of punches that either missed or ended up wrapped round my neck. He seemed a bit tottery even from the mildest jab, and kept dropping his head to escape punishment. When he straightened, two minutes into the second, I landed one on his jaw. It wasn't particularly hard, but LaSaga fell, face down, on the canvas faster than the trees he chopped down back home. The crowd were quiet for a few seconds, waiting for him to get up, but when he didn't, and referee Harry Gibbs counted him out, they started booing loudly. And they were still booing when LaSaga reached the dressing room. It was all highly unsatisfactory and the British Boxing Board of Control took the unusual step of ordering the Master of Ceremonies to say, from the ring, that LaSaga's purse was being withheld, pending an inquiry. I wasn't thrilled to hear that because it suggested that LaSaga, like Hack and Moore, had been picked to ensure early wins for me and so build up my name. But there was nothing that either George, or I, could do about it. Frankly, I'd have preferred it if I *had* been matched against someone more formidable: another £1,000 in our pot for less than three minutes in the ring was terrific, but I'd gained nothing in what I needed most – experience.

Not one to hang about when I hadn't broken sweat and there was money to be made, George had me back in action, a week later, in Leicester, against a former Spanish champion Jose Gonzales. At 13st 11lb, I had an 11lb weight advantage, but couldn't make this work, because Gonzales kept close to me, elbows tucked well down, gloves hiding his face, which nullified most of my heavy punches. In desperation, I started going for the ribs, but the referee, Austin O'Connor, judged I was too low and gave me two warnings. I was biding my time in the second, waiting to land a big punch to finish matters, when Gonzales went down for a count of eight, gesticulating to O'Connor that I'd hit him low. I was the only one working in the third when, suddenly, Gonzales dropped to the canvas, theatrically holding his groin. I was convinced it wasn't a low blow but O'Connor disqualified me, amid loud booing from the crowd, who clearly thought the Spaniard was conning the ref.

The verdict ruined my unbeaten pro record and it hurt. But only briefly. The good news was that the fight was over and we were going to get paid. Up to the moment I stepped into the ring, I had no dough. All the early morning running, the gruelling gym work-outs, didn't count for a penny. I couldn't say, I've done all this hard work, pay me for it. I didn't get anything until the fight was over. Then the money was guaranteed: win or lose. Well, the fight *was* over. And now, it was pay day, and the fun could start. That was the point, after all. For me, at least. Of course, I wanted to win; every fighter did. But, as George had told me all those years ago, you can't win 'em all. And if I did lose, what was the point in being depressed? It was the same with after-fight inquests. What was the point of whingeing about a ref's decision you consider unjust? It's done and dusted; no one was going to change it. Like with Gonzales. I thought the referee was wrong to disqualify me, but he had. And it was in the record books that Walker had lost for the first time as a pro. No amount of complaining was going to change that. I'd never been the type, even as an amateur, to get upset when I lost. And I wasn't going to start now. I'd go all out to win, and celebrate like mad when I did. And when I lost I'd do precisely the same. I didn't want any talk about what had gone wrong in the ring; that could wait for another day. I'd turned pro for the money. And the big money I was getting guaranteed a great time. All my mates knew the score: no matter what the result, we'd have a good laugh over quite a few drinks, usually at Tommy McCarthy's flat, off Edgware Road. From early on, it was always: *win or lose, plenty of booze.*

The following Monday, I was due to fight Peter Bates, a fifteen-stone publican from Chesterfield, at Manchester's Belle Vue stadium, but he withdrew at the last minute through injury and George quickly arranged a return with Gonzales. This suited me fine: I hated losing my unbeaten record and was eager for revenge. Ironically, on the night, I was warned for a low blow with my first punch and, after that, was reluctant to go 'downstairs'. I was always the aggressor, though, and battered Gonzales with everything I had for eight rounds. Although I hadn't found the big punch to finish him, I felt I'd done enough to win, but when the referee raised my arm, the crowd started booing. I didn't know what to make of it. If I knocked someone out quickly, the guy was a bum, only there to make me look good; if I worked hard for a points victory, I should have finished it sooner.

That was a strange night in Manchester but, in the main, I enjoyed fighting in the provinces. The crowds were far smaller than what I'd become used to, but they had plenty to say and always lifted my spirits. I felt loved and respected, which compensated for not being fired up by those awesome Wembley attendances. And there was the money, of course: we always got between £1,500 and £2,000, which meant by the end of November, I'd earned more than £15,000. This staggering fact was not overlooked by Peter Wilson, who told *Daily Mirror* readers: 'Despite the most disastrously overplayed professional debut of all time . . . this handsome hercules, with a Greek god haircut, has earned as much as the Prime Minister, a Scotland Yard chief superintendent and a major general earn together in one year! Even Floyd Patterson, the richest heavyweight of all time, got just £2,600 from his first six fights.' Not that I saw much of my so-called fortune. As the business brain, George held the purse strings – and his grip was very tight. He gave me a few quid when I asked for it, but said it was important to plough most of what I earned into the company.

As always, I trusted George's judgment. He had even been right about me not going to Australia. The British Empire and Commonwealth Games Gold medal was, indeed, won by a very large gentleman from Uganda, named George Oywello – and, who knows, he may well have done to me what I'd done to Cornelius. How different my life would have been if I had hung on for that trip to the sunshine. As it was, I was now in a position to pay to go anywhere in the world.

But, day to day, as long as I had money in my pocket to have fun, I was happy. And, I was delighted to discover, I'd become even more famous. People stopped me in the street to congratulate me on a good fight and wish me luck. In packed restaurants, head waiters always found me a table, and other diners would come up, wanting my autograph. And there was TV: I took to it very well. I wasn't shy or embarrassed in the least; I loved being interviewed and given the chance to talk about my achievements. And I loved being invited to appear on game shows and going out to dinner with other celebs. I never forgot who I was, or where I came from, but I was only twenty-three, for heaven's sake, and I'm sure my head was turned a little. Idolised is a funny word, but that's how all the attention made me feel. And, quite honestly, I revelled in it.

What was a surprise to me was that I'd found the killer instinct. When I caught someone, and they were cowering, I didn't stop and back off. I went in to finish them off. The gentle side of me says it's disgusting to enjoy hitting someone so hard that they fall down, but I enjoyed hurting. I *did* get pleasure out of it. I've never been an aggressive person and always viewed professional boxing as a job. I didn't like getting my face bashed in one little bit, but it was an occupational hazard. I was always so focussed on winning I never felt any pain.

All I ever heard in the ring was the constant noise of the crowd. I rarely had any real idea how I was doing and sometimes I couldn't even remember what round I was fighting. I was lucky in that I had the stamina to go the distance, if necessary. I didn't really worry about ending up punch-drunk either; if I'd thought for one minute that fighting was affecting my mental clarity I would have quit.

Ultimately, if I knocked someone out, I felt great. I never thought about the damage I was inflicting, just the money. And, for a young man just four months short of his twenty-fourth birthday, I had lots of it, bearing in mind the average bloke was earning under £16 a week, dreaming of buying a house for £2,950, or a new Mini for £495 19s 3d.

And then, as I was dreaming of Christmas at home with mum and dad, and my mates at the Palais, George dropped a bombshell: I was a good fighter, he said, but not good enough to go all the way and challenge for the British title. I was brave and had a big right hand that had got me through my first professional year. But even inferior opposition had exposed a basic weakness: my defence was poor and I was taking far too much punishment. I needed to be taught how to box, not just rely on my punching power to get me through. He'd been speaking to someone who could do that, he said. Someone named Harry Wiley. He was a boxing trainer, but not any old trainer – for more than fifteen years, he'd trained arguably the greatest middleweight of all time, the legendary Sugar Ray Robinson, who, only four years before, had won the world title for the fifth time. If anyone could improve my technique, George said, it was Harry; he would sharpen me up for my next fight, against Peter Bates, at Olympia, at the end of January 1963.

That was the good news. The bad news was that Harry's gym was in New York.

And I was going there next week.

***

I was more than happy to go to New York on my own, but felt it would be fun if Melvyn went, too. I wasn't going to be pounding Manhattan's streets, or in the gym all the time; I was bound to have spare time on my hands, and who better to share it with with than my sophisticated, well-mannered mate? Apart from anything else, I wanted to see what the Yanks made of his cravat! Melvyn's mum and dad thought the trip would be a wonderful experience for him, so, early in December, the two of us – and Harry Wiley – set sail from Southampton on the luxurious liner, the Queen Elizabeth. Getting hold of any of the posh birds en route was out of the question, unfortunately, because I was already in training – even on the ocean waves – and Harry made sure I spent a lot of time, between meals, in the ship's gym.

Harry's gym was on 132nd Street in Harlem, the notorious black quarter, in up-town New York, and Melvyn and I seemed to be the only white faces there. We were warned not to go out walking at night but, to be honest, we weren't frightened. It was bloody stupid, thinking about it now, but we thought that if there's a punch-up, we could hold our own. We were young and didn't think about knives, much less guns. I didn't think about racial discrimination either, until Harry took us on an early walkabout. I spotted what looked like a nice restaurant and suggested going in, but Harry shook his head. 'No, no, I can't go in there,' he said, hurrying past. I couldn't believe it and felt so sorry for him that a colour bar, as it was called, still existed in such a cosmopolitan city. Personally, I could not understand racism: I'd got on great with black guys I'd met in gyms and at the Palais, and considered them mates.

After a couple of days, Harry made our day: he took us to Sugar Ray's bar, on 125th Street – Harlem's Broadway – to meet the great man. Harry must have phoned, asking him to meet us, because Sugar Ray – or plain Sugar, as New Yorkers called him – knew all about us and chatted away as though we were long-lost buddies. After half an hour or so, he said: 'Come on, I'll walk you along the street,' and off we went, with Sugar taking us into various bars, introducing us to the managers or, in some cases, owners. 'These are my friends from England,' he told them. 'If they come in, look after them.'

Out of the ring, Sugar Ray was an unlikely fighter. I'd read about some of his fights and thought he'd be bashed up, but he was barely marked, and was so dapper and immaculately dressed, and handsome, he looked more like a business tycoon or movie star. I think Sugar was doing Harry a favour being so nice to us, so that Harry looked the big guy, but it didn't matter a damn: for Melvyn and I, it was fantastic, an honour, being treated so respectfully by such a legend and we were very, very impressed by him. I couldn't wait to tell George when I got home.

Naturally, Melvyn and I made sure we went to the bars and restaurants Sugar had taken us to. And such was the man's reputation that we were remembered and always got a warm, friendly reception, not only from the people in charge, but customers, too. Being the only white faces in a sea of black, and always dressed in suits, we probably looked like cops. We'd get some funny looks, then a buzz would go round and someone would say: 'Hey, you're Billy and Melvyn – Sugar's friends from England. How ya doing?' And then we'd be off, telling them what I was doing over there.

What I was there for was to learn how to be a skilful boxer, not an aggressive fighter; how to stand back, defensively, and use more left jabs and right crosses, rather than wading in, head down, shoulders up, prepared to take two or three punches to get one of my big right hand ones in. George had tried coaching me to protect myself, because I did lead with my face and got clobbered a lot. But it was the only way I knew how to fight and, to be blunt, it hadn't done me that bad: I *was* the British amateur champion, after all, and had knocked out some pretty tasty customers along the way.

Having been sent 3,000 miles to learn what George thought I needed, I did my best, but without him there, I didn't have the necessary bite and enthusiasm and got more and more fed up being told I was doing it wrong. As I said to Melvyn after one particularly unhappy session: 'If I'm not doing it right, I wonder how I've got as far as I have!' I kept at it though, but couldn't help thinking that what I needed was someone to mould my natural ability, strength and punching power into a formidable fighting machine, not change my style completely by trying to improve a left hand that had never been any good.

With night after night of gruelling, boring gym work amid the build up to Christmas, I began to get homesick. New York was an exciting place, but I was doing precious little, apart from train, eat, sleep and go to the pictures with Melvyn, and the thought of being at home with mum and dad, and seeing my mates, became more and more appealing.

To break the monotony, I asked one of the guys at the gym if he knew any pretty ladies who would like to spend an evening with me and Melvyn. It was no problem, he said, and a couple of days later we were having dinner with two gorgeous black girls. We went on to a club and gladly accepted an invitation to go back to their place. We paired off and I was getting into bed with my one, when she said: 'What do you say to $50?' Suddenly, the dime dropped. 'Where's my clothes?' I said, quickly. I dressed hurriedly then banged on the other bedroom door to retrieve Melvyn. We laughed all the way back to Harry's. There we were thinking it was our English charm that had worked so well!

Finally, a week before Christmas, I plucked up the courage to tell Harry we wanted to go home for a break. He was very understanding and said that, as my next fight was five weeks away, a few days off wouldn't do me any harm; in fact, it might do me some good.

Suddenly worried that George would put the block on me going back, I asked Harry not to tell him. He promised not to but, surprise, surprise, George was at Heathrow to meet us.

'Harry said he wasn't going to tell you,' I said.

George grinned. 'You may be 3,000 miles away, Bill, but I know everything you're doing. Everything!'

'So who did I meet in New York?' I asked.

George grinned. 'Sugar Ray Robinson.'

I was thrilled, being home at such an emotional time of year and I know mum and dad were pleased to see me. But I couldn't get too cosy, and so, after a moderate blow-out, I teamed up with Melvyn and we flew back to Manhattan and saw in the New Year in Times Square. It had been an exhilarating year: I'd lost only one of my first seven professional fights – and even that was a dodgy decision, in my view. And the money had rolled in.

What, I wondered, would 1963 hold?

10

I was the only white guy in the gym but, from the moment I walked in, I didn't feel any resentment, much less hostility. No one, apart from Harry, knew who I was, or why I was in New York. None of the guys who walked in the door would have given a monkey's anyway: nearly all were on the breadline and there only to spar for a few rounds, then walk out with some dough. Harry would give them the once-over and if someone looked like he could handle himself, he'd be told to strip down and get some head-gear on. The guys were paid by the round. Sometimes I might spar against two for two rounds each, but generally I did no more than three rounds. Although they were there for the money, that didn't mean they took things easy: none of them pulled their punches, which was good, because if they hit me hard, I could hit *them* hard. I wasn't hurt in all the time I was there, but did knock down one of my hired help. He was about my size and build, and he was leathering into me for all he was worth, when I came up with a left hook to the chin and down he went. The point in sparring is that you punch hard, but don't follow up if you hurt someone, and I didn't this time: I stopped and waited for the guy to get up. His trainer went potty, accusing me of taking a liberty, by trying to knock his boy out. But, I didn't care. The guys weren't there to do me any favours; they were there for the money – and George and I were paying them.

The trainer complained to Harry that I'd taken a liberty, but a few days later they were back for another session. Before we started, the trainer pulled me to one side. 'Go easy,' he said. 'The kid's only an amateur.'

'This time last year, I was an amateur,' I said, brusquely. 'I'm still learning to be a pro.'

I couldn't afford to be soft or sentimental. Boxing was a tough business, particularly in the States. And all my sparring partners were tough buggers.

One evening, around seven, I was having a rub-down when I was aware of one tough guy, still there when everyone else had gone.

'What's he hanging around for?' I asked Harry.

'You're on his bed,' he said.

'What do you mean?'

'He works for me. I pay him to keep the gym tidy. He sleeps on the rub-down couch.'

'He's a good fighter,' I said. 'He could go places.'

Harry shrugged. 'Good fighters round here are two a penny. He's going nowhere.'

Suddenly it hit home to me how lucky I was. At just twenty-three, I'd had four pro fights in Britain's most prestigious stadium and was earning a fortune, while being groomed to take on some of the country's best-known fighters. Yet, here was a guy of roughly the same age, who was one step up from a bum, with nowhere to live and no hope of ever achieving in his life what I'd achieved in a matter of months.

***

With the Bates fight looming, I stepped up my training. The highlight of my day, after evening gym work, was to go to the cinema with Melvyn, then it was bedtime for me while he went out on the town. Often, I'd be getting ready for my run around Central Park at 5.a.m., just as he was arriving home. Usually, he was knackered and went straight to bed, but sometimes he joined me and tried to make me jealous by describing in detail what had happened with whatever lovely lady he'd seduced with his suave English charm. More often than not, he succeeded – the bastard!

***

We flew home six days before my Olympia date with Bates and, while I'd enjoyed being in a city I'd seen only in the movies, I was relieved to be out of it – not least because of the heat of Harry's apartment. He was kind to let Melvyn and I stay there, and his wife couldn't have made us more at home, cooking meals, morning, noon and night, without the slightest complaint. But the heating in that apartment was something else. Because of the bitter January chill – and the New York winter is far colder than ours – the heating was always full on, and the room I shared with Melvyn was stifling. It got so bad that we had to turn it off and open the window. Harry's young son, also Harry, loved popping in for a chat and it never ceased to amuse us that when he did, he always wore a hat, coat and scarf. He must have thought we were nuts!

✱✱✱

The BBC wanted to televise my battle with Bates live – which gave Harry Levene something of a headache. Receiving 45 per cent of the £3,000 fee – the same as the split between the boxers – was attractive, but would live coverage affect sales of his 7,000 tickets? Finally, Harry agreed to let the screening go ahead, which was great news for me because it provided a marvellous shop window for me to do well and show what I'd learned in America. It was also good news for a young lady from Hackney, named Greta Warden, who wrote to me before the fight, wishing me luck. Admitting she had followed my career for some time, she said: 'It is rather unusual for me to be writing a fan letter, as I am now more accustomed to answering the many letters sent to pop singer Helen Shapiro, for whom I work as a secretary. Helen and I unfortunately missed seeing you after a contest in Liverpool last September, as I believe you also stayed at the Lord Nelson Hotel during the time we were there. However, the purpose of this letter is really to wish you the very best of luck on Tuesday evening and to tell you that I am so pleased I shall now be able to watch the match on television.'

I hope Greta – and God knows how many millions of other viewers – were in their armchairs early that night, because I knocked the portly publican out in the second round. Not that I got much credit for it. I thought the left hook that did the damage was legitimate, but Bates collapsed, clutching his stomach, grimacing with pain, and the next day I was monstered in the papers. My arch critic, Peter Wilson, was particularly damning. He coupled my fight with Brian London's clash with an American Tom McNeeley, and said it was 'the worst advertisement for sport' he'd seen in years. 'Wretched, wretched, wretched fighting . . . was the miserable fare at Olympia last night,' he wrote. Strong stuff! But he had more venom for me, personally: 'Walker was all right . . . well, if it's all right to leave your opponent writhing after a punch he clearly thought was nearly low enough to give him water on the knee. I, as no water diviner, certainly thought it was not included in the register drawn up by the late Marquess of Queensberry whose grave must have been doing the twist last night.'

Normally, George took a philosophical view on what boxing reporters wrote. 'Take no notice,' he'd tell me. 'As long as your name is in the papers, and it's spelt right, that's all that matters. If they don't write about you, you're not in the public eye and you might as well be dead.' This time, though, he spotted an opportunity to use Wilson's attack to our advantage – and make the journalist look a prat at the same time. He contacted Peter Dimmock, who produced the live Wednesday night programme, *Sportsview*, and suggested I went on to look at a re-run of the relevant stage of the fight with the programme's presenter, David Coleman. I loved the idea of being interviewed on national TV and, naturally, Dimmock was thrilled with some topical controversy to spice up his programme. George and I drove to BBC Television Centre at Shepherd's Bush and watched carefully as film of me landing the contentious blow was slowed down and shown frame by frame. At one stage, even George and I thought the punch was going to land low, but it became clear, that it was fair. That's where George was so bright: by setting the record straight on TV, we reached not only *Mirror* readers, but millions of other fight fans who might have mistakenly thought I'd won on a foul.

Two months later, I was back before another sell-out Wembley crowd, facing my first American pro opponent – Joe Di Grazio. I started the first round as I had with Bates, gloves held high, the way I'd been coached in New York, and moved around the ring more smoothly than in any fight I could remember. But then I got caught with a couple of hard left hooks to the head and, a few seconds later, two right ones. Just before the bell, I got home with a few jabs to the face, but didn't feel right and knew I'd lost the round. Di Grazio was obviously encouraged, because he steamed into me in the next round, and caught me with two painful hooks to the head. Then he switched to the body and a swinging right, from way down low, crunched into the side of my chest. It hurt like hell and, instinctively, I retaliated. All that Harlem teaching went out the window as I pushed the pain aside and ripped into Di Grazio, hooking to the body and swinging to the head. My onslaught surprised him and slowed him down and, after being warned for using his elbow, he trudged back to his corner, wearily. I slumped on my stool, trying not to grimace with the pain in my side, as Joe Lucy went to work on me. 'I think he's broken my rib,' I said.

Joe felt it. 'Doesn't feel like it,' he said. 'I think it's just bruised.' He turned to George, standing just a few feet behind, and told him. George called out to me: 'Tuck your elbow over it and do him with the right.' I didn't have time to consider whether this was good advice or not because the bell rang for round three. What I did know was that I was in such pain I had to finish the fight quickly. I rushed at Di Grazio like a man possessed, hurling as many punches as I could. He was punching back at me, but the power had gone and he was no longer hurting me. I was all over him and finally doubled him up with a right to the body. He turned away from me, clutching his stomach, but referee Harry Gibbs didn't rule it a low blow, so I leapt in with a right to the jaw that sent Di Grazio crashing to the canvas. The noise from the crowd was deafening as he was counted out. And they were still cheering as I climbed from the ring, doing my best to hide my pain.

In the dressing room for the post-fight medical check, the doctor confirmed that one of my ribs was, indeed, broken. I glared at George. 'I knew it was broken. Why the fuck did you let me carry on?'

'We thought it was just bruised,' he said, matter-of-factly. 'What did you want me to do? Pull you out the fight?'

'Bollocks,' I yelled. 'That was *dangerous*. If he'd hit me there again, I could have been fucking hurt. And badly.'

It was true. If Di Grazio had hit me on the same spot, with the same force, who knows, he might have punctured a lung. And where would we all have been then?

I was taken to hospital to be strapped up and it gave me time to think. Why had George dismissed my pain so lightly? Why had he not asked for time out, for a doctor to check me? That would have been the safest course to take. And it wouldn't have been a problem: we could easily have got Di Grazio again, because a broken rib is not considered a knockout, and the end to a fight. It would not have cost us anything; in fact, we would have earned from a re-match. But, surely, my health and welfare should have been the priority for my manager – ignoring the fact, that I was his kid brother and he should have been looking out for me.

The more I thought about it, the more it struck me that, maybe, George didn't love and adore me for myself, as much as I'd always thought. Maybe he loved me only because I was earning him money. That night, the seed was sown that maybe I was being used; that George was fixated by money and in his mind, I was merely a commodity that could earn him lots of it.

After a couple of weeks in London, I returned to New York to prepare for a second fight with Mariano Echevarria in June. The pain had eased in my rib, but not in my heart. That George might think of me as a money machine hurt me deeply.

✳✳✳

When I came home, I found that George had been busy on our behalf: he'd invested £16,000 of my latest earnings in a run-down filling station – in the village of Corringham, about three miles from the house he was renovating, at Fobbing. And that was only part of the good news: with two garages, it made sense to sell our own petrol, he said, and he'd set in motion plans to sell our own brand. We'll call it Punch, he enthused, and have a big boxing glove as our symbol on each of the four pumps. He'd already bought a small tanker and, he said, we'd buy the petrol in bulk from the oil depot at Thames Haven, a few miles from Corringham. It all sounded great to me: I was doing the business in the ring and he certainly was doing good business out of it. If the first sixteen months of my pro career were anything to go by, we were going to be sitting pretty in a few years.

My worry that George viewed me more as a money machine than a brother eased. That awful night at Wembley was a one-off, I consoled myself. He'd been caught up in the moment, not thinking straight for once. Of course he cared for me. Why wouldn't he? We'd been through so much together. I felt even better when George said he also had some plans for mum and dad. They weren't getting any younger and he thought it would be good for dad to give up his drayman's job and run the new garage for us. There was a three-bedroomed flat above it, which would be ideal for them. And for me.

As if this wasn't enough to take in, George then outlined a plan that excited me even more. The cost of sending me backwards and forwards to America, plus all the other expenses incurred, had been worrying him, he said, and he felt it made sense to have our own training camp on our doorstep. His father-in-law's farm was ideal, George said. And the two of them were working on a plan to convert a barn into a gymnasium – equal to the best in the country – with extensive live-in quarters, where I could stay with Harry and a specially-imported American sparring partner.

I was thrilled. I was just twenty-four and lived for the moment. But George, the one with the brains, had an eye on the future, and he obviously wanted to make it as secure and happy as possible. Not only for himself, but all the family.

All doubts about him gone, I prepared myself for the second encounter with the tough guy from Spain, and agreed with George and Harry Wiley: I had to use the skills I'd learned in New York and box, not fight. I'd stood toe to toe with the guy for eight rounds at Wembley and got nowhere: he was so thick-set and strong, I could have whacked him with a hammer and he'd still have come after me. He'd never once been knocked out, so we'd be daft to think I'd win by trying to out-punch him. 'Keep throwing out the left, then get away,' I kept being told. 'Don't try to hurt him, just keep building up the points.'

George always wanted to be there when I sparred, and he was furious when he arrived at Joe Bloom's gym, a few days before the fight, to discover that the session had not only started, but finished – after an angry dust-up. My sparring partner was a former Empire champion, Joe Bygraves, who I'd sparred with many times as an amateur. He always went a bit mad – and this day was no exception. We had a lovely first round, but he started to make a fight of it in the second, and kept punching me after Harry called 'Time'. We traded several fairly tasty blows for nearly a minute before Joe's manager, Al Phillips, climbed into the ring and dragged us apart. Unfortunately, Steve Fagan, the *Daily Sketch* boxing reporter, was there with photographer Monty Fresco and, of course, the altercation was blown up the next day. Bygraves claimed I always got mad because I couldn't hit him, but that wasn't the case: it was always Joe who got the needle. Either way, the session shouldn't have flared up like that. Joe was flying to Rome the next day for a fight, and I needed to have my mind firmly on Señor Echevarria. Joe and I had far too much on our minds to have got involved in something so stupid.

My fight with Echevarria, at the Albert Hall, turned out just the way George and Harry planned. I kept jabbing my left and, for once, didn't go back to my corner at the end of every round, spattered with blood. But we had a right go at each other for the full eight rounds and the crowd loved it. Apparently, I was 10/1-on, coming up for the final three minutes, yet there was still some boos, among the cheering, when I got the verdict. I couldn't understand that.

Before the fight, my chief rival as Britain's best young heavyweight prospect, Johnny Prescott, was introduced from the ring. Johnny, a good-looking Brummie, had also had a points win over Echevarria, and George was already talking to Harry Levene about the two us fighting at Wembley later in the year. First, though, I had to recover from Echevarria and get ready to take on Kurt Stroer, the German No.5, in Carmarthen, South Wales, in just thirteen days.

And there was something else I had to do as well – buy myself a new car. I'd tired of the Jaguar saloon and felt I needed something sleeker and faster, more eye-catching, perhaps. I decided on the Jaguar E-type. More expensive but, what the hell, I was young and famous and could afford it. And, anyway, Melvyn and I needed an impressive motor to impress the birds when we went on holiday in Italy after the Stroer fight.

For once, I was not fighting in a town or city, but in the open air, several miles from Carmarthen itself. When we arrived, the place was virtually deserted, which worried Harry. He said: 'Gee man, isn't anyone coming to see this fight?'

'Don't worry,' George told him. 'They'll come from all the villages over the hills.'

And they did: the stadium was packed. Unfortunately, they did not see a good fight. Stroer and I fiddled around, not doing much in the first round, then I dumped him on his backside with a beautiful right cross in the last minute of the second. Stroer got up at six, but then looked at the time-keeper and seemed confused. He looked towards his managers, Al Phillips, and Arno Kolbin, a former European champion, seemingly for guidance, then removed his gumshield. I had no idea what was going on but the referee, Ike Powell, took it to mean that Stroer was unable to continue, and stopped the fight. Afterwards, we learned that the German thought a compulsory eight count, which applied in Europe, did not apply here, and was confused when he saw the time-keeper continuing to count when he got up. Unfortunately, for Stroer, that moment's confusion cost him the fight. Not that George and I gave a monkey's: we headed back to London, delighted to have pocketed £1,500 from my five minutes in the ring and my confidence boosted by Prescott's first-round defeat, by Alex Barrow, on the same bill.

✳✳✳

I now had enough money in the bank to do something that had been on my mind some time: treat mum and dad to a luxurious holiday. I suggested two weeks in Rimini, on the Adriatic coast, but they were apprehensive because they had never flown before and feared they wouldn't know what to do when they arrived.

'Don't worry,' I said. 'Melvyn and I will already be in the country. We can be at the airport to meet you.'

Dad was far from convinced. 'You won't be there,' he said.

'Of course, I will,' I assured him. 'Promise.'

After touring through France and Italy for a couple of weeks, Melvyn and I were at Riccione Airport when mum and dad's plane touched down. The look in my eyes must have given me away, because almost the first thing dad said was: 'You're skint, aren't you?'

I hated admitting it, but I was. So was Melvyn. We'd blown everything we had. We'd stayed at the hotel where they were booked, eating and drinking on tick for three days. Dad settled our bill and loaned me enough to get us home. Naturally, I made sure he was repaid in full when they returned home. He was not a bad lad, my old dad. I liked him and, at times, felt close to him, but he was not a father I could grab and hug. I would have loved to, and I'd like to think he would have loved to have hugged me, but the war years had robbed us of being able to openly display our affection.

✳✳✳

I returned to London to discover that Prescott had avenged his Barrow defeat in a re-match, and I was to fight him in a big pay day at Wembley in September. George had transformed Blue House Farm at Pitsea into a training camp and, through Harry Wiley, had arranged for Freddie Mack, a very accomplished American light heavyweight, to fly in from New York to stay with me as my resident sparring partner. The memories of my sojourn in the Italian sun quickly faded as I knuckled down to Harry's strict regime.

I may not have been the most skilful boxer, but, apart from one occasion, I was always in the best possible shape when I went into the ring. I found training very boring, but that didn't stop me throwing myself into it for four weeks before a fight. My routine at Pitsea ensured that the half a stone I'd put on in Italy quickly came off. I'd get up around 5 a.m., then run five or six miles with Freddie across Pitsea Marshes, then go back to bed for a couple of hours. I'd get up for breakfast, then go for a walk, or do some physical labour – such as chopping wood – around the farm, before having a light lunch and another sleep. Around 4 p.m., I'd go to the newly-converted gym and work on the punchbag, then spar with Freddie – always under George's watchful eye, of course.

My battle with Prescott was one every fight fan wanted to see, but, just in case ticket sales were slow, Harry Levene pulled a PR master-stroke to ensure the Empire Pool was full on 10 September: he arranged for the current world heavyweight champion, Sonny Liston, to box a couple of exhibition rounds between bouts. George got Sonny to come to the farm, too, and invited the national Press to take photos of him skipping in the ring, and, naturally, Sonny made an appearance at the weigh-in.

On the night of the fight, Sonny was introduced by the great radio boxing commentator, Eamonn Andrews, and climbed through the ropes in green tights and purple shorts. For nearly a quarter of an hour, he entertained the crowd with a round of shadow boxing, three rounds' sparring with another black fighter, named Fozedo Cox, and a couple of minutes' skipping to his favourite song, 'Night Train'. He may have been unpopular in his own country, but the Wembley crowd gave him a rousing cheer at the end of his 'act'. Personally, I didn't like the man: he was very rude and arrogant and had the most appalling habit, which I found unforgivable. When he was introduced to someone new, he would extend his right hand, supposedly for a handshake, and when the other person leaned forward, and proferred their hand, Liston would say: 'Take a bow,' and hit them in the crutch with the hand they'd been expecting to shake. For some reason, he never did it to me. I wonder what would have happened if he had.

At 13st 13lb, I was a stone heavier than Johnny and was a firm favourite, with most so-called experts predicting I'd win inside the scheduled ten rounds. When I dumped him in the first few seconds, I thought they were right, but Johnny got up almost immediately and started to box me, countering my wild, swinging punches with left hands that landed on target, albeit with little power. Johnny and I knew each other well from our amateur international days and fought in the right spirit. When I landed a left hook that was a little low, I held up a glove, apologetically, which Johnny acknowledged. There was nothing matey about the rest of the battle, though, and when we went to our corners at the end of the ninth round, we were both almost out on our feet from continual slugging. Waiting for the bell to go, I looked at George, standing behind Joe Lucy. He'd seen Johnny staggering back to his corner, like a drunkard. 'He's gone, Billy,' George said. 'But you're behind, you've got to stop him.'

Johnny must have known he had only to survive those final three minutes to get the verdict, but, instead of keeping me at long range, he came at me, as though it was he who needed to win the round. I weathered the storm and started getting in my right hand. Then, with only a minute or so to go, I caught him with a left, then a right to the jaw and he went down. He got up at seven, but was very groggy. He was at my mercy, but as I went forward to finish him off, referee Tommy Little stepped in and stopped the fight. Johnny went barmy, stomping about the ring, banging the ropes in anger and frustration. His supporters didn't like Little's decision either, but I think the ref did Johnny a favour that night because I could have seriously hurt him in the time left.

If the first Prescott fight had lit the touch-paper of the public's enthusiasm, the re-match, two months later, was explosive: it was hailed as the fight of the year and the Empire Pool could have been sold out several times, I'm sure. The spivs must have made a bomb with black market tickets that November night.

I went into the ring a 3/1-on favourite and certainly felt I was too aggressive and strong for Johnny, who hadn't seriously hurt me in the first fight. I should have finished him off in the third round, after I jerked his head back with a right uppercut. Johnny fought back gamely, but was stunned and, towards the end of the round, I rocked him with a similar punch. He wobbled and tried to pull me into a clinch, but I pushed him away and knocked him down with a cracking right to the jaw. I felt sure he wouldn't beat the count, but he got up at eight. He was unsteady on his feet, vulnerable to one solid punch, but I couldn't find it before the bell went and gave him time to recover. Although I kept going forward in the fourth, Johnny counter-punched me beautifully and opened a cut on my right eye. I dabbed at it in the next round and Johnny held out a glove apologetically, thinking he'd thumbed me. At the end of the round, Johnny extended the hand of friendship again after the referree, Harry Gibbs, warned him for laying on me. But I was too fired up, focussed on fighting, that I ignored it and just stormed forward. In the seventh round, I had Prescott hanging on desperately, after left and right hooks to the jaw, and seemed able to hit him at will. But, frustratingly, I couldn't finish him off. It was like this in the eight, and ninth, but Johnny had dragged some energy and strength from somewhere and was fighting back. I'd done so much more of the work in the earlier rounds, I felt I was ahead, going into the final round, but you're never too sure, so I looked at George. 'You're a mile ahead, Bill,' he assured me. 'Coast it. Don't let him touch you and you've won the fight.' If he'd said: 'I'm not sure. Go all out to stop him,' I would have. And I'd probably have won. As it was, I took it easy, jabbing the left hand, to keep out of trouble, and lost.

I couldn't believe it when Harry Gibbs raised Johnny's hand, and I had a right go at George for mis-reading the fight so badly. He was dismissive. 'I was so sure you were in front, I didn't want you to take risks and maybe get hurt.' I was angry with George, very angry. But now wasn't the time for inquests. What was done was done and nobody could change it. And while I was gutted by the defeat, it was hardly the end of my career. In just two years, I'd had thirteen fights and this was only my second defeat. How bad was that? And how bad was the money we'd ploughed into Walker Brothers' Ltd? I reckoned it was at least £30,000.

True to the way I'd always behaved in defeat, I answered all the boxing writers' questions, downed a few beers with Tommy and the rest of our mates, then retired to a hotel room to get hold of an attractive young lady I'd arranged to be waiting in the wings. Having gone without sex for four weeks while training, I had some time to make up. After my first year as a pro, I'd always made sure I had a bird sorted; it was one of the perks of my big fights. Don't get me wrong: the lady was always someone I knew; I've never paid for sex in my life and never entertained the thought of hookers.

Sometimes if I needed medical treatment in the dressing room, we'd hold the Press conference in a nearby hotel, laying on food and champagne for the Press guys. Then I'd chuck the journalists out and get hold of the girl. Other times, I'd fancy a laugh and giggle with my mates first; it depended on how knocked about I was. But I always – but *always* – had a girl waiting for me at the end of the night. Train, fight, pay day, fun. My life was very uncomplicated, really.

* * *

When we *did* have the inquest, it was not so much the decision that bothered George and I as my performance. We both agreed I'd done enough to win, but what was worrying was that I'd had several opportunities to force Gibbs to stop the fight, and hadn't taken them. Why was that? As George said, I used to 'go in and bang 'em out', and I wasn't doing that any more. I'd had Prescott at my mercy, particularly in that third round, and I'd failed to finish him off. Had I lost the killer instinct? I didn't feel I had: my mind wanted to go for the knockout, but, for some reason, the body didn't respond. To be fair, George held his hands up and blamed himself – at least, partly, for my performance. Harry Wiley and Joe Lucy meant well, he said, but maybe my head was being filled with too much advice and it was confusing me. He was right: I felt like a schoolboy, preparing for the Eleven Plus, with well-meaning relatives and friends telling him how to pass. When he comes to sit the exam, his head is filled with so many theories, he fails.

I believed George had been wrong to send me to New York. And I told him so. I could see the sense in learning how to defend myself, but I'd always been a natural, instinctive fighter with a big punch, and having to concentrate on the finer points of boxing had robbed me of the power that had made me such a handful. We had to do something to get that power back. And quickly.

In the end, George decided to dispense with Harry's services and the enormous cost incurred. We went back to basics, with George training me like he used to. All right, he couldn't be in my corner on fight nights, but he'd make damn sure he got me in the right frame of mind and condition up to the moment I stepped into the ring. He was with me on my early morning runs. He was with me in the afternoons. And he was sometimes still in the gym with me at ten o'clock at night. I saw more of George than his wife – and it was a point not lost on Jean. Once, she said that she was left alone so much, it was like George was having an affair. 'If he was, at least I could have a go at the mistress,' she said. 'But *you're* the other woman!' I understood how she felt but, to be honest, I loved being the centre of George's world again.

Leading up to Christmas, all the fight talk was when and where Prescott and Walker were going to fight a decider. Harry Levene was offering each of us £10,000, but Johnny's manager, Jack Biddles, turned it down, saying that now his boy had beaten me, he should fight Joe Erskine, then, hopefully, Henry Cooper for the British title.

Johnny did fight Erskine, but lost and never got a shot at Cooper. To add insult to injury, he was paid just £2,000 for the Erskine fight. When he found out what Levene was prepared to pay us to fight a decider, Johnny did his nut and sacked his soppy manager. Quite right, too, in my opinion. It was a huge mistake by Biddles and it cost Johnny dear, and not only financially. By not beating Erskine, his career dipped dramatically and he soon dropped out of the ratings.

Naturally, George and I were disappointed at missing out on our big Prescott pay day, but we didn't dwell on it. I took the next six weeks off, enjoyed Christmas at home with the family, then got cracking under George's regime to prepare for my next fight at Olympia on 28 January 1964. It was against my old sparring partner, Joe Bygraves, who I hadn't seen since our scuffle six months before. It promised to be an interesting clash, to say the least, and I was looking forward to it. I wondered if he was.

✳✳✳

Three weeks before the fight, George suggested we went to the Boat Show, at Earl's Court. As the money was rolling in, he was looking to the future, with both of us indulging in a millionaire lifestyle, he said. Admiring the hundreds of thousands of pounds worth of luxury yachts, he smiled at me. 'Give us a few years, Bill. Then we'll have a big house each and we'll buy one of these boats and cruise the Greek islands together.'

He was fun in those days, George. We were so, so close, we were like brothers!

11

Thanks to George, I felt relaxed and more like my old self when the bell rang for the first round at Olympia. Naturally, the Press had hyped the contest into a grudge affair, but you wouldn't have guessed it by Joe's attitude in those first three minutes: he threw only one worthwhile punch and was warned for pulling me around in a clinch. Before the fight, most experts seemed to think his only chance of victory was to stop me inside three rounds, but Joe didn't seem to be trying too much and in the third, was warned again – first for misuse of his head, then for not keeping his hands up. I was fighting the way I had in my amateur and early-pro days, not standing stiffly, throwing out tentative left jabs, but steaming in and throwing lots of leather with both hands, hoping one punch with either of them would land and be powerful enough to finish things. My onslaught seemed to wake Joe up and, in the fourth, he slowed me down, first with short, snappy punches to the head, then long-range jabbing. Sensing he might be able to stop me, he pinned me against the ropes in the fifth, pummelling my face with both hands. Ignoring the pain, I threw rights and lefts and forced him off and we stood in the centre of the ring, belting each other, at close quarters, with the crowd roaring. In the sixth, Joe was warned yet again for a low blow, but then had me wobbling at the knees with a barrage of punches. Halfway through the round, he went, bosh!, right on my protection gear, covering my cobblers, and Harry Gibbs stepped in and disqualified him.

The crowd booed loudly and Joe draped himself over the ropes, head hanging in supposed disappointment. But I'd seen him give me a sly smile as Gibbs disqualified him and I'm sure he'd decided to cop his dough and walk away, rather than tire and take a pasting in later rounds. The disqualification cost him a £100 fine by the British Boxing Board of Control, but that was a fraction of what Joe earned from the fight and he, most certainly, would have thought it a good move. He left the ring, almost unmarked, while I had a black eye and a cracked lip. The black eye worried me less: have you ever tried kissing a girl with a cracked lip?

The victory was a terrific morale-booster for me, after the disappointment of losing to Prescott. Okay, it wasn't the way I'd have chosen to get the verdict, but having Joe Bygraves in the 'Win' column on my record was no mean achievement and could only help in my quest for the British title. The guy had mixed it with very good boxers, including Henry Cooper and the Swede, Ingemar Johannson, and although, at thirty-two, his best days were behind him, Joe was still a force to be reckoned with and he'd had almost a stone and a half weight advantage that night. Also, very pleasing were the Olympia takings. It was another sell-out proving that, despite my Prescott setback, I was still a crowd-pleaser and a box-office hit – even though the fight was televised.

Drained by the Bygraves battle, I'd have loved to have taken off in the E-type and bummed around for a couple of months. Unfortunately, George had me back in action at the Albert Hall on 10 March, against a tall, rangy fighter from Nebraska, named Bill Nielsen. So, after a brief blow-out, I was back in the gym, honing my fitness. My twenty-fifth birthday was a week before the fight and, naturally, I put all celebrations on hold while I prepared.

My return to winning ways was short-lived: I lost to Nielsen, stopped because of a cut right eye, twenty seconds from the end of the eighth round. It was the first time I'd been beaten inside the distance since turning pro, and it hurt my pride. But that was only part of the story. To read some of the following morning's papers, you'd have thought I was bashed up beyond recognition and on my last legs. My old adversary, Peter Wilson, so behind me in my amateur, Bull of Belgrade, days was the chief culprit. 'Where is Walker – where is me darlin' Billy boy?' he wrote. 'That's him, floundering in his corner. Handsome Billy, unrecognisable with a nose that is a swollen toadstool flaring red, a right eye that is a dark cavernous socket and a mouth agape, dribbling a subterranean river of blood.'

Graphic stuff. And, no doubt, thrilling to *Mirror* readers. But it gave the wrong impression, and George and I were so angry, we went on *Sportsview* again that night, to set the record straight. The camera zoomed in on my relatively unmarked face, correcting the *Mirror*'s impression that I'd been cut to ribbons. What rankled even more, though, was that Wilson reckoned I was still a three-round amateur fighter and should consider giving up fighting unless I learned to defend myself. I was brave, with great natural strength, he said 'but it didn't profit a man to prove his face is tougher than his opponents' fists.'

'The man they can't gag' is the line the Mirror used to champion their top sportswriter. From what I saw, in The Albion, 'the man they can't stop drinking' would have been more appropriate. He was a good writer, Peter, and certainly a Fleet Street legend in his time, but he did like a drink! Unfortunately, I never got to the bottom of why he started to knock me so cruelly. I asked George if he'd had a row with him. 'No, I haven't,' he said.

'Maybe he has a daughter I've got hold of,' I joked.

✱✱✱

Probably sensing an easy pay day, Nielsen's advisors grabbed the chance of a re-match, at Wembley two months later. I was eager for it, too: despite the pounding I'd taken before being stopped, I honestly believed I was getting on top and could have done Nielsen in the last two rounds. I was convinced I'd beat him in the return. I had a month off before I started training again, and one of the first things on my agenda was to have a drink or three to celebrate my belated birthday.

I was at the bar in the Log Cabin, with George, Tommy and a mutual friend, Albert Rothman, when two attractive young women walked in. One of them was just my type – dark-haired, good form, lovely to look at – and I sent them over a couple of drinks, inviting them to celebrate my birthday with me. The one I fancied was a bit of a sourpuss, but she and her pal accepted the drinks and, after a while, I suggested to Albert that we went over and chatted them up. The dark one's dour expression belied her personality and we all got on well enough to go on a little pub crawl. Afterwards, I took my dark-haired beauty home to her flat, off Cromwell Road, west of Knightsbridge, and got the shock of my life. She was in the kitchen, making us coffee, when I looked through and saw her dark wig fall off, revealing just a tuft of hair on the top of her head – blonde hair! Spotting that I'd seen her, she quickly put the wig back on, then came into the lounge with the coffees. I didn't say anything, but I was a bit lairey then, and, when I got up to leave, half an hour or so later, I gave her a ten-shilling note. 'Here,' I said. 'Have that little tuft cut off.' It was a crass thing to say, very nasty and insensitive, and I got the reply I deserved: 'Fuck off, you arsehole,' she said, and slammed the door behind me.

What I'd said played on my mind and the next night I went to the Whisky a Go-Go Club, in Wardour Street, where she had told me she played the records. By way of an apology I said: 'Come on, you've got to laugh, haven't you?' Eventually she came round. 'I'm naturally auburn but I wanted to go blonde,' she said. 'My hairdresser advised me to do it slowly over a few weeks, but I insisted on having it dyed on the spot. Reluctantly, he dyed it not once, but three times, and when he removed the rollers all my new blonde hair fell out, leaving the little tuft.'

That broke the ice and we both laughed. We started seeing each other, but never went out, as such, because she was a blackjack croupier as well, and, after her stint at the Whisky, would work at the the Playboy Club and other West End casinos, until the early hours. What fame I had must have gone to my head a bit because I was a naughty boy who took terrible liberties. Whenever I'd failed to pull and was at a loose end, around two or three in the morning, I'd turn up wherever she was working and ask for the keys to her flat. Invariably, her first words were 'Fuck off', but I always charmed her into handing them over and I'd be waiting, ready for a game, when she got home. In time, we became very close and I'd move into the flat and stay for a week or so.

It was an arrangement that suited me, because mum and dad and I had now moved to Corringham, and it saved me having to schlep twenty-odd miles down the A13. Not that I'd had to do that every night, anyway. More often than not – even when I was at Ilford – I'd kipped at The Albion in one of the rooms above the restaurant. If we got lucky, Melvyn and I took our conquest back for some games, unknown, so we thought, to his mum and dad, who'd be in the bar serving after-hours' drinks to nightworkers in and around Fleet Street. We thought we were so discreet, letting ourselves in through the pub restaurant – which was closed at night – then creeping upstairs without anyone knowing. Of course, Micky Barnett, and his wife, Rona, knew all the time: they used to peep through the curtains in the pub and laugh as they watched us all tip-toeing about. Melvyn's grandmother was aware of our shenanigans, too: she was a lovely, very fastidious, old lady, and if she saw any underwear laying around, she'd put them in the wash. Once, a young lady, who hadn't gone home after our games, went downstairs looking for her knickers, only to find them hanging in the kitchen!

It was a wonderful bolt-hole for me, The Albion, and never more so than when I found myself locked out of a girl's flat in the early hours – in my bare feet. I'd met the young lady in a West End bar, and she'd taken me back to her bedsit – one of a maze of little rooms on the fourth or fifth floor of an old building, off Earl's Court Road. We had a few drinks and she ravished me – as they did, the rascals! I dropped off to sleep and woke up around 3 a.m., busting to go to the loo. The young lady told me the toilet was a communal one on the floor below and I slipped on my shirt and trousers, and went down. I found the toilet all right, but when I came out, I was so drowsy, I couldn't remember where the girl's room was. I wandered along the corridor and tapped lightly on what I thought was the girl's door, but a male told me, gruffly, to: 'Fuck off.' I got similar reactions from three other tenants and when a fourth – a woman – told me to go away, or she'd call the police, I panicked. The last thing I wanted, as a famous face, was to be arrested. Thankfully, I'd kept my money in my trouser pocket, so I decided, late as it was, I had no alternative but to get a cab to The Albion.

I crept down four flights of stairs, feeling a complete prat, and stepped out into driving rain, desperately hoping I'd find a cab driver willing to take a young man in bare feet to Blackfriars. Fortunately, I did. And, fortunately, Melvyn was awake to let me in. Don't ask me how I found my way back to that maze of bedsits the next day and discovered where the girl lived, but I did. She said she thought I'd walked out on her, but why she thought that, I don't know, because I couldn't walk very far without shoes! Anyway, the bizarre experience killed any desire I might have had to see the girl again, so I picked up my shoes and jacket and went off in search of pastures new.

✳✳✳

One day, George said: 'I've been approached by someone who wants you to make a record.'

'He must be out of his brain,' I said. 'I can't sing.'

'You'll have to take lessons,' he said.

I always did what I was told, so the next I knew I was standing in front of a guy on a piano, in a little Soho studio, learning the scales. Lo and behold, a couple of months later I was launched as a recording artist, with a jazzed-up old song, called: 'A Little on the Lonely Side'. The record must have made *some* money, because I was asked to make another and appeared on a TV pop programme, called *Thank Your Lucky Stars*, singing it. The song was called 'A Certain Girl', and I had four girls round me, singing: 'What's her name?', to which I sang back: 'I can't tell you.' It was banal, but hysterical. I was dancing about, waving my arms, as though I was shadow boxing, when I looked towards the wings and saw one of the girl solo singers, Anita Harris, doubled up laughing. I thought: I must be good.

I wasn't any good at all, of course, but that didn't stop a smart showbiz agent persuading George that I'd go down a bomb, touring working men's clubs in the north of England when I had no fights booked. The guy said he would teach me a few jokes, so that I'd be an 'act', not just a singer. George liked the idea, because he could smell money in it, but I didn't. Can you imagine the stick I'd have got, a Cockney fighter singing in front of a load of tanked-up northerners. How long would it have taken for me to lose my temper with some bloke taking the mickey? George knew better than to try to force me into it.

I wasn't asked to record a third song but I enjoyed my brief flirtation with the music business. Our company made some money. I got some publicity from TV appearances. And, just as important, I had a lot of fun.

✳ ✳ ✳

A few weeks later I was back at West Ham boxing club. But it had nothing to do with the fight game: I was making my debut in the world of TV advertising, promoting Vitalis, a grooming aid that was supposed to do wonders for men's hair. George would put my name to anything – as long as the price was right. And it was.

After a sparring session, I had to look at my opponent, grooming his hair, in the changing room and ask: 'What's that stuff you're using on your hair? It looks so messy.' I'd tell him he should use Vitalis and he'd put it on, saying something like: 'Yes, it makes the hair really great doesn't it?' I wanted to get one of my mates the part of sparring partner, but had to use a member of the actors' union, Equity. In fact, I had to join myself. The guy they brought in was a lovely person, but very limp-wristed and when I saw him in the ring, camping it up, I thought: 'This is never going to work.' But the production team edited our 'fighting' brilliantly and when the commercial went on the telly, George and I were really pleased. We were delighted with the fee, too: another nice pay day for the pot we were building together.

On the back of Vitalis, I was asked to do another commercial, Pop Into Your Local, promoting pubs and, this time, I was able to row in some mates, as they did not have more than one line to speak. All I had to do was walk into a pub, greet two of my pals, Tommy, and Bobby – who worked at the Log Cabin – then turn to the camera, and say: 'Isn't it great – your local? Where you can see your friends.' Then we'd pretend to drink beer from our half-pint mugs. Tommy and I only sipped our drinks, but Bobby had no idea about filming and downed his in a couple of gulps. That would have been okay if the director had been happy with just a couple of takes, but he wasn't, and kept re-shooting. By the tenth take, Bobby was so boozed he could hardly stand up, and his greeting of 'All right, Bill?' had become a slurred 'Errallrightbill.' Sadly for Bobby, his TV debut ended with the sack and I had to wheel in another mate.

✳ ✳ ✳

Everything was fun to me then, even work. I enjoyed playing the field, and there was a rich, juicy harvest of long-legged mini-skirted beauties that year. But the more I saw of my blackjack lady, albeit mainly for pre-dawn sex, the more I grew to like her, and the closer we became. Her father was Norwegian, but she was born in Manchester and had that Northern bluntness you could easily mistake for rudeness. She was certainly a tough, no-nonsense, in-your-face lady, who liked a good row and she often gave me stick for treating her like a doormat. But I admired her for that, because I probably needed it. Beyond her vile temper and foul-mouth lay a heart of gold and, if I hadn't been so full of myself, I'd probably have seen that we were something akin to soulmates, and perfect for each other. As it was, I was too busy indulging myself in all that Swinging London had to offer a rich and famous twenty-five-year-old, and did not see it until much later. Then, in those wonderfully promiscuous days, she was just Pat.

Pat Furoborg.

12

Five days before I was due to face Bill Nielsen for a second time, the British Boxing Board of Control passed a new rule that George had been campaigning for since I turned professional: for the first time in thirteen years, blood relatives were to be allowed in a boxer's corner. It was a decision I knew would help me: much as I admired Joe Lucy and Bert Spriggs for their expertise and encouragement, no one could ever replace George as my mentor and inspiration. Another rule that was scrapped was one forbidding boxers to wear white shorts. In the past, they had been banned because of their transparency, but new and better materials had overcome this. I was the first to take advantage of the new rule and climbed into the Empire Pool ring, on 12 May 1964, proudly wearing pure white satin shorts.

After my previous defeat, many people had written me off, suggesting I was never going to be a serious title challenger and should quit before I got seriously hurt. So I knew the re-match with Nielsen was arguably the most important fight of my pro career. I had to win. And I had to win big.

It took only a minute or so for me to benefit from the blood relatives' rule: I'd bulldozed Nielsen into my corner and was battering his body and head with both hands when he butted his head against mine, trying to bore his way out. In the past, I'd have stayed there, slugging it out at close quarters, but George, fearing a cut eye again, yelled at me to step back and allow Neilsen to straighten up. I did and we moved to the centre of the ring, where I found him easier to hit.

For some reason, in the second round, Nielsen mistakenly decided to fight, not box. He caught me with a left, right, left to the jaw, which only made me retaliate. I hit him with two lefts and a right to the body, then a crunching right to the head, and he went down. The crowd were cheering and stamping their feet so loudly, I couldn't hear the count until it got to 'nine' and Nielsen staggered to his feet. I pounced on him, pounding and clubbing him on the ropes. Fearing I'd push him out of the ring, referee Harry Gibbs pulled me off, but, sensing victory, and sweet revenge, I rushed Nielsen and pinned him in a neutral corner. Surprisingly, he dropped his hands, inviting me to go at him, and I smashed a right cross on his chin, sending him down again. He got up without taking a count, but went down a third time under a shower of punches and was counted out. The crowd went nutty and so did I. It was my first knockout victory since Di Grazio and even more satisfying that I'd achieved it with George in my corner at last. Surely I was now at the front of the queue for a crack at the skilful Welshman Joe Erskine – the only obstacle, it seemed, between me and Henry Cooper and the British title.

✳✳✳

Staying at The Albion, or at Pat's, was all very cosy but I felt at twenty-five I should have a place of my own, so that I'd be able to booze to my heart's content without worrying about driving. And it wouldn't do my love life any harm, either. The Kings Road was *the* place: the dollybirds in their mini-skirts were gorgeous, with legs up to their armpits, so, when I heard about a property going on the market a mile or so away, in Belgravia, I jumped in quick. It was a Georgian conversion, in Ebury Street: just one bedroom, but big, with an even bigger lounge. It was ideal for a wealthy young man in his prime, who wanted nothing more than to spend his money, indulging himself in all the fun London had to offer. I didn't give a monkey's that the lease was for only five years. When it ran out, I'd be a lot richer than I was now, and buying another place wouldn't be a problem. Anyway, I wasn't thinking about tomorrow; there was too much fun to be had today. I signed the lease, agreed the £13-a-week rent, and happily moved in that summer.

If I'd bothered to think about it, I'd have considered myself a very lucky guy. I was good-looking, strong and healthy, with an enviable physique that suited fine, fashionable clothes; I drove an expensive car and now had a smart flat in an exclusive, wealthy part of town. With enough money from George to fund a carefree lifestyle most men my age only dreamed about, I was what the newspapers called an eligible bachelor. But marriage could not have been further from our minds – even when Pat became pregnant. We felt we were too young and had all our lives ahead of us. Neither of us had any illusions about our relationship – so I paid for her to have an abortion at the London Clinic. I *did* want to get married one day, however, and when I did, I wanted to enjoy a long-lasting loving relationship like my brothers and parents. Right now, though, I had everything in place to become what I'd always wanted, what I'd gone into the fight game to become – a dashing man about town, with no responsibilities; a fun-loving playboy, who could have anything he wanted, when he wanted, and had no one to answer to. And, boy, was I going to revel in it.

I knew nothing about champagne, but someone told me Dom Pérignon was the most expensive and the best, so I started stocking some for the ladies. Why not? I could afford it. I met some guys who could get it cheap, so I bought dozens of bottles and filled a huge rack with them in my kitchen. Whenever I invited anyone back for a drink, it was always 'Care for a drop of Dom?' And when the rack was getting empty, I'd fill it up again. Maybe I was a little uncouth, but I was an ordinary bloke who'd been a fish market porter only four years before, and I wanted to show off my success. Can you blame me for going a bit mad?

The beauty of it for me was having a brother for a business manager. You heard all those stories of fighters earning bundles during their career, then mysteriously ending up broke, but I knew that wouldn't, couldn't, happen to me. I was able to relax, knowing that, apart from ensuring we got the best deals on my fights, George was pouring all my earnings into the pot, to be used for money-making ventures – like the garages – he felt worthwhile. It was everything a simple, easy-going guy like me could wish for: all I had to do was work hard and perform well in the ring, and enjoy myself out of it, while George secured our futures. He wanted me to live well, but was not going to allow me to blow my money and have nothing to show. So I was not on a salary: whenever I needed spending money, I just asked him for some – a bit like a kid asking his dad for pocket money, I suppose. There was so much coming in I could have more or less anything I wanted but, apart from the expensive car and flat, all I spent my money on were immaculate, made-to-measure suits and wining and dining. I was a quiet, smart dresser, and certainly never a slave to fashion: my trousers were slightly flared, but I never went in for those hideously wide, ostentatious 'kipper' ties that were so popular. And I never ate in the posh restaurants, such as The Mirabelle, in Curzon Street; I prefered little Italian places, such as Roberta's, La Stampa and Topo Gigio's, in Soho. I didn't like eating on my own and would go out mainly with Tommy.

If wearing expensive suits, driving a luxurious car and not worrying what I spent in restaurants and clubs is flash, I hold my hands up: I *was* flash; I got a buzz showing off what I had. But I was never flash in that horrible 'don't you know who I am?' way that a lot of celebrities have. I may have used my fame to give myself an edge at times, but I never played the 'Big I Am' with my mates. That's not to say I didn't pose sometimes, particularly when I was out in the E-Type. There were no yellow-line parking restrictions and you could leave the car outside where you wanted to go, and I got a buzz seeing the faces of people as, first, they clocked the car, then the smartly-dressed, handsome hunk getting out of it. Mind you, such a striking motor didn't go down well with everyone, and one Saturday night I foolishly got involved in something that could easily have seriously wrecked my career. I came out of the Whisky a Go-Go with a young lady – not Pat – and found three guys sitting on the bonnet. I got in the car, thinking they'd jump off when I switched on the ignition but, before I could do that, one of the guys held up the petrol cap. 'This yours?' he said, arrogantly.

'Don't be daft,' I said. 'Put it on.'

'Put it on your fucking self,' he said.

No pro boxer should ever get involved in a punch-up outside the ring but I lost it completely. I dived out the car, grabbed the petrol cap, smashed the guy on the jaw, knocking him into the road. Before his mates could do anything, I gave them both a couple of whacks, then jumped in the car and zoomed off. I thought I'd got away with it but, on Monday morning, George called to tell me a newspaper reporter had been on, saying that three guys had come to the paper, wanting to sell a story about being beaten up by Billy Walker. With my reputation, and all that went with it, at stake George told me we had to meet the guys at the newspaper office to try to keep the story out of the paper.

When I saw the state they were in – black eyes, cut lips and looking a lot less cocky than they'd been on Saturday night – I thought: 'Fuck it. I don't care. They were trying to take a liberty and deserved what they got.' But I was under pressure to keep what had happened between the four of us, so I apologised and agreed to pay them £1,000 to forget about it. Fortunately, the newspaper was on my side and didn't run a story of any kind. I wasn't happy paying those idiots a penny – let alone a grand! – but George felt it was worth it. And it probably was.

✳✳✳

Later that summer, I was invited to judge a beauty contest at a seaside resort. Naturally, I got chatting to the winner and when she said she had to go to London to catch a train home to Birmingham, I offered her a lift. The young lady was married, but she was up for a game and happily rang her husband to say she wasn't coming home because she'd won the contest and had been offered other work. After a lively night at Ebury Street, she told me she was competing in another beauty contest the following week – would I like to go? Yes, I would, I said, and I did. And we had the same again, which was very nice. But then she asked me to go to the next one, the following week, and I thought: 'Hold up – this is getting a bit heavy.' At first, I thought I'd cracked it: a dark, slim, married bird, with big boobs, coming up to London to see me every so often. I hadn't realised there was a beauty queen circuit and she was available every bloody week.

I told her I was busy but she said not to worry, she would find her way to Ebury Street. I did see her one more time because she was very exciting in the snore, but she was over the top and, in the end, I stopped taking her calls. I've got to hand it to her for cheek, though: when she turned up at the flat and was told by the landlord I'd gone away, she somehow found Tommy's address and went round there, wanting to know when I'd be back. Summer County, Tommy called her, because she came from Devon.

To be frank, it didn't bother me, getting hold of married women. I suppose it was a rascally thing to do, but I was very young then and didn't realise the repercussions it could have. At the time I thought it takes two to tango. Anyway, it wasn't as if it was my mates' or associates' wives. I had rules about that: it's not nice and I wouldn't feel right.

Anyway, in those heady days, I didn't need married women unless the opportunity presented iself: beautiful, young sexy girls were all over the place and, for someone like me, they were easy to get hold of; easier than getting a free drink, which my name guaranteed in every club I went to. Fame and power are strong aphrodisiacs and I made full use of both. But I never took advantage of women. Not once did I ask anyone to do anything they didn't want to do. I never pretended they were the only one I was seeing, and I'd learned my lesson about telling anyone I loved them. They knew where they were with me and seemed happy to be in my company for how ever long we found each other fun.

Not that I scored with every bird, mind. I got lots of knock-backs – bundles. I'm sure many didn't find me attractive but, at the same time, I suspect that others who didn't want to know blanked me for effect, so they could boast: 'Billy Walker tried to pull me, but I told him to fuck off.' I never took it personally. I'd think, Okay, shame you feel like that, and move on to the next one. If the same happened, I'd move on again. What was the point in wasting time? There's a party going on and we want to be there! If you're pissing about, move over and I'll find someone else. And I always did. If that sounds arrogant, I hold my hands up. I probably was. But instant fame, and more money than sense, can do things to a young bloke and it did affect me. No doubt about it. I was like a spoilt kid who wanted everything he could lay his hands on and didn't want to waste time.

If not all the ladies liked me, the club owners did. Being a popular 'Face', I was good for business and was welcomed into every establishment. Every one, that is, except Annabel's, in Berkeley Square. Unaware that its clientele included royalty and the aristocracy, I rolled up, hoping my famous face, if not my charm, would get me in. No luck: it was an exclusive strictly members-only club, and I needed to be recommended and sponsored by an existing member. As I didn't know any, that was the end of that. The rest of clubland welcomed me with open arms, though, and I have to admit I basked in the warmth of the doormen who greeted me by name. One who knew me was the main man at the Crazy E, a basement club in Jermyn Street, which, after Annabel's, was the hardest to blag your way into. One night I was at Brad's disco in St. James's, chatting to a photographic model, named Melanie Hampshire and, after a while, I suggested we move on to the Crazy E.

'We'll never get in there,' Melanie said.

'We will,' I assured her. And Melanie's photogenic face was a picture when we arrived at the club and the doorman greeted me with a smile. 'Good evening, Mr Walker,' he said, ushering us in. I'd only been to the club once before, with Melvyn, but I'd made a connection with the doorman and felt sure he'd recognise me. I would not have taken the chance otherwise.

Melanie was a lovely girl, very beautiful and great company, if a bit scatty, at times. She really enjoyed the big occasion and was the perfect person to accompany me to dinners, premieres and formal functions. Although, I can't say we were ever in love, we made a good-looking couple, and went out, on and off, for a couple of years. For most of that time I believed Melanie Hampshire was her real name, and that she was a wealthy girl, with a father 'in shipping.'

But, then, one of my East End girlfriends enlightened me.

'You're going out with Sandra Walters, aren't you?'

'I don't know anyone by that name,' I said.

'Yes, you do,' she said. 'She's a model. She goes under the name, Melanie Hampshire. She's from East Ham. And her dad's a docker.'

I found that funny. And couldn't understand it. Why would anyone who'd made a big name for themselves, who'd been on the front cover of *Vogue*, not once, but twice, want to deny where they came from? And why would anyone be embarrassed at saying their dad was a docker? For some reason, it seemed clear that Sandra had moved on in life. And it was dawning on me that I had, too.

As I'd become richer and more famous, I kept going back to Ilford, wallowing in the adulation of my mates, revelling in the witty cockney banter we'd always found so amusing. I was the 'local lad who'd done good' and I thought I'd never lose touch with the people and the place. But after tasting even a little of the sweet life the West End had to offer, I was aware of a change in me. The more I saw of my mates, the more I became aware of their limitations, and I no longer found them stimulating company. That was down to me, not them: I'd had the luck to be a good fighter which had opened doors for me and transformed my life. My new friends were worldly, exciting and forward-thinking, always up for something at a moment's notice but, then, most of them weren't ordinary wage-earners, with families to keep. My old mates were great guys and we'd had lots of fun together, but I'd moved up a gear and was living on a higher plain. Once, Ilford had been my world and I loved it, but I no longer fitted in. My fame, and the money that went with it, had opened my eyes to a new world I found exhilarating; where I never knew what was going to happen next; where people's expectations were endless.

I feel terrible admitting it, but the more I went back to Ilford, the less I liked it and, inevitably, it reached a point where I couldn't stand going back at all. Ilford had been good to me and I'd had very happy days there. But I was a West End boy now.

I would never betray my roots and certainly never deny my dear old dad was a poorly-paid drayman. But, like Sandra Walters, I had moved on.

13

Early in that summer of 1964, George and Jean moved into the Old Rectory, which they'd renovated into the most spectacular, sprawling mansion in Fobbing. Naturally, such a magnificent home required a swimming pool and George rang, asking me to help him and some friends put in the concrete base. I got Melvyn to come with me on the pretext that I was judging a beauty competion and he might get lucky with one of the contestants. Poor Melvyn! He's not the type who likes getting his hands dirty and he was well miffed when he discovered that the only thing he was going to get hold of was a shovel! A couple of the guys poured quick-drying concrete into one end of the pool and Melvyn, George and I had to shovel it into barrows and carry it to the other end. We'd been working at a hectic pace for about half an hour when I noticed George was laughing. He motioned to me to look at Melvyn. The poor bugger was so unused to physical labour, he'd fallen asleep, standing up, leaning on his shovel! We were tempted to leave him there, but George said he didn't want him decorating the pool for the rest of his life. We woke Melvyn up from his siesta and continued working until it was so dark we had to shine our car headlights on to the working area.

When we finished, around ten, we switched the lights off and were about to go indoors for some much-needed beers when we heard eerie sounds coming from the graveyard, the other side of a high wall, at the end of the garden. We were all a bit jittery because George had made a big point about the house being haunted, but it turned out the ghostly sounds came from George himself. He'd quietly disappeared in the darkness and crept behind the wall to give us a bit of a scare. That was typical of George then: full of fun, always wanting to laugh. On another occasion I remember us going to a Licensed Victualler's Fancy Dress Ball, dressed as clowns, and filling up water pistols with wine, and squirting each other like a couple of naughty kids. He was my adorable, fun-loving, dependable big brother. And I could see us growing old together, still laughing at the same silly things.

✳✳✳

All I wanted was to have fun, a laugh, and my Ebury Street flat became THE place to go for a party when the clubs closed. One of the clubs me and my mates went to a lot was The Latin Quarter, next to Tommy's place. It was a very well-known cabaret club where 'hostesses' earned money encouraging naive punters to buy champagne at exorbitant prices. In a corner of the club was a room where the girls sat and chatted before going to join men at their tables. It was called the Sin Bin and because I knew the club's owner, Peter Telany, I was allowed to take my pals there and talk to the girls while they waited. If there were any girls not doing anything when the club closed, I'd invite them back to my place for a party. We'd play records and dance but, before long, we got down to business with a sexy game called Truth or Action. We'd sit in a circle and, in turn, tell a self-appointed Master of Ceremonies, if we wanted Truth or Action. If one said Truth, for example, they might be asked if it were true that they fancied a particular person in the room. If, next time, they chose Action, the MC would tell them to get hold of that person. We were all drunk, so embarassment or shyness didn't come into it. It was a lot of fun. One big laugh. I was always a bit crafty. There was one particular girl I fancied and we'd agree to get together later on. We'd join in the fun and games, but when we'd had enough, we'd stagger into my bedroom for some games on our own, leaving the rest to see themselves out. Nine times out of ten, there'd be a couple of drunks still there, comatose, when we got up around lunchtime!

✳✳✳

I'd made friends with the guys at the music label Decca and we often met up in pubs around London's Oxford Street to play darts. One of the crowd was Terry Oates, who looked after overseas recording artistes when they were in town, and one evening he introduced me to a tall, slim and scruffily-dressed American singer/songwriter, named Harry Nillson. I liked Harry on sight and suggested we partnered up for the ritual darts match. Being American, he hadn't thrown a dart in his life, so I told him to concentrate on just hitting the board while I went for the doubles. When we won, Harry was very enthusiastic, but he drank brandy and his enthusiasm may have been down to the trebles he guzzled between throws!

When Harry learned he was unable to come to my next fight, he sent me a copy of his latest album, with an amusing cartoon he'd drawn on the sleeve: I was in one corner, he, flat on his back, in the other, and written across the top was the message: 'Sorry I can't make the fight, Champ.' Harry *was* in town when George and I opened our latest business venture – a Soho restaurant, named Isows – however. And he turned up looking so scruffy he nearly got thrown out.

George took one look at the unshaven guy in a dirty T-shirt, with holes in his jeans, and odd running shoes, and whispered to me: 'God, who's that? Get him out of here.' When I explained how successful Harry was, and how much he made from his music, George moved towards him quickly and the next I heard was: 'Harry, how lovely to meet you. How are you?'

That was George – fast to judge a book by its cover until he thought there may be money inside the jacket!

✳✳✳

My win over Bill Nielsen earned me the right to fight Joe Erskine – by far the biggest challenge of my career. If I could beat Erskine – who had beaten Prescott, who had beaten Brian London – who else was there to take on Henry Cooper for the British title? Harry Levene came up with the right offer to stage the fight at Wembley, on 27 October, and I roared off to the South of France in the E-Type with Melvyn, to have some fun in the sun before starting the hard work. I found I could always switch off and have a few beers without worrying about my weight. I never came back from holiday more than half a stone heavier, which was nothing to shift in a month. In fact, I preferred it if I was carrying a few extra pounds, because it gave me something to sweat off.

I didn't need any incentive to beat Erskine but, shortly before the fight, he stupidly presented me with one. 'If I can't beat Billy Walker,' he announced, 'I'd feel so bad, I'd retire.' In a way, I could understand why he said that: he was the former British and Empire champion, had had fifty-three fights – thirty-seven more than me – losing only seven. And, earlier that year, he'd out-pointed Prescott, who had beaten me. But it still seemed a rash, provocative statement to make, and it served only to stoke me up – which was the best possible motivation, because no one in the country gave me a chance. Although I was five years younger than Joe, and, at fourteen stone, had a weight advantage, all the so-called experts, bar none, said that while Erskine did not pack a hard punch, he'd be too clever and experienced for me: the wily 'Old Professor' would outbox the brave, but unskilful 'Pupil'. The bookies reflected this, making the Welshman an odds-on favourite to win on points.

Throughout our month's training, George convinced me I could pull off a sensational shock win. We had to accept that Erskine was a better boxer, and try to prevent him outclassing me. The only way, George said, was for me to be all over him from the first bell to the last, going forward, throwing as much leather as I could, so Joe didn't have time to get into his skilful rhythm. We knew he didn't have the power to stop me, much less knock me out, so who knows what would happen if the fight went the distance and I'd done most of the work? I threw myself into training at Pitsea and when I climbed into the ring I felt terrific. It was the most crucial contest of my career, more so than the Nielsen fight, and I felt fitter and stronger than ever. I was ready for half an hour's fighting that might decide my destiny; thirty minutes to make Erskine feel so bad he *would* want to retire.

The bell went and I was on him immediately, both fists flailing. Few punches found their target, but that was less important than stopping him from getting settled. For the full three minutes I stormed forward, with reckless abandon, and at the end of the round George was pleased. All I had to do now was keep it going. To be fair, Joe survived my relentless onslaught in the early rounds, but he began to tire in the fifth and got caught by some wild punches he'd previously found easy to slip. This encouraged me and I kept going forward, driven on by the incessant roar from thousands of my supporters, willing me to finish it with one big punch.

But Joe was by far the cleverest boxer I'd faced, and he always bobbed and weaved his way out of trouble. When I did find my way inside, he tied me up, then hit me on the counter as we broke free. Once, he rattled my face with three or four straight lefts and I heard George yelling: 'Work with him. Stay close. Don't let him settle.' And I did my best and went forward, kept going forward, taking Joe's blows, but not feeling them, not letting myself feel them. My left eye was now sore from the constant jabbing, but I ignored it and steamed forward again and again, throwing punch after punch from all angles.

In the second half of the fight I got a bit desperate and was cautioned several times by Bill Williams, for misuse of my head and hitting low with two left hooks. But Joe was warned for various fouls, too. It was that sort of fight: untidy, but all action, and, for the crowd, thrilling. I thought I'd finally got Joe in the eighth: I clobbered him with a left and right to the jaw and he swayed over the ropes. I hurled myself at him, eager for the killer punch, but Joe was fooling and turned me round and danced away. Before the bell, I bludgeoned him several times about the head and he came out for the ninth with a dressing over his left eye. Throughout that round, and the tenth, I carried on as I'd started – going forward all the time, driving Joe around the ring, pummelling him upstairs, downstairs, round the neck, on the arms and on the elbow, anywhere I could. He was still on his feet when the bell ended the fight, but my non-stop aggression got me the verdict.

It didn't please many people, who thought Erskine deserved at least a draw, but George and I didn't give a monkey's. I'd followed his tactics from the first bell to last and scored the most important win of my pro career, confounding the critics who said I was nothing more than a strong novice with a big punch. It was a triumph that would, surely, give me a crack at Cooper, and as Williams raised my hand, George hugged and kissed me on the cheek – thrilled he'd guided me to a famous victory, but, no doubt, also thinking of the monster pay day ahead.

✳✳✳

George loved keeping me in the public eye between fights and he set up a marvellous double-page spread in the *News of the World*, in which I was interviewed by the sexy British actress Diana Dors, as part of her popular, long-running series, Dors and Men. Diana was a fervent boxing fan and regularly came to my fights with other major stars of the day, who saw televised fights as an unmissable opportunity to get all dolled up – ladies in fur coats, gents in tuxedos – and be spotted at ringside.

The newspaper interview went so well, Diana invited me to a party at the London home she shared with her husband, Dennis Hamilton, and I was getting friendly with a tasty bird when Dennis pulled me to one side and nodded towards one of the bedrooms: 'If you want some privacy,' he whispered, 'slip her in there.' I thought that was a a handy thing to know and I was just going to take advantage of it when someone I knew warned me: 'Don't go in there. There's a two-way mirror inside and they all gather outside and watch you.' I immediately changed course, darted upstairs with the girl, and locked ourselves in another bedroom. Dennis and some of his guests came running up after me and banged on the door. 'Not in there, Billy, not in there. You've got to go in the other room.'

I said something along the lines of 'Bollocks'. And I heard them all laugh.

Another beauty I was thrilled to meet was Diana Rigg, who played Emma Peel in the hit TV series, *The Avengers*. George had agreed for me to do a 'Beauty and the Beast' publicity shot for a newspaper – and, because I was still sporting a black eye, I was in make-up longest. The photographer wanted Diana to sit on my shoulder, but the pose didn't work. After a few awkward minutes, the wonderful Miss Rigg took over: 'Sit there, Billy. Put your legs together and put your hands on your knees. Now, keep a straight face.' With that she draped herself, seductively, over my lap. How I kept the self-satisfied smile off my face while the photographer got his shot, I'll never know!

***

A few weeks after the Erskine fight, I was asked to write an article for the *Boxing News 1964 Yearbook*. I said there was always room at the top – and that's where I was heading. A Walker–Cooper clash – Experience versus Strength, Skill versus Strength – would be a battle that would fire the public's imagination and fill not only the Empire Pool, but the famous 100,000-seater football stadium nearby. I'd had only seventeen pro fights, but honestly believed that, by beating one of the country's finest boxers, I'd earned that golden chance, and that it would happen the following summer.

Sadly, it was not to be.

✳ ✳ ✳

For some reason the Cooper camp didn't feel I was ready, so, instead of 'our 'Enery', my next fight, on 26 January 1965, was against an American few people in Britain had heard of. Charley Powell was his name: a 6ft 4in black guy, with eleven years' experience, who had once been rated fifth in the world. I wanted to put on a good show to capitalise on my Erskine victory, but Charley Boy didn't seem as if he'd come for a long battle. Right from the off, he held his hands surprisingly low and backed away, apprehensively, whenever I went forward. He brought a slight trickle of blood from my nose with a couple of long lefts, but I made him wince with a heavy right to the body and he seemed glad to hear the bell. He offered little resistance in the second round, but showed a glimpse of the classy fighter he'd once been when he landed two beauties on my jaw after I'd caught him with a left, then a sharp, clubbing right. It served only to drive me on and I landed two chopping rights to his unguarded chin, which sent him, face first, to the canvas. He got to his knees at 'seven,' but slumped down again, appearing to be in some pain and, after he was counted out, his seconds worked on him for about a minute before getting him back to his corner. The Olympia crowd's reaction was mixed: cheers for me, who'd done my best to give them their money's worth, but boos for Charley who, they clearly felt, had come only for the money. Predictably, the papers called the fight a fiasco, but, as I always say, you can only fight as well as the other guy lets you. And, that night, I did as well as I could. Was it my fault that Charley didn't get up after taking those rights on the chin?

One of the few loyal and trusted friends allowed in my dressing room after fights was Billy Adair, a good pal of George's, who ran a fast-food restaurant in the West End. He was there after the Powell fight and was keen for me to meet a friend named Jack Stevens, who, he said, owned a small boarding house on the Channel Island of Jersey. Jack seemed an agreeable sort of bloke and, in the brief chat we had, he was at pains to tell me that I should check Jersey out: it was a fun place, he said, and was sure I'd like it. From the way he described it, I was sure I would, too.

Billy Walker

***

The fight was great for our bank balance, but not for my career. I was able to trade in my E-Type and treat myself to two new cars – a nippy green Mini Cooper for zipping about the West End, and a silvery blue Aston Martin to impress the ladies. But, career-wise, I clearly needed a formidable, more credible, opponent. And I needed him fast if I wasn't to lose the clout and impetus the Erskine fight had given me. George came up with the answer: Brian London, a hugely-experienced boxer, from Blackpool, who'd had forty-four fights, including an unsuccessful challenge for Floyd Patterson's world title six years before. A non-title fight against a dour Northerner didn't have the same appeal as an all-Cockney clash for the British championship, but you wouldn't have guessed it from the reaction when the Wembley contest was announced: it caused the biggest ticket stampede for years and, besides being a sell-out, was shown live on closed-circuit TV in two theatres – in London and Birmingham – and as a top-of-the-bill feature for a boxing tournament in Manchester. Brian had fought in the capital several times, but none of his bouts had tickled the fight fans' fancy as much as this one. Despite the disappointing Powell affair, I was obviously still someone the public wanted to see.

At twenty-six, I was six years younger than London, and 5/4-on favourite when we entered the ring on 30 March. If the bookies had known about my physical condition, however, they would have had second thoughts about those odds, for I'd gone down with a nasty flu-like cold a week before the fight and felt so weak I wanted to pull out. But George said it was too late and we had to go through with it. A few hours before setting off for Wembley, I'd even had to have my sinuses drained.

The boxing writers were sure I was going to win, too: more than one said London would not withstand my onslaught and the fight was unlikely to last two rounds. But it didn't turn out that way. I rushed into war, as usual, and forced Brian to the ropes, chopping him about the head with short clubby rights, then pumping away with left and rights to the body. But I went to my corner disappointed at not catching him with one of my right-hand hammer blows and finishing it, because the way I was feeling, I didn't think I'd be able to last the distance. I rushed out for the second in the same way, willing to take two or three punches to the head just to get in one of mine, but Brian was too clever for me and quickly got on top. Many had been expecting a real brawl, but Brian had obviously decided to box, not fight, and he did it magnificently. By non-stop aggression, I'd managed to blunt Erskine's skill, but I couldn't stop Brian hitting me at will. He leapt at me at the start of the third and, before I knew it, I was trapped in a neutral corner, being battered about the head, unable to do anything but duck and hide behind my gloves. Eventually, I got out and stood toe-to-toe, swapping punches, but Brian hurt me with a hard right under the heart, and I went back to my corner dejected, wondering whether I'd be able to summon the strength to get back in the fight. The minute's rest brought me round: Brian rocked me with a left, right, left, right, but I forced him on to the ropes with far heftier swings and was all over him. Although he kept jabbing out his left, he couldn't keep me at bay and I felt I was back in the fight. But in the fifth and sixth, he monstered me and my left eye started to close. Tiredness was making me careless and after a couple of wild swings landed on Brian's kidneys, referee Harry Gibbs warned me for punching low. To his credit, Brian took the punches without complaint. I was lucky to get through the last four rounds. I kept going forward, looking for that big punch, but Brian out-classed me and, on several occasions, I was so bemused, I ended up with my back to him. Each time, Brian turned me around and spanked me about the head; the teacher admonishing the pupil. I felt a little hopeful at the sight of a cut at the side of his left eye, but it didn't affect him because, in the last three rounds, he seemed to hit me with every punch in the book, and I took a lot of punishment before the final bell. It was no surprise to me, or anyone, that Brian got the verdict. I'd been odds-on to win, but the way I was feeling that night, I should have had my money on him.

My despondent mood was not helped when I heard Jack Stevens come in with Billy Adair and start going on about the fight. I couldn't see him, but he started crying – which is hardly the thing to do in a fighter's dressing room. He really got up Tommy's nose, and the next I heard was Tommy bellowing: '*He's* lost – not you, you prick! Get out of here, you fucking idiot!' Shaken by the ferocity of Tommy's fury, Jack swiftly dried his tears and made himself scarce.

How Jack had the nerve to come back to the dressing room again after that, I don't know. But he did and would go on and on about paying for me to go to Jersey and see for myself what a great place it was. I never took much notice, because people were always trying to get into me, offering all kinds of things for their own ends, but there was something about him that made me think he might be genuine.

❊❊❊

The defeat was terrible for me. Where did I go from here? If I couldn't beat London, how could I expect to have a go at Cooper? But that was a worry for another day. Right now, in keeping with my 'win or lose, plenty of booze' policy, I had the eye patched up, had a few drinks and went off to sort out the young lady who'd been waiting so patiently in the wings. Then, it was off to the Continent in the Aston Martin for three months lazing around with Melvyn, before returning to get in shape for my next fight, against an Italian, Eduardo Corletti, in San Remo, on 19 August.

At the time, I was having an affair with a beautiful woman, named Josephine. As luck would have it, Josephine was going to be in Sardinia on holiday, with her three-year-old son, when I fought Corletti. San Remo was less than an hour's flight away, on the French–Italian border, so, naturally, I said I'd fly in and spend a few days with her after the fight.

I didn't expect to spend too much energy on Corletti: he'd had two ten-round and two six-round fights in the last four months and George assured me it would be an easy outing that would put me back on the winning trail. Quite where he got that information from I don't know: Corletti proved a difficult customer and, after a gruelling ten rounds, in which my face took a right battering, I was happy to get a draw.

Although I was physically knackered and not a pretty sight, that didn't mean I wasn't going to keep my promise to join Josephine for some games. I'd arranged to see her the day after the fight but, by the time I got to Genoa Airport, and waited for a flight to Sardinia, it was two in the morning before I got to her hotel. My first, totally selfish, thought was to find her room and wake her. I'd gone without sex throughout my month's training and, despite my black eyes, busted lip and aching limbs, I was rampant and up for anything Josephine could provide. The gentleman in me won, however, and I checked into another room and slept the night alone. The next morning I discovered Josephine had been next door all night: she'd deliberately booked adjoining rooms to make it easy for us to get together, but hadn't told me. Needless to say we made up for lost time.

✳✳✳

Shortly after I returned from Italy, George said that he'd decided to invest some of our money in a disco. 'They're all making bundles, Bill – we've got to have one of our own,' he said. So we opened Dollies, in a basement in Gerrard Street, in partnership with an American entrepreneur, Oscar Lerman, and a guy named John Gold, who George had known since the late fifties. George went to see Billy Adair about some building materials to renovate the property. And while he was there, Billy started enthusing about the success of one of his other ventures – a fast-food restaurant, off Regent Street, which provided baked potato lunches for West End workers in a hurry. The restaurant, which Billy called Baked Potato, catered for fifty people every day, but George quickly saw a potential for expansion and suggested opening another one in the City of London, using my name to promote it. Billy didn't have any spare capital to invest but we did, and he could see the sense in joining forces with us to expand his idea. Through his connection with a businessman well known in boxing circles, George found an ideal property for the restaurant – a basement in a very large building in Foster Lane, near St. Paul's. And that Autumn, just before my return fight with Eduardo Corletti, we started transforming the basement ourselves. The company was called Waldair Limited. And the restaurant, which we planned to open early the following year, was to be called: Billy's Baked Potato.

✳✳✳

If the fight with Brian London had been crucial in my quest for a title shot, the return with Eduardo Corletti, at the Empire Pool, on 19 October, was even more so; not only to keep me in the championship hunt, but also to silence those who felt I was finished. After the exhausting draw in San Remo, I should have appreciated what a tough, resilient, clever opponent Corletti was. I should have knuckled down to a month's training, listened to what George had to say, and got myself in tip-top condition and the right frame of mind. But I didn't. And I paid the price.

If determination and aggression were the only things that mattered I'd have won easily. I chased Corletti for nearly eight rounds, but, apart from a right to the jaw in the second, I never hurt him. And what points I scored for my work rate were more than cancelled out by Corletti's crisp counter attacks; sometimes two or three to one of mine. It takes two to make a fight and if I hadn't made the running, there wouldn't have been one. But it was down to me to wear the guy down, then catch him with my famed right hand. And, again, I failed to do it.

Going into the eighth round, I thought I was doing well and might yet be able to find a big punch. But then Corletti caught me with a hook that sent me reeling into the ropes, and as I bounced off, I walked into a peach of a right hand and went down. I managed to get up at eight, but was all over the place. Corletti came in for the kill, pounding away at my face with both hands. I tried to hold on, but I was still dazed, and unable to defend myself. I was as sick as a pig when Bill Williams stopped the fight, but I don't think he had a choice. Our faces told the story: mine was bloodied and swollen; Corletti's was virtually unmarked. Afterwards, the reporters all wanted to know whether I was now going to hang up my gloves. George and I told them no. But we both knew it had been a bad result for me. And while it was a small consolation that Henry Cooper also lost on the same bill – to an opponent he was expected to beat – it was clear that if I was to prove the doubters wrong, I needed to change my attitude.

As George said the next day: 'Make your mind up. If you want to stay in boxing, start living the game again. If you don't, pack it up.' George was right as usual.

Having won only one contest that year – against an over-the-hill fighter who fell over rather too easily – I didn't deserve a holiday on the company. But George wanted to take our mum and dad, and Jean's, on a Christmas cruise round the Canary Islands, and who was I to argue? It promised to be a lot of fun and I took Susanne, a nice-looking lady I'd been seeing on and off for a couple of months. After just two days, however, I was bored: George had booked us all in First Class and I couldn't bear all the formality that went with it. I made an excuse that I needed to do some training. The gym was in tourist class, and I got chatting to a tasty bird, who was the ship's hairdresser. She invited me to the crew's quarters and, having a drink with her and the crew was a welcome relief from the stuffiness of the upper decks. And, naturally, I crept down to the hairdresser for some games a few times on the pretext of training in the gym for a couple of hours.

There are things I've done in my life I wish I hadn't. My behaviour on that cruise is one of them. I was a right horrible bastard then, quite insensitive to anyone's feelings. And, much as I'm ashamed of my arrogance and conceit, you can't put the clock back, can you?

14

I needed a comfortable fight to restore my reputation, and my confidence, and George arranged one for me, at an Anglo–American Sporting Club tournament at the Hilton Hotel in Mayfair. It was one of those posh, black-tie events, where an expensive four-course dinner preceded the action, and this year the Duke of Edinburgh was among the ringside VIPs. I'd always fancied the idea of performing for royalty, but I had an important task to fulfil before I could do that. Throughout the winter, George had orchestrated the transformation of the Foster Lane basement and, with an eye on the maximum publicity, delayed the opening of Billy's Baked Potato restaurant until 22 March, nine days before the Hilton date. With my training all but over, I was to attend the opening and pose for photographs with the various celebrities George had invited. The opening went better than he and I expected and did achieve a lot of publicity. But no one there that night could possibly have imagined just how profitable Billy's Baked Potato would become, much less that its success would spawn a business empire that would threaten my loving relationship with George.

The restaurant had seating for 500 and catered for City workers wanting good, simple food, served quickly. It majored on baked potatoes, filled with minced beef, cheese and bacon, bacon and onion, even curry. We did serve 'specials', such as shepherd's pie, steak and kidney pie, steak and fish, and omelettes, but in the main it was a baked potato place and quickly became known as that. We priced our meals at 2s 9d – under the 3s value of the luncheon vouchers that most of our customers used. As giving change from these was not allowed, we made 3d on a meal in most cases. Often, knowing it would cost them only 3d, people would order one of the 6d puddings on offer, too. It doesn't sound much, but with the volume of people packing the place, it added up to a nice little earner every weekday. We opened at 11 a.m. and closed no later than 3 p.m., using as waitresses mainly mothers wanting to earn a bit of pin money while their children were at school. The food was cheap. It was fast. And it was the recipe for the most spectacular success. Within months, George was already thinking of opening another one.

As the 'Face', my role was to greet people and show them to their seats. I'd have a run in the early morning, go back to bed until 11 a.m. or so, then potter off to the restaurant as the customers, mainly young office girls, started to come in around midday. What a lovely job it was: 'Hello, how are you? You look lovely – what's your phone number?' I'd stay there for a couple of hours, then go home for another little nap before starting the serious business in the gym at four o'clock. If I wasn't in training, I was out with the lads, having fun, naturally.

Unfortunately, at the Hilton the following week, Prince Philip and the other illustrious guests did not see much of me. I was far too strong for my Swedish opponent, Lars Norling, and stopped him midway through the fourth round. I was very trim and fast after my five-month break and never gave him a chance to get in the fight. My left eye was nicked after a heavy right, but it didn't bother me and, in the third, I opened a cut between Norling's eyes with a right of my own. His seconds worked feverishly to repair the damage, but I went to work on it in the fourth, and referee Harry Gibbs had no option but to step in. Later, I had to go to the top table to present the Duke with a cheque for charity. I felt a bit of a prat because he and everyone else at the table were in DJs and I was in my dressing gown, still sweating from bashing the Swede. 'Don't worry, Billy,' the Duke said, with a charming smile. 'We don't expect you to dress for dinner.' As I turned to go, he said something else, but I didn't catch it. Maybe he'd heard of my reputation and was telling me: 'Please stop phoning my missus!'

✳✳✳

With his mind now more on business than boxing, George did not have time to train me and put the word out that he was looking for someone to take over. The first guy to come on was my namesake who had not been impressed with me as an eighteen-year-old at West Ham. Remembering how Billy had said that I didn't have what it took to make it, George told him: 'Fuck off. If I'd taken your advice Billy would never have got in the ring.' Instead, George and I went for Freddie Hill, a former amateur boxer, who'd trained such eminent fighters as Alan Rudkin, Bobby Neill and Frankie Taylor at his legendary, but strict and traditional gym above the Craven Arms pub, in Battersea, South London.

'How would you like to train Billy?' George asked him.

'Well, I don't mind giving him a month's trial,' Freddie joked, well aware that I was earning far more than all the other fighters under his wing and he'd be on a big cut.

'Saucy bastard!' I said, returning the smile. 'I like you. We'll get on all right.'

And we did. Fred had his own way of saying and doing things, and often upset people by being so dogmatic and effing and blinding all the time, but I thought he was a lovely man and I liked him. I really didn't need a trainer, but it was great to have someone to goad you on, make you do that extra little bit that makes the difference, and Freddie was a past-master at it. If George was too busy, I was more than happy to let Freddie take control. Not that George took his eye off the ball completely: when we stopped training at Pitsea and I said I'd be staying in Ebury Street, George threw a wobbler: 'I'm not having you stay there on your own while you're in training. You'll have a bird there every night!'

That wasn't quite true, but I could see his point. I'd always found it difficult to resist temptation, particularly where nice-looking ladies are concerned. In the end, Tommy McCarthy solved the problem. Although he and the lovely Ann had only just got married, Tommy volunteered to let me stay with them and make sure I didn't go off the rails.

I must admit, Tommy's flat in Oxford and Cambridge Mansions, held an embarrassing memory for me. For some reason, shortly before he got married, I didn't want to take Josephine back to Ebury Street for a game, and Tommy allowed me to use his place, while he and Ann were at work. Josephine and I were in bed when we heard someone come in the front door. We weren't unduly disturbed, thinking it was probably Tommy or Ann, but then this tall, very statuesque young woman, with an unbelievable figure, walked into the room and stared angrily at us. She was an American girl, named Jane; she worked at the Windmill Theatre and posed naked on stage. In those days, any naked person on a stage was not allowed to move and she had obviously got the job because she was so stunning. And Jane was not best pleased – because I was having games with her, too, and she knew nothing about Josephine. There was a bit of an argument, which ended with Josephine and me getting dressed and leaving because, unknown to me, Jane was living in the flat for a while. It was all very embarrassing, not to say inconvenient, but that wasn't the end of the matter. When Tommy and Ann got married, the three of us came face to face again – because Jane and Josephine were bridesmaids! I felt somewhat awkward, because the two girls were not speaking, and, to add to the situation, I was accompanied by my cruise guest, Susanne. But I quickly got over my embarrassment: to me, sexual encounters were harmless fun. Pure and simple. I never said to any girl: I love you to death, darling – get your gear off!

Staying with Tommy and Ann was a great set-up for me: in the mornings, Tommy and I would get up at 5 a.m. and go running, under Freddie's watchful eye, along Sussex Gardens, into Hyde Park, then follow the south side of The Serpentine round to the south-east corner, at Knightsbridge, before running up the park, towards Marble Arch. Freddie would be waiting in his car there, with towels and blankets and bobble hats to keep out the early morning chill. He was a tough taskmaster, always bellowing at us to do this or that, faster or better, and one day, I'd had enough and decided to get my own back by winding him up. Instead of running up to Marble Arch, I persuaded Tommy to double-back with me across the park, to Sussex Gardens and home for a nice cup of tea, leaving Freddie wondering where we had gone.

We were lounging back in our armchairs, enjoying our second cuppa, when there was a knock on the door. The air was blue that morning and I was left with the image of a policeman asking Freddie what he was up to, standing in the middle of a deserted Hyde Park, and Freddie, dead-pan, telling him: 'I'm just waiting for my boys, officer!'

In the afternoon and early evening, while Tommy was at The Log Cabin, I'd work out in the gym and sometimes join him for dinner at one of our favourite Soho restaurants. Most nights, though, I'd go home and spend the evening with Ann. She would cook a meal and we'd either watch TV or she'd teach me chess. Tommy and Ann were like a family to me: they made me very comfortable and at home, which is very important to a boxer when he is preparing for a fight. And, of course, their flat was nearly always the place where we put 'win or lose, plenty of booze' into practice!

Although I liked a drink between fights, I never touched spirits, only beer or wine. And I always kept myself in shape by running off the booze every other day. If Tommy and I staggered away from a party at 1 a.m., for example, we'd get up at nine, drive to Parliament Hill, on Hampstead Heath, and run six or seven miles. To be honest, if it had been down to me, I'd probably have stayed in bed, but Tommy, bless him, gave me a reason for getting up. He was my best buddy and had my interests at heart. He was my mentor, nearly as much as George, and I couldn't let him down.

∗∗∗

While I was having fun, making the most of my money and fame, George was beavering away behind the scenes, doing business to benefit us both. And an offer that appealed to me enormously was a sponsorship deal he struck with Pontin's, the holiday company, shortly before I went into the ring for my twenty-third pro fight. In return for a Pontin's Holidays name-check on my white satin shorts and dressing gown, the company were prepared to provide complimentary accommodation at any of their holiday camps or hotels anywhere in the world. For a fun-loving guy, who liked nothing more than lazing in the sun with a beer on one side and a tasty bird on the other, it was ideal – particularly as one their hotels was on Sardinia, which had become my favourite holiday destination. My old mate, Pat Booth, was thrilled at the idea of joining me on a free holiday in such a relatively unspoiled location and I looked forward to spending a couple of weeks with her there once I'd got over my fight with Bowie Adams, at Manchester's Belle Vue stadium on 2 May.

Adams was a large gentleman from Arizona, a blond Adonis, who had worked in Hollywood as a double for Jack Hawkins and Robert Mitchum in *Rampage*. He was several inches taller than me and, at 16st 1lb, more than three stone heavier. The good news, as I discovered in the first round, was that he couldn't fight, and I pummelled him for the full three minutes without taking a serious punch in return. It was the same in the second round and although the crowd cheered me for giving the guy a hiding, they started booing him for not making more of a fight of it. I put him down for an eight count with a right and left to his somewhat overfed belly and, when he got up, I gave him more of the same, plus a few blows to the head, and he went down again. He got up once more, but he was an open target and I steamed in, with a left to the body, a right to the chin, then the hardest left I could muster to the ribs. He went down a third time and never looked like beating the count. It was just as well he didn't because there was still a minute left in the round and he would only have taken unnecessary punishment.

Although I got a great ovation, the crowd booed Adams out of the ring, which I felt detracted from my own performance. He'd come into the fight on the back of seventeen quick wins in twenty contests, so he was no mug. Okay, he hadn't thrown a punch in anger, but he was a big lump and I still had to put him away – which I did – powerfully and convincingly. I was worried what the cynics might say about my disappointing opponent, but I needn't have been. The boxing writers were far more concerned with another boxing encounter taking place at Arsenal's Highbury stadium in less than three weeks – Henry Cooper's world title challenge with Muhammad Ali. I was grateful for the distraction: it would take the spotlight off me for a while and let me continue my boxing rehabilitation without all the ballyhoo.

✳ ✳ ✳

That summer, I took advantage of Mr Pontin's hospitality by spending a month at the company's hotel, in Sardinia, and took Freddie Hill and his wife, Sarah, along too. He watched me carefully, bless him, to ensure I didn't over-indulge myself before my third fight of the year, in September. Pat Booth duly arrived, wearing the shortest mini-skirt I'd ever seen: a Pussy Pelmet, I called it. Minis were all the rage in Britain, but had not caught on in Europe yet, so you can imagine the heads Pat turned when we went sight-seeing in the Sardinian capital, Cagliari. We were watching half a dozen Italian guards going through a marching drill in the city square, when the men at the back spotted Pat. They were staring, open-mouthed, at her when the leader copped an eyeful, too, and stopped in his tracks, causing all the other soldiers to bump into each other, dropping their rifles. It was so comical. Pat and I were doubled up, laughing hysterically.

What *wasn't* funny on that holiday was the self-inflicted accident that could have ended my career. I was leaning on a fishing gun when my hand slipped and the gun went off, hitting me just under my right eye. There was no hospital on the island and I had to have it stitched – with no anaesthetic – by some nuns, who ran a medical centre. When I got home, George sent me to Harley Street to get the wound stitched properly, but the specialist I saw said there was no need: the nuns had done a perfect job. I was a very lucky man, he said: I could so easily have been blinded. Odd, isn't it? My worst cut by a long way – and it happened outside the ring!

Unfortunately, Pat, who liked to party as much as I did, had a modelling assignment in London and could stay for only one week. But we made the most of it.

I returned home in August to find that not one, but two, opponents for my fight at Wembley, on 20 September, had been substituted. First, I'd been due to face Dick Wipperman, but he dropped out. Then Billy Daniels came into the frame. But he fell by the wayside, too, and a third man was wheeled in – a German, named Horst Benedens, who, surprisingly, had been fighting cruiserweights until then. At the weigh-in, we all got an even bigger surprise: Horst was 14st 4lb, roughly nine pounds heavier than me. As it turned out, weight didn't come into it on the night: I was shaken by three left hooks to the face after less than a minute, but immediately retaliated, cutting Horst's eyes, then knocking him down for a count of eight with a ferocious two-handed attack. I was so pumped up and eager for an early finish, I fell over him as he went down! When he got up, Horst didn't seem to know where he was and Harry Gibbs wisely stepped in. The crowd roared their approval. They'd seen the 'old style' whirlwind Walker chalk up his third successive win of the year, all inside the distance. That was immensely satisfying to me, but equally pleasing was the way I'd taken those punches to the face. They'd hurt, but I'd brushed them aside and got on with the demolition job. If and when I got my chance at the European title or, better still, Cooper's British crown, that was going to stand me in good stead.

✳✳✳

What pleasure I took from the Benedens victory was wiped out the following Sunday, however, when I saw *The People* newspaper's front page: there was my name, in huge type, linked to an alleged bribery scandal. Billy Daniels, it appeared, had gone to the paper, claiming he had been offered money to lose against me. The paper made it clear the Walker 'camp' had nothing to do with the alleged bribe, but the insinuation was highly damaging to my reputation. Daniels had been employed as a sparring partner for Henry Cooper and when he told the newspaper that Cooper's manager, the highly-respected Jim Wicks, knew of the bribery attempt, a reporter phoned him and tape-recorded the conversation.

Wicks admitted he knew Daniels had been offered money, and told the reporter that he'd advised Daniels to have nothing to do with it. That was all very well, but where did that leave George and me? The paper had millions of readers and many of them were bound to think: 'No smoke without fire.' What annoyed us was that Wicks should have reported what he knew to the British Boxing Board of Control, which would most certainly have launched an inquiry. But he didn't. Over the next two days we were considering what action to take when we got whiff of another damaging story. To our horror, in the following Sunday's *News of the World*, Joe Erskine admitted that he, too, had been offered £5,000 to lose his fight with me.

Although the newspaper also stressed that neither George, nor I, had anything to do with the bribe, the insinuation was the same. Erskine told reporters he was asked to feign a fifth-round knockout, by his manager, Benny Jacobs, and was tempted to do it, not just because £5,000 was £2,000 more than his purse for the fight, but he would have cleaned up in a gambling coup, since the odds against me winning were so high. Joe said his weight ballooned by more than three stone because he didn't see the point in getting in shape if he was going to take a dive. And it was only when his trainer noticed his heart wasn't in it that he confessed what he planned to do. The trainer, Ernie Hurford, told the paper he immediately confronted Jacobs and told him the deal was off. Holding out his arms, he said he'd sooner lose both arms than Joe would throw a fight.

This was all very well, but the story, coming on the back of Daniels' allegations, was extremely damaging and hurtful to us. The next day I went public, offering to fight anybody who fancied their chances against me.

The 'anybody' turned out to be another Argentinian, Jose Menno, and our scrap was fixed for 25 October at the Albert Hall. First though, we had to deal with the bribery allegations and, two days later, we held a Press conference at Foster Lane at which I read a statement George had written. Referring to both articles, I said: 'I am furious that these newspapers should try to make capital and enlarge their circulation at the expense of my career.' I also read out a sworn statement by Peter Bates, who we'd learned, had been approached by two *People* reporters the previous Tuesday. They said they had been round the country, investigating Billy Walker's fights and asked if he could help them. Peter, who I'd knocked out in 1963, said in his statement: 'They said: "Were you offered a bribe to lay down, or anything like that, when you fought Billy Walker?" I said: "No, I wasn't and even if I was, I wouldn't discuss it with you." They then said: "Wouldn't you discuss it for £1,200?" – giving me the impression that if I said I had been offered a bribe they would pay me that sum. I said: "If there was anything in your suggestion, I wouldn't even discuss it for £12,000." '

I told the assembled journalists we were sending Peter's statement to the Press Council, in the hope that 'the unfair attacks . . . are stopped, and that the newspapers in question pay more regard to accuracy in reporting.' I also said we were taking counsel's advice to see if any legal action could be taken. It wasn't so much that we wanted to make money from a libel action as clear our names. The papers stated that I was not party to the alleged bribery attempts, but that didn't stop the gossip. If I won a fight people would now say it was bent. And if I lost, they'd say I couldn't fight. What was particularly annoying was that neither newspaper approached us during their investigations. If they knew we were not involved in any alleged corruption, why didn't they? The answer is simple: neither wanted to jeopardise what it felt was a juicy story. Both papers knew that if they alerted us, we'd slap injunctions on them and the so-called stories wouldn't see the light of day.

With the odd exception, I'd always enjoyed a good relationship with the Press: they had praised me when I was good, and criticised me, usually fairly, when I was poor. I could handle that. But I didn't care for the way *The People* and the *News of the World* tarnished my reputation in such a big way when the so-called stories they ran were based on what might have happened, not what did. That was unfair. And unforgivable.

✳✳✳

I had something to prove when I took on Jose Menno at the Albert Hall. And I was going to prove it *big*, just in case there were people out there who *did* believe the bribery allegations. My opponent had fought three times in Britain and had a 100 per cent record. He'd stopped Chic Calderwood, out-pointed John Hendrickson and, more significantly, had conquered Carl Gizzi, a Welsh heavyweight who was one of my rivals for a crack at Henry Cooper. I was more pumped up for this fight than any since turning pro. I was going to war. And I was determined there was going to be only one winner.

The Albert Hall was sold out for the first time in three years and it seemed virtually all the crowd were cheering me on, but they applauded the plucky Argentinian for catching me with several brilliant counters. I thought I was going to score a sensational victory when I floored Menno in the first round, but he got up without taking a count. I was on him at once, clobbering him to the face and body, but he hung on until the bell and somehow found his way to his corner. He was a brave boy, Jose. For the next five rounds, I hit him with everything I had but, desperately wanting to preserve his record, he took it all and came back with clusters of jabs, crosses and the occasional right uppercut. Menno's left eye was cut. My right eye was cut. But we took no notice, just stood toe to toe, trading punch for punch, amid a deafening din. In the seventh, I rocked him with swinging left and rights to the head and body, and thought I had him. But he came back at me, with several classy counter-punches I honestly didn't see coming. Nothing was going to stop me, however, and I went forward, bludgeoning and belting him with everything in my locker. In the ninth, Menno was reduced to walking pace and, as he shuffled round the ring, trying to hold me off, the sole of his right boot came away from the upper. He was an easy target, but somehow managed to survive. George asked for Menno's seconds to tear off the flapping sole and he came out for the final round with only the top half of the boot. It made no difference. I knew I was going to win the fight. The only question was how. I wanted to knock him out. Menno, proud never to have taken a count, was interested only in trying to keep out of trouble. In the end, I was hitting him at will and referee Bill Williams rightly stepped in and ended it. The crowd went barmy. They had come, sensing I had something to prove. And I hadn't disappointed them.

After that, let anyone dare suggest that Señor Menno had been paid to let me win!

Six weeks later, I took on former world champion Floyd Patterson's brother, Ray, knowing a win would complete an unbeaten year and put me in line to fight European heavyweight champion, Karl Mildenberger. And who knew where that would lead if I won. Okay, Ray was not in the same league as his brother, but he was a talented boxer, who had out-pointed Carl Gizzi and stopped Johnny Prescott. He wasn't a devastating puncher, but he was tough and durable and won a lot of his contests by wearing down his opponents. I was going to have to be at my best at the Albert Hall on the first Tuesday in December.

I was an odds-on favourite and the bookies seemed right when I caught Patterson with some good body shots and a left and right to the jaw in the first round, and looked on course for another swift victory. But Patterson cut loose with left and right swings which made my head spin. He was warned to mind his head in this round, and again in the second. But it didn't bother me and, when the bell rang for the third, I raced over and drove him against the ropes, hammering away at the ribs. He got away and caught me easily with a left and right to the head, and then we were in the centre of the ring, slugging it out. The war had started. And I had the heavy artillery to win it. I was bruised about the face, though, and as I was about to come out for the fourth, the referee, Roland Dakin, ordered my corner to wipe away some of the Vaseline they'd smeared on it. I boxed Patterson for a while, jolting his head back with a stiff jab, but the traditional style was still alien to me, so I abandoned it and I started going forward again, belting him with both hands, forcing him backwards. He bounced back, surprising me with a swing and vicious uppercut, but I steamed on, not letting him know he'd hurt me. Patterson was warned again to mind his head in a clinch but, before breaking away, landed three fast uppercuts. I was shaken, but not so much as a few seconds later when he knocked me down with a left hook to the jaw. I got up almost immediately, but had my back to Patterson and he smartly hooked me again. I was relieved to hear the bell. Showing no effects of the knockdown, I kept going forward in the fifth and sixth and, gradually, my superior strength began to dispirit Patterson. He looked distressed as I drove him into a neutral corner, but I was too slow to catch him, and when I did get in close he forced me off with stinging left and right hooks. I lost some of my aggression in the seventh, but I heard the crowd roaring: 'W-A-L-K-E-R, W-A-L-K-E-R,' in the style of the football terraces and it spurred me on. We had a bit of a rough-house in the eighth and Patterson emerged from one close-quarters' clash with his nose and mouth bleeding. I was all over him, sure I could finish it, but he hit back, driving me on to the ropes, and we stayed there for several seconds, hooking each other to the body. Then we were in the centre of the ring, heads locked together, like two stags, each not yielding an inch. The fight was going the distance, I was sure of it. But, as Patterson caught me with a peach of a right to the jaw, Roland Dakin came between us and stopped the fight in my favour. It was an unexpected end and there was a lot of booing and whistling. Patterson had been warned so much for laying on and careless use of the head many of the crowd thought he'd been disqualified. Patterson was furious at the decision and when he was sent to his corner, he ducked under the ropes and tried to leave the ring. But he was persuaded to come back and pose for photographs, and when he was interviewed by the reporters, he paid me a lovely compliment: 'That Walker! I hit him again and again. He's still there. I belt him. He won't give an inch. I knock him over. He gets straight up and wades into me.'

✳✳✳

With Dollies putting a nice few quid in our pot, George felt we should open another club, but one that capitalised on the ever-increasing popularity of the music market. While I'd been busy enjoying myself, he'd been scouting around for a property, and had found one, in Woodgrange Road, Forest Gate. He'd come up with what he felt was the ideal name – Billy Walker's Upper Cut Club – and, four days before Christmas, we launched it with what George proudly announced as a 'Fabulous Opening Week.' The 'Grand Opening Night' featured The Who, one of the country's biggest bands, and guests had to pay 17s 6d (gents) and 15s (ladies) for the privilege of seeing them. To this day, The Who's lead singer, Roger Daltrey, laughingly calls me a 'tight bastard' for paying the band just £20 for the opening night gig. I was there only to have fun, to play Mein Host and make sure all the punters were having a good time.

Two days after opening, we featured Dave Dee, Dozy, Beaky, Mick and Titch, but The Animals, who'd been booked for a Christmas Eve Gala nearly didn't appear – all because I didn't recognise the lead singer, Eric Burden.

A week before they were due to perform we were at the same party, but I didn't introduce myself because I had no idea what the band looked like, and was too embarrassed to ask. I was on my own and chatting up a girl when this guy came up and warned me off. Confident I was in with the girl, I said: 'She's coming with me, so don't cause any trouble.' That seemed to do the trick and half an hour or so later, I took the girl to my flat.

At eight o'clock the next morning, we were in bed when the phone rang. It was George. Not in the best of moods.

'What the fucking hell are you playing at,' he bellowed.

'Hold up, 'I said. 'What are you on about?'

'Eric Burden,' he screamed. 'You've only threatened Eric Burden.'

'Who the fuck is Eric Burden?' I wanted to know.

'The Animals is who he is. He's the lead singer. He says he's not doing the gig now. And he says it's down to you.'

After a while I calmed him and asked what he wanted me to do.

'I'll get his number,' he said. 'Ring him and apologise. Tell him what you like. But we want him to do the gig.'

I wasn't mad about doing that, because I didn't think I'd done anything wrong: the girl had made it clear she fancied going off with me, not staying with Eric. But I had no choice: The Animals had had a number of Top Ten hits and meant good business for The Upper Cut. So I rang Eric and ate humble pie and he was okay about it and did the gig. But we never became the best of friends. Odd that!

That Christmas of 1966 was the most exciting time for me. I'd bounced back spectacularly and was now in the frame to challenge Mildenberger. If I could beat him, George reckoned there was a chance of fighting Muhammad Ali for the Heavyweight Championship of the World.

What a thrilling prospect for an East End kid who'd never wanted to fight in the first place.

15

I was doing my best to get in shape for my next fight, against an Italian, Giulio Rinaldi, in Manchester, on 13 February, but something was playing on my mind, eating away, making it hard to concentrate. It was George. He had changed. And I didn't like it. He'd always insisted we never started training without him there to oversee things, but now, that seemed unimportant. Freddie and I would be waiting in the changing room with a couple of sparring partners, when the phone would go. It would be George, saying he wasn't going to make it and to start without him. When I'd ask him about it, he'd just shrug dismissively, and say he'd had a meeting that had gone on longer than expected. I couldn't complain, I suppose: in the ten months since our Baked Potato had been open, we'd cleared our investment and George was busy planning to open more restaurants, which was obviously good for me, as well as him. Nevertheless, over the years, I'd grown used to him watching over me and, now he wasn't, I missed him dreadfully. Freddie was great, dedicated, focussed, and trained me with 100 per cent professionalism but, like Joe Lucy, he wasn't family. *George* was my mentor, my inspiration, my reason for always wanting to do my best. And I wanted him by my side, as he always had been. Even when he *was* around, he wasn't the same old George, though; the George I adored and was close to; who revelled in going out and enjoying himself when the work was done. He didn't want to have fun any more, it seemed. And he wasn't fun himself: he was withdrawn, distant and always seemed to have something on his mind that was more important than me. It was the business, of course. I worked to live, but George lived to work. And the more money we were making, the more he loved the work involved in making it. Suddenly, business had become more important than boxing. And I didn't like it. I didn't like my brother not having time for me when it was my fighting that had got us started. I knuckled down: getting fit to face Rinaldi, but I found it hard. I worried that I was losing my brother.

As it turned out, I needn't have trained at all. Rinaldi may once have been European light heavyweight champion, but he certainly didn't come to fight that Monday night at Belle Vue. He seemed intent only on head-butting me and was rightly disqualified eighteen seconds from the end of the first round.

Fight fans in Britain went barmy when it was announced I was to fight Karl Mildenberger at Wembley on 21 March. And I must say I was chuffed when I read what Harry Levene wrote in the 2s 6d programme that night: *'I have promoted many major tournaments in my time, including many world championship fights, but never in my experience have I known such a rush for tickets as I had for tonight's battle. All tickets for this big arena were sold before I had announced a single supporting bout. This is ample proof, if it were needed, that Walker is the biggest box-office attraction in British boxing history.'*

Mildenberger was by far the most formidable opponent I'd had to face in twenty-seven pro fights. Hailed by many as the best German heavyweight since Max Schmeling, a former world champion, he'd gone eleven rounds with Muhammad Ali before being stopped in the twelfth in a world title fight the previous September, and had defended his European crown only seven weeks before our fight. So, he was going to be ring sharp, to say the least!

The stampede for tickets prompted Harry to agree a deal with a company transmitting major sporting events on giant screens and, in addition to the capacity Wembley crowd, the fight was shown in thirteen British cinemas and theatres, and beamed to Germany, France, Italy and other European countries – a total audience of 75 million, apparently. As our share of the takings was 23.5 per cent, George and I came out of the fight with the best part of £30,000, more than enough to buy and renovate the property for our second Baked Potato restaurant, which George planned to open in Chancery Lane that summer.

I wish I could say I gave the watching millions value for money, but I can't. I did my best, as usual, went at Mildenberger from the first bell, and kept going forward, trying to land the big one, but I took a hell of a beating and I'll admit it was the first time in my career – amateur and pro – when I was grateful that the referee called a halt; when I wanted a fight over and was content to lose.

Mildenberger was 14st 3lb, more than half a stone heavier than me, and the first southpaw I'd fought since that other German, Erwin Hack, in my first pro year. I hadn't given Hack any time to worry me, hammering him to defeat within minutes, but I was worried about Mildenberger. I'd never coped well with southpaws, and I feared I wouldn't be able to work him out and get in close enough to hurt him. I tried my customary early blitz, but Mildenberger didn't retreat, just stood there, fighting it out and caught me with rights and lefts to the jaw, giving me an early taste of what was to come. In my eagerness to get in close and to break up his attacks, I grabbed his neck with my right hand, then hooked him with my left, and was duly warned by Dutch referee, Ben Bril. I didn't think I'd done too badly, but when I got back to my corner I learned my left eye, which I'd damaged in training the previous week, was cut. My seconds did their best to treat it, but I was gutted because I knew it would give Mildenberger something to focus on, and encouragement he clearly didn't need.

I had the crowd yelling in the second round when I had the German backing on to the ropes, but he boxed his way out of danger and hit me with a couple of punches that re-opened the cut. At the end of the third, though, I got in a few big ones of my own and sent him back to his corner, grazed over and under his right eye. Until now, Mildenberger had been happy to slug it out with me, but he seemed frustrated at not being able to nail me and, in the fourth, started to box, not fight. Two right jabs and a left cross smashed me in the face, further aggravating my eye injury, but I forced myself to keep going forward, hoping I could stop him in his tracks with one big punch. In the fifth, though, a terrific left hook to the solar plexus made me gasp and I shuffled sideways away from him, in pain. Mildenberger knew he'd hurt me badly and came at me again, hooking me in the same spot. I wobbled a bit and got caught with jabs, hooks and crosses to the face. I tried to respond, but couldn't get to him and I started thinking: 'I'm going to lose this fight and I'm going to lose it bad.'

When I got back to my corner, George told me to keep throwing punches and not let Mildenberger catch me. What tosh! As I've always said, you can only fight as well as the other person lets you. And Mildenberger wasn't letting me anywhere near him. I was so angry: it was as if George couldn't see I was getting an almighty hammering. The sixth round was terrible for me. I managed one good, short right cross that knocked Mildenberger back on the ropes, but then he doubled me up with two more crunching left hooks to the belly and caught me with a stinging left to the jaw. I forced myself not to fall down, but the referee saw that I was gone and, under European Union ruling, made me take a standing count. He had just reached eight when the bell went. It was just as well I couldn't see my face, but I could guess that it was a red mask by the state of Mildenberger's golden shorts: they looked like a bloody butcher's apron. During the minute break, Boxing Board Chairman, Jack Onslow Fane, left his ringside seat and came to my corner to tell George he felt I'd taken enough punishment and should not continue. I wouldn't have been unhappy with that, but George was having none of it, and I was back on my feet when the bell went. I don't feel I should have gone out for that seventh round. Soon my left eye was slashed open again and I couldn't see out of it properly – it was like looking through frosted glass. Somehow I survived the round, but the one-way traffic beating continued in the eighth and, after 1 min 40 secs, referee Bril had seen enough and, to my relief, called it a day.

I suppose it was some kind of consolation that Bril joined Mildenberger when the triumphant German led the crowd in applauding my courage, and that Mildenberger admitted I was so tough he'd hurt his shoulder hitting me. But, quite honestly, all I could think was that I'd let myself down and blown any chance I had of fighting for the world title.

❊❊❊

Jack Stevens was in the dressing room again and when I was patched up and getting ready to leave, he cornered me and said he had a proposition to make: at Easter, the school which his daughters attended in Jersey – Beaulieu – was holding a fête in aid of charity, and he would like me to open it. He was unable to pay me a fee, but was prepared to pay for Tommy and Ann to go with me as his guests. An all-expenses paid weekend on a holiday island with my best friends was too good an opportunity to miss, so I said yes.

When we arrived I quickly discovered that Jack had clearly done himself a lot of favours by getting a famous face for nothing, but I didn't mind that: he was a good host and kept booze flowing all the time we were there. And he also fixed me up with a long-legged, dark-haired beauty, who made my stay even more enjoyable. Her name was Lesley. I wanted to see more of her. 'Any time you want me,' I told Jack, 'I'll be happy to fly over.'

And that's how my love affair with the beautiful island of Jersey began.

✳✳✳

On 3 June, Henry Cooper fought Jack Bodell, for the British title in Wolverhampton, and George had promised me that if Cooper won, as was expected, I'd be his next challenger. Cooper *did* win, stopping the Swadlincote farmer in two rounds. And, a couple of weeks later George's promise was made public. I would have my chance to take Henry's crown, at Wembley, on the first Tuesday in November.

✳✳✳

Earlier that year, I'd grown tired of my Aston Martin and commissioned a made-to-measure racing car, the AC Cobra. And, that August, I couldn't resist the temptation to drive to Sardinia in it and meet Tommy and Ann there. I wasn't keen to drive all that way on my own, so I thought about who I could take. I was so smitten by the lovely Lesley that I invited her to Ebury Street for a long weekend. We got on so well that I invited her to Sardinia.

She jumped at the chance. And after some fun and games in Ebury Street, to get to know each other better, off we went. We spent a few days in various hotels on the French Riviera and everything was fine. But then, Lesley seemed to get bored and kept dropping off to sleep in the car. By the time we reached Genoa, to get a ferry over to Sardinia, I was wondering whether I could handle a fortnight with her – particularly as she'd made it plain she didn't like drinking much! After four days in the Roc a Ria Hotel, in Stintino, I realised I couldn't: she was so boring. She was a bit lazy as well; she wouldn't even wash my underwear!

I was sitting on the beach, telling Ann how fed up I was when we saw Tommy swimming towards us from the other side of a small cave, where he had been chatting with Lesley. He came up to me, looking worried, and whispered: 'Your voice is carrying. We've heard everything you've been saying.' At first, I was embarrassed; I don't like hurting people's feelings. But, then, I thought: Oh well, that's life. At least she now knows how I feel about her. With it out in the open, I decided I had to do something. I went back to the hotel and checked the flights to England. There was one at eleven o'clock the next morning. When Lesley came up to our room from the beach, I took a deep breath and came out with it: 'Lesley, we're not getting on, are we? I don't want to spoil a holiday for you or me, so . . . '

'I agree,' Lesley interrupted. 'I'll go home, if you like.'

'You're on the eleven o'clock plane tomorrow,' I told her.

And she was.

✳✳✳

A few days later, Tommy and I were sunbathing on the beach when a boat pulled in. As a small group of people prepared to step off on to the sand, one of the hotel beach attendants went up to a gentleman who seemed to be in charge of the boat party and told him that it was a private beach, for residents only. I'm even more patriotic when I'm abroad and when I heard the new arrival's English accent, I stepped in. 'It's okay,' I called to the attendant. 'They're with us. We invited them.'

The attendant smiled warmly at me, then at the people in the boat. 'Our pleasure,' he said. 'If you're Mr Walker's guests.'

As the group disembarked and strolled up to the hotel, the gentleman we presumed owned the boat came over and introduced himself as Howard Taylor. We chatted about this and that for a while and then he said that, as I'd been so kind, he would like to take me and my friends on the set of a film his sister was making in a nearby town.

'Who's your sister?' Tommy and I said, in unison.

'Elizabeth Taylor,' Howard said. 'I thought you'd twigged.'

Tommy and I shook our heads. 'No, we didn't,' I said. 'We had no idea.'

And we hadn't.

That evening, Howard drove Tommy, Ann and I to a hotel in Capo Caccia, near Alghero, where the film crew and cast were staying. We were drinking in the bar when Elizabeth Taylor walked in with her husband, Richard Burton, on the way to the restaurant. Howard told them who we were and Richard said: 'May I introduce my lovely fat Jewess.' Without missing a beat, Miss Taylor rejoined: 'And, please, meet my pock-marked Welsh miner.' We all laughed, but that was the end of that because the beautiful couple carried on into the restaurant to dine alone.

We stayed at the hotel overnight, but didn't see the Burtons again until the next day when we went to the set, where they were making a movie called *Boom*. Unfortunately, we arrived during a break for lunch and felt it best to sit discreetly on our own some distance away. A few minutes later, however, Burton spotted us and walked over.

'Billy,' he said. 'I've just realised. You're fighting Cooper this year, aren't you?'

I nodded. 'Yes. In November.'

Burton clenched his fist and gritted his teeth. 'Cut him,' he said, in that glorious accent I'd heard so many times on the screen. 'Cut him.'

'I'm going to do my best,' I said. 'But they're not going to let me carry a knife in there.'

Burton smiled that captivating smile. 'Good luck, Billy,' he said. 'Good luck.'

He went back to his table. I looked over and Miss Taylor smiled and gave me a little wave.

And that was that.

✴✴✴

George had been only too pleased to wave me goodbye on holiday so that he could concentrate on building up our business empire. Boxing had already earned us around £120,000, but Foster Lane was making a profit and even I could see that revenue from our restaurants and garages would eventually outstrip what my fists earned our company. Many will find it hard to understand, but I still took not the slightest interest in the business side. I had little idea how George ran the finances, much less what we were worth. And, by the sound of it, we were worth a fortune.

The spectacular success of the first Baked Potato, and the promising start of the second, had interested a City merchant bank who were keen to back George's plans for expansion, in return for a stake in the company. The firm, Close Brothers, raised £100,000 through private issue to wealthy clients and, by the time I returned from holiday, I learned I was part-owner of not two, but four, restaurants, and G. and W. Walker now had a head office in one of London's most famous and prestigious locations – at Piccadilly Circus, on the corner of Shaftesbury Avenue and Coventry Street.

In the build-up to the Cooper fight, a national newspaper ran a double-page spread – headlined 'The Golden Gloves' – comparing Henry's wealth with mine. It said that, with George, I was director of ten companies, handling revenue from the boxing, restaurants, garages, taxis, TV rights and advertising. And, according to George's estimates, I could sell my interests in the restaurants and garages alone for £160,000. The article would not have made any impact on me at the time. All I knew, and cared about, was that I had money in my pocket NOW; that George gave me what I wanted *when* I wanted it. As for selling out my interests, why would I even think about that? I was just twenty-eight and 50–50 with a brother who was determined to make us even richer, maybe millionaires. I was doing my bit in the ring and promoting our interests out of it. And George was using his business brain to maximise the potential of all we got involved in. We were a perfect team, always had been since he'd seen me put on my fighting gloves at West Ham Boxing Club. Why would I want to jeopardise all the exciting plans George had in mind for us? And, anyway, what would I do if I cashed in my share of what I'd earned? It wasn't as if I was married, thinking of retiring, and needed a lump sum to buy a house and start a new life. No, I wasn't concerned about what I was worth. I was content to live the carefree life of the playboy boxer: going on holiday, coming back to train and fight, then going on holiday again. It was Happy Days, all right, spending – even squandering – money when I felt like it, while letting George look after our future.

And then, a few weeks before the Cooper fight, I walked into our Foster Lane restaurant and got my first clue that what George had in mind for the future would tear us apart and ultimately destroy the love and respect I'd always believed we shared.

Even though I was in training, I'd usually go to one or two of the restaurants around midday for a late breakfast, then walk around for an hour or so, chatting to customers and staff. I'd always been the same – very friendly and most unlike a boss, let alone the guy who partly owned the place. On this day, I greeted one of the staff in my usual way, using her name, and she replied: 'Hello, Mister Walker.' I thought it a bit odd and when another young woman addressed me the same way, I asked what was going on. She produced a letter from head office, signed by George's wife, which made it clear that, in future, the three of us had to be addressed as Mr or Mrs Walker, not Billy, George or Jean. I went barmy and immediately drove to Piccadilly to confront George.

'What's all this Mister Walker bollocks?' I wanted to know.

Stern-faced, George said: 'Now that we're getting bigger, we've got to distance ourselves from the staff. If we let them get too familiar it'll be bad for business.'

Part of me wanted to laugh. I was giving the manageress one at the time, and couldn't imagine her laying next to me, in the aftermath of sex, sighing gratefully: 'Thank you so much for having me, Mister Walker!' Another part of me was angry. George and Jean might want to change, but I didn't. I'd always been the same; I liked people for what they were, not for what they had or how useful they could be. And just because I now had money and was an employer, I didn't want to be any different. Money and power, it was clear, had changed George. And I found it sad. I told him I wasn't going to have any of it: no one who'd been a friend was going to call me 'Mister'.

I'd always been Billy. And always would.

George looked at me, grimly. 'In business, you can't have employees treating you like you're a mate,' he said. 'They'll take liberties.'

His icyness shocked me. I'd seen how hard and tough he could be with people, especially where money was concerned, but suddenly telling people who'd known us for ages that we were now Mister Walker – how bloody stupid! I was free and easy with people, and didn't like tension, much less ill-feeling, which is what I could see George's attitude causing.

I stormed out, leaving him with a face like thunder. It was the first time I'd questioned anything George had done in our business relationship. And he didn't like it one little bit.

16

I hadn't planned to fall in love while training for the biggest fight of my life. But that's what happened in the autumn of 1967.

Her name was Susan Coleopy. She was dark-haired and beautiful, and I was smitten the moment I saw her in our Foster Lane restaurant. I wanted to go over and speak to her there and then, but she was with friends and I didn't think it would be too clever, in case she put me down, or didn't take me seriously. So I got one of the waitresses to ask for her phone number. Susan wasn't keen on giving it at first, but eventually gave in and, a few days later, I rang and asked her out. We went to The Terrazo, in Soho, and I learned she was just twenty and lived with her parents, who managed a newsagents near Woking, in Surrey. She was simple and down to earth and very easy to talk to. We clicked and, in the run-up to my Wembley fight, I took her to the pictures a few evenings after I'd finished working out and sparring at the gym. She was a lovely, sensuous girl and, while sex was definitely not on my mind with a fight round the corner, I did look forward to trying to get hold of her when it was over.

✳✳✳

Not surprisingly, Wembley's Empire Pool was sold out yet again, on Tuesday 7 November, when I climbed into the ring to face Henry Cooper, Britain's longest-reigning heavyweight champion, a much-revered veteran who'd won the title just twelve months after I'd faced Terry Drudge in my first amateur fight. Not one boxing writer gave me a hope and Henry was odds-on favourite to become the first fighter to win three Lonsdale Belts outright. But I honestly thought I could cause a sensational upset, particularly if I could land a few right-handers on Henry's susceptible eyes which had let him down so often in the past. He had a good left jab and left hook, but he'd be the first to admit his right was useless. And, as Henry was now thirty-four, I had age on my side. Okay, he'd beaten Brian London, who'd given me a pasting eighteen months before, but I'd licked Johnny Prescott and Joe Erskine, who Henry had also beaten. Obviously, I was keen to win and become British heavyweight champion but, quite frankly, it wouldn't be a disaster if I got beaten, because George and I were getting a fortune, win or lose.

We had a plan: I'd keep going forward for the first seven rounds and take what Henry had to offer. Then, hopefully, in the second half of the fight, the age difference would begin to tell and I'd be able to up the pace and wear Henry down, maybe stop him with my strength and punching power.

Unfortunately, going forward was easier said than done: within seconds of the opening bell, I was caught cold by a stream of left jabs and had to grab Henry and hold on, my head dangerously near his eyes. Henry clearly thought this was a deliberate tactic and lashed out viciously with a left and right hook, forcing me to hold on again, then hooked me on the break. He hadn't hung about showing me his class, and I went back to my corner, anxious for George's advice.

I rushed Henry to the ropes at the start of the second to try to rough him up, but failed to land a decent punch and was jolted back with a hook to the jaw. I forced myself into him and was encouraged when, instead of standing back and picking me off with that stinging jab, he pulled me in, trying to lock arms. I was further encouraged when he emerged from a close-quarter brawl with his left eye bleeding. It wasn't a big cut, about a quarter-inch, but it gave me confidence and I stepped up the pace, aiming several blows at the wound. Henry seemed to sense he needed to rob me of that confidence and nail me sooner, rather than later, and I felt blood gushing from my nose as he counter-punched me with several punishing jabs.

Those at ringside must have thought I was seriously hurt when I went to my corner at the end of the round, my face badly marked. But

Henry hadn't hurt me with any of his punches and I went out for the third round, determined to keep going forward, confident I could get on top. I got caught with two beauties on the jaw, but retaliated and forced Henry to back away. I left gaps in my defence, though, and as he peppered me with rasping left hooks, I heard George yelling: 'Grab him, Bill, grab him.' But I was too pumped up, and lunged forward, swinging wildly to the head. I landed two right-handers on the jaw, then brought up a left hook to Henry's ribs that left him open-mouthed, grimacing in pain. I steamed forward, forcing him back on the ropes with swinging rights and lefts and, at the bell, went back to my corner, confident I'd shaded the round.

Henry's seconds obviously said something during the break because he came out for the fourth, clearly intent on boxing, not fighting. If I'm honest, he did show up my limitations and the difference in class between us, but I kept going forward, catching him several times with my right hand, and I'm sure I won the round on aggression alone. In the fifth, I carried on where I'd left off, trying to make Henry fight, but I took two mighty left hooks to the jaw, which stopped me in my tracks. They hurt, but I didn't let Henry see that, and kept going forward, swinging left and rights to the head. I was being caught again and again with left jabs and, two or three seconds from the bell, knew that one of them had cut my right eye.

The cut gave Henry a shot of adrenalin and he opened the cut early in the sixth. Rightly, he showed me no mercy, but I still wasn't hurt and felt I could weather the storm. The referee, George Smith, was clearly concerned about the state of my eye, however, and when he ordered us to stop boxing, I feared the worst – and I was right. Smith felt the eye was so badly cut it was dangerous for me to continue. When he waved his arms, signalling the fight was all over, I was gutted and banged my gloves together in frustration and disappointment: the cut didn't feel that bad to me and I believed I was perfectly capable of carrying on.

Henry, as you'd imagine, was gracious in victory. He came over to my corner, kept pulling me round the neck affectionately, and said: 'Oh well, Bill, that's it. Makes a bloody change – normally I get the cut eye.' I liked Henry. He'd always been straightforward and not in the least aggressive, but his sympathy was little consolation to me, particularly when the doctor looked at the cut that had ended my title dreams and decided it needed *just one stitch!*

Could I have won that fight if it hadn't been stopped? No one will ever know, but I do feel I was in with a chance with Henry. I felt at the time, and still feel when I watch the video that, despite the punches I was taking, I was getting on top. I'd trained for fifteen rounds and, most definitely, had lots of energy in the tank. My gut feeling is that Henry would not have stopped me and I would have got to him later in the fight. What was so frustrating was being denied that chance by a soppy cut eye. It took me some time to get over that.

✳✳✳

When Susan and I made love I discovered, to my delight, that she was a virgin. What a turn-on! Could any young man find anything better than a gorgeous-looking young woman, untouched by any other male? It was the ultimate of prizes. I couldn't believe my luck.

Soon, she was staying at the flat so much I felt it sensible for her to move in, rather than me having to keep driving her home to Woking. Susan thought it a good idea, too, but her mother, who was a strict Catholic, could not bear the thought of her daughter 'living in sin'. So, in February, I suggested that we kept her parents happy by getting married. We'd known each other only six months or so, but Susan was all for it. And I was, too. She was unworldly and very inexperienced in bed, which worried me, but she was beautiful and a lovely person and, when I proposed, I genuinely believed she was the girl I wanted to spend the rest of my life with. My mum and dad and brothers had been happy with their partners for years and all seemed destined to grow old together. Why should I be any different?

Susan's mother wanted a big wedding at a local Catholic church, but when the priest there asked me to sign papers, confirming I'd bring up children from the marriage as Catholics, I refused, and said I would consult a priest I knew in London. I went to St. Peter's Church in Clerkenwell, and spoke to a priest, who had joined me and my pals on various nights out, drinking. When I took Susan to meet him later, he asked her if she intended bringing up any children as Catholics and she said she would. That was good enough for him to agree to perform the marriage. He didn't even ask me.

I'd arranged the church, but George then took over, firstly making sure that news of my engagement made the papers, then orchestrating the most lavish wedding he could. Ideally, one's wedding day should be

161

a wonderful, emotional and, above all, memorable occasion to be cherished forever. But I have only sour memories of that day, deliberately chosen by George on the last Saturday in March, so that I could claim my full marriage allowance. It was not so much a wedding as one massive publicity stunt and exercise in social climbing, organised by George and Jean for their own purposes. Susan and I were the ones getting married, but we had little say in who was invited. George and Jean took control of the guest list and made sure all the people they wanted to impress, who were useful to them, were there, while Susan and I were rationed on how many we could invite. At the reception, in one of our restaurants by the Tower of London, I looked around and saw that more than half the guests were business people I'd barely said hello to, let alone knew. The few pals I *had* invited were stuck away with Susan's family and friends in a corner, as though they, like me, were unimportant. In George's eyes, they clearly were.

It was a most disappointing day, which I remember more for the singing and dancing and laughing that went on after the stuffed-shirts and their boring wives had left. I have to thank Tommy for that: as soon as people started getting up to leave, he nipped down to a club he knew and came back with a band, a great bunch of lads, who were only too pleased to play for as long as we wanted. We finally rolled out of the restaurant at 3 a.m.

It was *my* wedding day. What a shame George was unable to put business to one side for once.

What no one, not even my closest friends, knew was that I'd walked down the aisle that day and pledged my love for Susan 'till death us do part', knowing I was making the biggest mistake of my life. For weeks, I'd known that marrying Susan was wrong, not only for me, but for her, too. I'd wanted desperately to get out of it but, by then, all George's carefully-laid plans and the publicity had gone too far, and I bottled it.

I desperately needed to talk to Pat. She understood me; she was the one person who would give it to me straight, sort out my muddled thoughts. I went in search of her late on the Thursday night before the wedding. I had to leave Friday clear to have my hair cut, collect my suit from the tailors and brief the ushers, so I decided to have my stag 'do' with Melvyn, Albert Rockman and Tommy on the Thursday. We all met up at the Log Cabin, then went on to Roberto's Italian restaurant in Greek Street, for dinner. When we called it a day, around midnight, the others assumed I was going home to Ebury Street, but I went to a club where I knew Pat was working. Cheekily, I asked for the keys to her flat but, as usual, she told me to get lost. I told her I didn't want to get hold of her, just needed to talk, and there must have been something in my tone that convinced her it was important, because she arranged to finish early, and we went for a drink. An hour or so later, we went back to her flat and – inevitably, perhaps – ended up in bed. I didn't feel bad about that; I had no conscience about it at all because Pat and I were still very close and I felt she was a part of me.

Laying next to her, I told her that I was making a mistake, marrying Susan. 'You know what, Pat,' I said. 'I love her but I see problems in the future. We don't have much in common. She's so young and naïve. I don't know if she knows, or even understands, the real me.'

'You've made your bed,' Pat said, typically bluntly. 'Now fucking lie on it.'

I knew that was what I had to do, of course. How could I possibly tell Susan: 'I'm sorry, darling, I know you've got your wedding dress and everything's all set for a lovely day, but I can't marry you, after all.' I couldn't do that to her. Or to her family. Or to mine. I just couldn't do it. No matter how wrong I knew the marriage was, I had to go through with it.

Obviously, I'll never know what would have happened if I'd been man enough to stand up and tell the truth, take the flak everyone, including the Press, would have chucked at me. But what I do know, what I'm certain of, is that Pat and I were right for each other, and Susan and I were not. I loved Susan but I was so close to Pat that I kept going back to her because, when we did actually spend time together, we were so, so happy. We were soulmates.

George controlled my life so much I believed all he told me. He thought Susan was perfect, which to all intents and purposes she was, and he was pushing hard for the wedding and all the ensuing publicity. But I was stupid. I should have been strong enough to say: 'NO. I love this woman. I like this woman. I love how I feel about this woman. And I want this woman. But I am not ready for marriage, I actually want to get to know her more and see if we are really suited. Cancel the wedding – let's take a raincheck.' But I didn't. I kept schtum, bottled up my feelings, and walked down the aisle of that magnificent Italian Catholic church that last Saturday in March 1968, all my misgivings hidden behind my wide wedding-day smile.

I had made my bed. And I was going to do my best to make it as comfortable as possible. For Susan, as well as myself.

✳✳✳

To outsiders, our marriage in those early days must have seemed idyllic. We were the country's golden couple – the good-looking Adonis sportsman and his pretty, enchanting young wife. Thanks to my fame and popularity, we were feted everywhere we went. And we went everywhere, it seemed. Film premieres, theatre first nights, restaurant openings – we did the lot, rubbing shoulders with the rich and famous, always to the accompaniment of camera flashbulbs and reporters, eager for a quick quote. Susan revelled in every exciting moment. She loved meeting other celebrities. And she adored being in the limelight, never more so than when a film crew followed us around for a BBC2 documentary about my life. *The Money Programme* began at a celebrity party at Billy's Dilly, our new nightclub on the site of the famous Piccadilly restaurant, Scott's, which we'd just bought and converted for £50,000. The programme traced my career, but focussed mainly on the financial success George and I had enjoyed, and showed us all – George and Jean and Susan and I – having fun in and around the swimming pool at George's mansion. Susan loved being on camera. I wasn't shy either, demonstrating my 'bombing' technique off the diving board. But George, filmed at the massive, stone-work barbecue, hardly cracked a smile. He was very serious and self-conscious, barely recognisable from the fun-loving guy who'd got so pissed on the wine I'd brought home from Sardinia one summer that he burned his stomach on the hot coals – and didn't feel a thing till the next day!

The Money Programme was a massive ego trip, naturally, but it was also a fantastic PR exercise, great for business, because we were filmed in the Foster Lane restaurant and all our other places got name-checks. And there was a revealing interview with one of the Close brothers, who had invested in our business. It was great to hear someone with such financial clout talk so glowingly about the money G. and W. Walker Ltd was going to earn in the future. And when, at the end of the programme I heard George say the company was now worth a quarter of a million pounds, I glowed with pride. For someone who'd gone into pro boxing for money, not glory, it was an extraordinary statement to hear. And for someone who, despite misgivings, saw himself married forever, it was immensely encouraging. I was only just twenty-nine and could yet have another shot at the British title but, even if I never boxed again, Susan and I had nothing to worry about, financially. We were, it seemed clear, set up for life.

✳✳✳

Most of the showbiz gatherings we went to were fun but, at one black-tie VIP function, I came face to face with a notorious showbusiness drunk and came within an ace of punching his lights out. He was sitting opposite me at a large table in a top London hotel, where six other celebs and their partners had just finished dinner. I had no idea who he was, and had no wish to find out, because he was loud and boorish and, by the way he was guzzling his drink, seemed determined to get drunker than he already was. To make matters worse, he was making it obvious that he fancied Susan. I would probably have ignored him, but he started staring at Susan intently, trying to 'stare her out.' After a few moments, I leaned over and said: 'If you want to stare at someone, stare at me.' He did, and, stupidly, I stared back. Finally, I said: 'This is ridiculous. You're drunk. Turn it in.'

He stared back at me, then at Susan, then at me again. He was playing his own drunken game and I wasn't amused. 'Enough,' I said, loudly. 'You're upsetting me now. I'm really getting the hump.'

'Yeah,' he slurred. 'What you goin' to do about it?'

'Don't make me lose it,' I said. 'Because I'll really hurt you.'

The guy must have thought he was a tough guy, or had a death wish, because he kept goading me until I could stand it no more. I got up and went to him.

'Look, I don't know who you are and I don't care,' I said. 'But I think you're an idiot and if I wasn't who I am, I'd knock you spark out.' Then I told Susan I felt it wise to leave, so we said our goodbyes to the other, highly embarrassed, guests and walked out.

I didn't know who the plonker was until someone told me that it was the actor, Oliver Reed, who was well known for getting into drunken brawls. A few months later, I would get my chance for revenge.

✳✳✳

We were happy enough in Belgravia but, in June, Susan announced she was pregnant and we knew we had to move: neither of us felt it right to bring up a baby in the middle of town. Both of us liked the idea of the country life and when Susan saw an advertisement for Gable End – a large Georgian house, at Dorney Reach, near Maidenhead, in Berkshire – we were excited. The asking price was a colossal £17,000, but the property was in one and a half acres, beside the Thames, and just what we were looking for. And, anyway, the company would be paying for it. I talked it through with George and, although even a small percentage of my earnings would have bought the house outright, George said it was best to pay just £7,000 and have the rest on a twenty-five year mortgage. I didn't think much about it at the time: George knew about these things and if he said that was the way to go, who was I to argue? I had more than enough on my mind, what with the baby, and having to get in shape for my next fight against an American former top boxer, Thad Spencer, at Wembley in November.

It was a big fight for Spencer and me. I was looking for a way back and Spencer had lost two bouts in three months earlier in the year. In February, he was stopped in the twelfth round by fellow American Jerry Quarry; and in May he lost in nine rounds to another American, Leotis Martin. The previous year, Spencer had been a heavyweight high-flyer, favourite to win the WBA title, but he was grossly overweight when he entered the Wembley ring to fight me. His reflexes and timing proved to be way out, too, and I belted him all over the ring before the referee called a halt in the sixth round.

Although Spencer was nowhere near the fighter he'd been, I was delighted to have won my only fight of the year. My anxiety about George, however, marred what pleasure I should have felt. In the build-up to the fight, my worries about him started nagging at me again. When he'd failed to oversee my training in the past, he'd always phoned to apologise, but now he just didn't show, and it hurt. Once, I'd been the big earner, the one to be nurtured, but the businesses had become more profitable than my fists and I wasn't that important any more. Okay, the money from boxing was nice as an extra but, to George, it wasn't the be all and end all. I had to face the truth, no matter how painful it was: my brother viewed me as a once-lucrative commodity that was fast approaching its sell-by date. It hurt badly, but I still made excuses for him.

✳✳✳

On 25 March 1969, I stepped into the Empire Pool ring again to fight Jack Bodell, a southpaw I knew well from our amateur days. But I hadn't been scheduled to face him. My opponent should have been Buster Mathis, who had beaten George Chuvalo in New York. On the back of this victory, however, Buster accepted an offer to fight Jerry Quarry on 24 March, which meant he couldn't face me the following night. As it happened Jack Bodell was stuck for an opponent in Harry Levene's bill and went public, saying: 'They keep talking about Buster Mathis, Floyd Patterson and Continental boxers, but they're not sure to get them. I repeat my offer: I'll fight Billy Walker any place, any time – and that includes Wembley, 25 March. Why won't Walker fight me?' There was no reason why I didn't want to fight Bodell if the money was right, so George got talking to his manager, George Biddles, and Harry Levene. Harry wasn't too sure, but decided to gamble. It paid off: Wembley was sold out again, prompting him to tell the papers: 'I'm astounded by the public's response to this contest. It seems the world and his wife want to see it!' The fight was built up as a needle match between Jack and I, but that was nonsense; there was more needle between the managers. Biddles accused George of belittling Bodell and side-stepping him, while George countered: 'Biddles and Bodell should be grateful to me for holding out so long. We were never offered anything like the money we're now getting for this fight.'

Three weeks before the fight, my son, Daniel, was born, and I took time off from training to be there when Susan gave birth. It was an exciting experience, but terrifying, too, and, although I felt a certain bonding with my beautiful baby, I knew I was far too squeamish to endure a similar ordeal in the future. Naturally, as the first-born, Daniel made me feel enormously proud, and I remember thinking how much I wanted him to have a happy life, with no problems, and not have to fight for a living.

I also took a couple of hours off from training for the Bodell fight to go to a London gymnasium to do some make-believe sparring with Oliver Reed to publicise a forthcoming film, in which he fought another actor, Alan Bates. As soon as I arrived, I recognised Ollie as the obnoxious drunk who'd annoyed me so much. But he didn't recognise me and I decided to give him a fright. We got changed into boxing gear, not saying a word to each other, them climbed in the ring and started posing for the photographers. I waited until he was relaxed and enjoying the moment, then grabbed his arm and pulled him towards me, locking the arm tightly under mine. 'Right, you fucking arsehole,' I said. 'Remember me? The guy you pissed off at that dinner?'

Ollie screamed like a kid and jumped out of the ring, frightened, saying I was going to hit him. George was there that day and he looked at me, angrily. 'What the fuck you doing?' he said.

'He was out of order with me once and I just reminded him,' I said.

George insisted I ate humble pie. And to save the shoot, I did. I told Ollie, I'd only been joking and he got back in the ring and we posed for the snappers. I'd heard he fancied himself as a bit of a tough guy, who could handle himself but, that day, he showed himself up for what he was.

✳✳✳

In a way, it was odd that Jack Bodell wanted the fight so much. He'd already won an eliminator to challenge for the British title by stopping Carl Gizzi, four months before, and it would set him back if he didn't beat me. As for me, I knew I *had* to win to keep my career alive. And when I stepped into the Wembley ring, rated No. 3 British heavyweight and odds-on favourite, I genuinely thought I *would* win, even though Jack had won his last eight fights.

By their deafening noise, the crowd were expecting fireworks from the off. I'm sad to say they got them – but not from me. I took four jabs in the face before I'd landed a punch and after a one-sided first minute when I couldn't get going, I was knocked down for a count of eight. I got up, but Jack piled in again, shifting his attack to the body, and I was relieved to hear the bell. In the second, I took a lot more punishment, almost all to the head, and was felled by a right to the jaw. I took a count of eight and fought back angrily. But, in that round and the next, I took an awful pasting and George gave me a right talking-to. I came back into it in the fourth, but the punishment I'd soaked up had slowed me down and I didn't seem to be punching my weight. I went for broke in the fifth, thrashing and crashing and smashing at Jack, praying one of my right hand beauties would land on the money. Finally, one did, right on the jaw, sending him headlong to the canvas. I went to a neutral corner and looked at him, on one knee, listening to the count. 'Stay down, you bastard,' I thought. 'If you get up, I'm fucked. I'm knackered.'

But he did get up and I had to summon up what little strength I had to go forward again, to try to keep the advantage. We slugged it out in the sixth, barely able to stand, and I honestly thought my superior strength had worn him down. But he came out for the seventh as if someone had injected him with some wonder drug that restores lost energy, and knocked me all over the ring. I came out for the eighth, more exhausted than I'd felt in my life, and was knocked back with three or four hard blows to the head. I tried to fight back, I really did. But, for the first time in my career, I couldn't drag any strength from my guts and could only stand there, taking what Jack threw at me. He switched his attack to the body and I was finally dumped to my knees by a thumping right under the heart. I managed to get up at eight, but was out on my feet and referee Harry Gibbs wisely stepped in. I was gutted. I was so sure I could win, but all the years of over-indulgence had finally taken their toll and I couldn't produce the goods when it mattered.

I was wiped out, zonked, knackered, call it what you will and, in the seconds after Jack's arm was raised, I knew that I'd had it with the fight game; that I never wanted to get in the ring again. I shuffled disconsolately to my corner, bruised and battered, and told George: 'That's it. That's me lot. I'm finished. I can't do it anymore.' George pulled me in close, his mouth against my ear. 'Shut up,' he whispered. 'We'll sell the story.' So, when the newspaper reporters gathered in my dressing room, expecting a 'retirement' story, I sat back and let George do most of the talking. 'Retire? Why should he retire?' he asked. 'He's not hurt. We're going to have another couple of fights, then challenge Cooper again.'

We both knew it was bollocks, of course. My chance of the title had gone and would never come again. But George had told me to keep quiet about quitting, so I went along with it, to the Press *and* Harry Carpenter, who had commentated on the fight, to be shown on BBC TV the following night. When he asked the same question, I said, cheekily: 'You're always asking me about retiring. Do you think about retiring when you've given a bad commentary?'

The next days' papers were full of it, of course. They called the fight 'an ugly, primitive battle, not a boxing match – a battle of such ferocity, savagery and teeth-gripping all-out desperation, it belonged to the days when men wore animal skins and fought with clubs in caves.' And, to a man, the writers screamed: 'Walker should retire – NOW!'

The following night, I was interviewed by BBC TV presenter David Coleman, whose show, *Sportsnight With Coleman*, had replaced *Sportsview*, and went along with the same story. 'You keep talking about punishment,' I told him. 'I have a slight mark around my eye. That's all I've got. I'm a professional fighter. Why should I turn it in? Other boxers have been knocked out cold, but never got as much publicity as me. And I wasn't even counted out. Why do I carry on fighting? For the money! All my money goes into the business, but we still have to pay our taxes. Also, I recently bought a house.'

Asked for his views, George said: 'Why should we quit? We can still earn a fortune, the public want to see Billy and we know he's still fit. I'll make up my mind about Billy retiring when he's made up *his*, and we've talked it over. It will be our decision, not influenced by pressure. If anything, pressure will make us carry on.'

The 100 per cent media campaign for me to quit did bother George, however, because he felt it looked as if he was forcing me to fight and take unnecessary punishment that could endanger my health. So, the following week, we went to the British Boxing Board of Control, armed with a medical certificate, proving I was in sound condition and fit to box. Mr J. Onslow Fane made his point strongly that, in view of the heavy punishment I had taken from Bodell, the Board felt it wise for me to retire, but it would leave the decision to us. To everyone in the boxing business, it looked as though I *was* going to carry on, because George wrote to *Boxing News* and, the following week, the paper published his letter under the headline, 'Nothing Wrong with Billy':

I thought I would write to you on the question of Billy's last fight, because of the unusual clamour, from some of the Press, for Billy's retirement. This, I think, they actually want to force upon him, not giving him credit for having the ability to make up his own mind as to when he should quit the fight game.

I would like to assure all the readers of Boxing News *that Billy is one of the most medically examined boxers in Great Britain today and that as far as any medical opinion is concerned, Billy is A1 both mentally and physically. I have, in the time I have been associated with boxing, seen fighters take much more punishment than Billy received in that last fight. In fact, at one stage it was touch and go as to who would be the winner.*

I do feel that the Press are sensationalising and greatly exaggerating the amount of blows that Billy received and I think this is wrong and grossly unfair to a boy who has been such a credit and inspiration to the boxing game.

George Walker, Manager of Billy Walker, Coventry St., W.1.

George tried to make me change my mind. He said he'd get me a couple of easy fights and maybe I'd have another go with Cooper. But I said: 'No, I'm out of it. I've seen too many guys walking on their heels for having one fight too many.' As for another shot at Cooper, we both knew that whatever slim chance I'd had of a title had gone and would never come again. Even the money I could earn from another couple of fights did not concern me; I had more in the pot we'd been building than most men my age would earn in a lifetime. And anyway, I was going to cop a packet from a newspaper for my retirement exclusive and rags-to-riches life story.

I wanted nothing more now than to enjoy the financial rewards of seven years' hard graft. I'd seen it all, done it all, on the celebrity circuit and it held nothing for me any more. What was supremely appealing was a life of domesticity in the country, raising more children with my beautiful young wife, in a magnificent home to die for and I had no money worries. I'd taken up boxing purely for the money and the gruelling early morning runs, exhausting gym work and the batterings and bruisings had paid off. I was set up for life. It was indeed Happy Days. And, boy, was I going to enjoy them.

The Sunday after the Bodell fight, our dear friend, Frank Butler, revealed to *News of the World* readers and, in turn, the country, that I'd called it a day. Over the next few days, it was clear that nearly everyone in the fight game was pleased – and not a little relieved. In a way, I was, too. I'd enjoyed my time in the spotlight, revelled in all the adulation, but I knew in my heart that the time was right to leave the stage.

What I didn't know, and didn't give a thought to, was how the dramatic change in lifestyle would affect Susan. How she would react when I wasn't the golden boy of British boxing, the nation's hero any more, but simply Billy Walker, ordinary bloke and family man.

17

Stepping out of the ring into an office, and sitting behind a desk for eight hours a day, wasn't me. But when all the hoo-ha about my retirement died down, that's what George told me I had to do. I'd be based at Piccadilly, he said, and I'd take charge of the catering side of our businesses. I knew a lot of people, he said. And I knew how the markets worked. Buying food for our chain of restaurants was the perfect job for me, apparently.

Well, it wasn't. It was totally the wrong job. My image was my strength and George should have appreciated that more than anyone. He should have given me a public relations role, where I'd be out and about, meeting influential people, and creating publicity for the company and all its interests. Since leaving school, I'd never been asked to use my brain much. I wasn't dense, not by a long way, but for ten years my life had revolved around physical exercise and doing what I was told – and now George expected me to become a businessman, like him. Almost as soon as my boxing gloves had come off, it was like: 'Now, Billy boy, get your suit and tie on and get in the office and do some work!'

That life was all right for him: he loved the pressure, tension and stress that came from big business, revelled in doing deals and bossing people around. But I wasn't like that: I didn't want stress of any kind, never had. I wanted to be one of the boys and have fun, not problems. Unlike

George, I didn't get a buzz from barking out orders. And, apart from anything else, I felt I'd done my bit for the company. It was my blood and sweat and guts that had put us in this enviable financial position, and I believed I'd earned the right to enjoy the easy life with my wife and baby, in our new home, not have to commute to London to do a job I didn't even understand, much less like. And it didn't end there. The company had bought Marlowe House, a big banqueting room in Sidcup, Kent, where we'd also put in a Billy's Baked Potato, and George made me go there most Fridays and Saturdays as a PR exercise. It was about a 100-mile round trip and I couldn't stand it – particularly as I had to be on my best behaviour and not drink too much.

If I wasn't in Sidcup, I was expected to be in Southend where we had another place, called Garons Number One, where the same rules applied.

So, I wasn't ever able to switch off at weekends.

I wasn't even on a salary: George still treated me like a father handing out pocket money to his son. The company paid all my household bills, including the mortgage, but whenever Susan and I needed money for, say, a new washing machine or fridge, I'd have to go to George, cap in hand almost, and ask for the money. It would drive Susan nuts. And, of course, it was very embarrassing for me.

Yes, I know I should have stood up for myself, but making one's point with George had never been easy and I'll admit I was a bit scared of him. Not physically, but he had a way of making me feel inferior, even inadequate; that he knew it all and I was a mug who knew nothing. I was worried, too, about rocking the boat: there was loads of money in the company and the last thing I wanted was to upset the man who controlled the purse strings – and my life.

So, without a minute's training in man-management, I gave the business life a go. I'd drive to Taplow and join the bowler-brigade on the 8.10 a.m. to Paddington, get a cab to Piccadilly, and be behind my desk by nine. But, frankly, I wasn't sure what I had to do, and I'd sit there, twiddling my thumbs. After a couple of hours, I was so bored I'd go out for a drink, then find it was time for lunch. Going back and sitting behind that desk again didn't appeal to me, so I didn't bother to go back. After a few weeks, of course, George got to hear and hit the roof. But I told him I couldn't handle it. He loved being in an office, making decisions, but it was alien to me, and I couldn't hack it.

If George had shown some patience, handled me with kid gloves and explained, in simple terms, what he expected of me, I might have reacted differently. But he didn't: he was confrontational, bullying almost, and just kept giving me orders as though I was an underling. Not an equal partner.

'Do this! Do that!,' he'd bark, pointing at me. Seriously, it gave me the hump so much I'd feel like biting his finger off.

When I'd been fighting and earning money, George was always on the phone. Even if he didn't turn up to oversee my training, he always wanted to know how much I'd done. He'd go on and on about my condition, like I was some racehorse: keep that horse in good nick, he may have another race in him yet! But, now we were in the business world, he only spoke to me to tell me what to do, or when he wanted something. He'd always invited me to VIP functions, but he was now moving in higher circles and didn't want me there.

I found it hard to take and would get very upset, particularly if I was on my own at home and had been drinking. The more I drank, the sorrier I felt for myself and I'd find myself feeling very low, as I thought back over the years and how good it had been: how I'd looked up to George, loved him, trusted him so much. I began to think that I'd been used, used all the way along the line. While I'd been earning money he was always there, but now that I was nothing, now that I wasn't earning him anything, he didn't want to know. I'd been a business venture that had collapsed. He'd put me on a sheet of paper and gone: 'Ah, Bill Walker, he's not on the sales ledger any more, he's on the purchase ledger. What are we getting out of Billy boy now? Zilch. So let's look around for something new.'

From being so close, George and I had become strangers. Clearly, I'd been dropped – like a hot baked potato. And it broke my heart.

✳✳✳

Life at home could have been better, too. In the months after Daniel was born, Susan and I were too wrapped up in him to take a close look at our lives. If we had done, we would have realised that, now we'd got down to the nitty-gritty of living under the same roof, we weren't really suited. If Susan had moved into the Ebury Street flat and we'd lived together for a year, say, I'm sure we would have found this out and split up. But we didn't.

Don't get me wrong: I thought Susan was great – a lovely person, with many qualities I admired. But sex was important to me and it became more and more apparent that we were not at all suited, sexually. Her inexperience had been a great attraction and a real turn-on, at the beginning, but I did think she would get better and understand that, sometimes, a man – particularly one with a big sexual appetite – does want his sweet, demure lady to become a tart in the bedroom. And Susan didn't. She simply was not in the slightest adventurous, or worldly, in that way. Maybe it was my fault. I've always been very physical, robust, in my love-making. Who knows, maybe I was too rough for her. Maybe my whole personality was too rough and ready for her.

Certainly I'd begun to get that impression with our choice of friends. I was happy to be with people I liked, no matter how they spoke or what they did for a living. As long as they were fun, I wanted to spend time with them, even invite them to dinner with their wives. But Susan wasn't like that: she was more concerned that they suited the image she had of herself. They might be pompous, boring social-climbers, but if they spoke with a posh accent and had a bit of money, that was fine. Consequently, I didn't like her friends and she couldn't stand mine. I started to suspect that she didn't like me as a person, maybe never had; that perhaps she'd fallen in love with the image of Billy Walker, famous fighter, but now that I was just a family man – albeit a wealthy one – and she could see me at close quarters, she saw things she didn't like. It got to a point where I didn't get much of a welcome when I came home from London, so I didn't bother what time I got there.

I met a guy on the train, who said: 'Aren't you that boxer chappie?' I told him I was and he was charm himself. 'Nice to meet you,' he said. 'How are you?' And, after that, it was chat, chat, chat. Geoffrey was his name. He was sixty-odd and in insurance. He'd been an RAF pilot in the war and when he heard where I worked, he invited me to lunch at the RAF club, just down the road in Piccadilly. We got on so well that lunch became something of a habit and, with neither of us at the beck and call of anyone, they became longer and boozier. We'd end up on the vintage port, fall on the train, then roll into the Railway Arms, at Taplow, to continue drinking. More often than not, I'd still be there at closing time – which presented a problem when it came time to go home.

I always drove my car to the station and I'd find it hard getting the ignition key in, let alone driving the couple of miles home and parking when I got there! Finally, I decided to get a bike: not only would it ensure I didn't get nicked for being drunk behind the wheel, it would keep me fit. All was well until, one night, I got so plastered I fell off, not once, but three times. In drunken petulance, I hurled the bike as far as I could into a field and walked home.

Far more worrying for both Susan and me was Daniel: he had a urinary problem and needed an operation. He wasn't yet two and I was terrified about him going under anaesthetic. I kept my fears to myself and was stunned when Susan's mother insisted we see her priest before Daniel went into hospital. Why? I wanted to know. 'The child isn't christened and if he dies, he won't go to heaven,' she said, coldly.

I didn't go to church now, but my religious beliefs were rooted in my Sunday School days and, as far as I remembered, God loved all little children, and a man-made ceremony was not going to colour His view of my darling boy. I was tempted to tell Susan's mother what I thought of her, and her shuttered religion, but now wasn't the time. Thankfully the operation was a complete success.

✳✳✳

That November, 1969, Jack Stevens invited Susan and me to Jersey and made a most astonishing request: he was getting married and wanted me to be his best man. For once in my life, I was lost for words: I barely knew the man. When I told him this, he pooh-pooed it saying he'd chosen me because he liked me and felt we got on so well together. I found it hard to turn him down, particularly as Jack had been so generous to me and my friends over the years, so I agreed to do the honours at the wedding, the following January.

Jack's bride-to-be was just twenty – more than twenty years younger than him. Her name was Susan Farley and she was beautiful and dark-haired, with long legs. Although she was my type, I didn't think for a moment of trying to get hold of her. After all, she was about to be married – and I was the groom's best man!

Around this time, Tommy's wife, Ann, said her father had become too ill to look after his three-year-old golden Labrador, Bruno, and asked if we would be interested in taking the dog in? Susan isn't interested in animals and wasn't keen, but I agreed immediately: I'd been to the father's farm, near Rugby, and knew the dog. He was a bundle of fun and very obedient, and I thought he'd be great company for Daniel. And I liked the idea of taking him running with me, three miles along the towpath to Eton and back.

Having been raised on a farm, Bruno hated being indoors, so I turned one of the outhouses into a huge kennel and put a wire fence under the hedge to give him the run of the huge garden. He loved it. And I loved him. He was an adorable dog and I grew very, very fond of him. He was great company and at least *he* was always pleased to see me.

One morning, however, I took Bruno for his usual run, then went into Maidenhead for lunch. When I came back in the evening, I couldn't find him anywhere. I reported him missing to the local police but he didn't turn up and I spent a sleepless night, worrying. The next morning, I got a call saying Bruno had been found, dead, on the hard shoulder of the M4. He had been taken to Maidenhead police station, where I could collect him. Dreading seeing poor Bruno's dead body, I drove there and gently put him in the car boot. I drove back, sobbing my heart out, and went into the garden and dug a grave under the hedge. I laid Bruno in it, tears streaming down my face. God, how I loved that dog. God, how I was going to miss him.

✳✳✳

Although I'd been out of the spotlight, someone must have remembered me, because, early in 1970, I got a call from a showbiz agent, asking if I wanted a non-speaking part in a send-up of a Roman orgy in *Up Pompeii*, a comedy movie, starring the gay comic, Frankie Howerd. All I had to do was walk on in a toga, pick up a nubile maiden from a stone slab and carry her off. It sounded fun. So I said yes immediately. After all, I wasn't doing much else.

Whether it was Frankie who wanted me in the film, I never found out, but he certainly showed a liking for me. We were chatting in his caravan dressing room when he made a cheeky remark and touched between my legs. I knew he was gay, but I was not prepared for that.

'I didn't realise you wanted to be knocked out, Frankie,' I said, as politely as I could.

'What do you mean?' he replied, feigning surprise.

'Do that to me again and I'll have to hit you.'

'Ooh, you wouldn't do that,' he said in his camp manner.

'I bloody well will,' I said, not so politely.

He laughed loudly. 'I think you would an' all.'

It's possible Frankie may have fancied getting hold of a brawny ex-

177

boxer, but I don't think so. I'm sure he was just larking about, seeing how far he could go, because he was as good as gold after that and, in fact, arranged for me to appear in another film with him that year, *Up the Chastity Belt*. We became good friends and he came to Gable End for lunch with his partner a few times. Off-stage, Frankie was not the wise-cracking funny man you'd expect him to be; he was very serious and, at times, morose, actually. He was very opinionated and, like me, loved a good discussion. We'd sit in the garden, drinking tea in the sun, and have a right good go at each other. But neither of us ever got cross. Unlike many people, who get stroppy or personal when they're losing an argument, Frankie simply went off on a different tack. He was very good company and I liked him a lot.

Although I'd had only a small part in *Up Pompeii*, the experience gave me a taste for acting and I enrolled at the London Guildhall School of Music and Drama, seriously determined to learn the trade and try to break into the business. While I was there, someone suggested I took fencing lessons, 'to give you poise', but it was all for publicity purposes and it never went anywhere. However, I did land a part in a comic sketch in Leslie Crowther's ITV series – telling him 'That's my handbag,' and mincing off like a poof! – and appeared in a modest Guildhall production of the musical, *Irma la Douce*. I played a 'heavy', who sang as well as threw punches.

After getting in the ring in front of 10,000 yelling fans, performing in front of a theatre audience held no fears for me, but, being a lazy sod, I got fed up with drama lessons, and what dreams I may have had of becoming the next James Bond quickly died. The little acting I did was a lot of fun, though. And, as usual, I made sure I had a laugh.

✳✳✳

George never missed an opportunity and when he learned I'd become friendly with Frankie Howerd, he was in quickly. 'Billy,' he said. 'I want you to take Frankie to Sidcup. The punters will love him.' Frankie was up for a free dinner and some fun, so I picked him up and drove him to Kent. He didn't think for a minute he'd have to sing for his supper, but soon after we arrived at The Marlowe Rooms, in Sidcup High Street, he saw his name on the menu, as 'After Dinner Speaker'. Titter, he did not! He thought he had a night off. He asked me what had happened and I said I'd told the banqueting manager that he would be there, but certainly not that he'd be speaking. Embarrassed and angry, I was all for walking out, but Frankie would have none of it. 'Now my name's there, I've got to do something, Bill,' he said. 'I can tell you or the manager that it's a liberty, but the punters don't care. They've paid to see me, so I've got to do something.'

What a true pro and nice guy Frankie was. At the end of the dinner, he stood up and spoke, very amusingly, for twenty minutes or so, without giving the slightest clue that he was due there solely as a guest. To this day, I don't know if anyone pulled a stroke to get him there for nothing.

✳✳✳

My daughter, Clare, was born on 30 March 1971, and I adored her as much I did Daniel. I was determined to be a good dad, and spent lots of time at home with them, filled with hope for their futures. I felt I owed it to them, and Susan, to try to get more involved in the business, but when I tried to put my oar in about something, George would shout me down. 'You've been boxing while I've been building up the business, what do you know? You know nothing.' Maybe he was right. As I didn't want to be involved, maybe I should have left him to it, just taken the money. But I owned half the shares in the company and, if I saw something I didn't like, what was I to do? Just say: 'I don't care' and walk away?

What George was saying, of course, was that he was the boss, the ultimate No. 1 Guv'nor and I should keep quiet – the *very* silent partner! – and do as I was told. Just like I'd done in my career. Again, I kept schtum: if I'd dared to say my boxing had given us all we had, he'd have said we wouldn't have got anywhere without his ideas and business acumen, and we would have had a slanging match. And I knew I wouldn't be able to handle the tension and bad feeling.

Anyway, money was not really the issue. The point was that all I'd ever wanted was enough money to live happily and have fun, whereas that had never been enough for George. He craved power, wanted to be in control of everything. Money obviously came into it, because that bought the power, but being Mister Big and calling the shots was the real turn-on. And he was never satisfied. He once told me: 'If we can get a hundred grand we'll retire and really enjoy ourselves – it'll be fantastic.' Well, we got the hundred grand and then it was: 'If we can get a quarter of a million . . .' George never stopped. He always wanted more.

Without doubt, he resented me having a fifty per cent share of the business. I don't think he ever looked on me as an equal partner. And, now that I was no longer a valuable commodity, lining his pocket, I'm sure he viewed me merely as a member of staff, taking money from the till.

For most of 1971, I kept going to the office. Why, I don't know. I never did anything, just hung around for a couple of hours to show my face, and then went off again to enjoy myself.

And then, one day, I needed to discuss something important with George and was told to make an appointment.

And I knew then that I'd lost my brother for ever.

✳✳✳

We had a blazing row about the way 'our' company was being run and George, the Big Boss, steamed into me, laying down his brand of law.

'It's not *our* business,' he yelled. 'It's *MY* business.'

'And I own fifty per cent,' I yelled back.

'Yeah, but I built it up,' he said. 'And I run it, not you. It's nothing to do with you.'

I felt like he was looking on me as he would a bank manager; someone who would never have part of the business as long as they got their loan back. The row blazed on and, in the end, I did my nut, as I suspect George knew I would. 'Fuck you. And fuck the business,' I screamed. 'I can't handle any of this bollocks any more. I want out.'

I've often wondered whether George had planned it all from the start. Certainly he knew me well enough to know that if he stuck me in an office all day, I'd rebel, and that it would be only a question of time before I'd blow a fuse. Who knows, maybe he thought that if he bided his time until I could stand it no longer, he'd be able to grab the business for himself.

For my part, I needed to get away from George – fast. If I stayed, I knew I'd have to change, adapt, swallow a lot of pride, and start living my life as he led his. I didn't want that. I wanted to live my life as I wanted to live it. I didn't want to be a slave to the business. So he came up with a deal – one that suited him, and got me out of his hair.

Diana Rigg draping herself across me for a publicity shot – lucky me!
She set the pose up; a really fun lady and very professional.
(Author's private collection)

In New York, 1963, at ex-heavyweight champion of the world Jack Dempsey's restaurant, with the man himself, my American trainer Harry Wiley and the well-known BBC commentator Harry Carpenter.
(Author's private collection)

Banging the drum at a charity function in 1966 with Floyd Patterson, ex-World HW champion, and Sir Henry Cooper.
(Author's private collection)

A lovely photo of the family together in 1968: Mum, Dad, George, John and myself.
(Author's private collection)

The day of my marriage to Susan Coleopy, with my brothers John and George. Don't we look smart!
(Author's private collection)

I was best man at the wedding of Susan and Jack Stevens. Little did I know that 33 years later we would meet again and I would make Susan my fourth wife.
(Author's private collection)

ACTION PACKED PHOTOS PLUS FULL PAGE AUTOGRAPHED PICTURE

BILLY WALKER

By Award Winning Columnist of the Evening Standard **GEORGE WHITING**

FIVE SHILLINGS

The *Evening Standard* produced a magazine about my life, written by George Whiting. It sold for five shillings in 1969.

(Author's private collection)

My favourite photograph of me fighting.
(Author's private collection)

The punch that made me: Cornelius Perry knocked out in the first round in the Amateur International Boxing Tournament, Great Britain v USA contest, at the Empire Pool, Wembley. We beat them 10–0 – what a great day!
(Author's private collection)

My favourite publicity photo – I send this out to fans.
(Author's private collection)

Billy Walker

I always liked this picture taken in about 1988 in Tenerife, where I lived for a while, with my two children from my second marriage, Kelly and Tom.
(Author's private collection)

With my third wife, the lovely Patricia Furuborg, who tragically died of cancer in June 2003. (Author's private collection)

In a reflective mood on holiday in Skiathos, our favourite escape, in 2004. It was there that I proposed to Susan, again! (Author's private collection)

On holiday in Lipari, in 2005, with my life-long friends Tommy and Ann McCarthy and my beautiful fourth wife Susan.
(Author's private collection)

23 September 2005: Susan and me outside Chelsea Registry Office on our wedding day – one of the happiest days of my life.
(Arnold Slater)

The agreement was that I would now own Hobart Wharf at Silvertown, East London and receive £6,500 a year rent that a building company paid – in quarterly instalments – to G. and W. Walker. The rent was guaranteed for life by our company, and George made a big point that the deal was really worth £65,000.

In addition, he said, the company would pay me £4,500 a year to run the purchasing division from a warehouse in the City. That part of the deal didn't excite me, obviously, but, in practice, the purchasing company was run very efficiently by our brother, John, and he was quite happy to continue running it, with me as his boss in name only. The arrangement suited us both fine: I'd roll in around mid-morning, ask John if everything was okay, then go out and enjoy myself with my mates when he said it was. Soon, I was living the life of Reilly: not only did I have money in my pocket, but George had also given me carte blanche to charge all my restaurant and bar bills to the company.

In his eyes, it was an incredibly small price to pay for getting rid of me.

✳✳✳

Of course, I feel I should have got more out of the business. It was my blood and sweat that had brought in the money. But I was happy with what I got. In fact, I was so desperate to get away from all the pressure and George's moaning, that I would have taken a lot less to go. There's no doubt he did me a favour making me want to sell. I'm sure I'd have had stomach ulcers, maybe a heart attack, if I'd been subjected to the sort of stress he was under.

Some might say I should have stayed and put up with it because he went on to form the leisure company, Brent Walker, and become a multi-millionaire. But it would never have worked because George lives to work and wanted me to be a clone of him, whereas I work to live, and always put my enjoyment first. We're so different we could have ended up killing each other.

Maybe I shouldn't have been surprised at George's change in attitude towards me. Over the years, I'd begun to see cracks in his affection as the money rolled in and he and Jean started climbing the social ladder. Money changed him, no doubt about that. Suddenly, he didn't want to go out with me any more, mixing instead with people he thought were useful to him. That surprised and disappointed me because I'd always thought he was like me. I feel, with people, please like me, I want you to like me, I'm *begging* you to like me. But if you can't – tough. I'm not going to turn into a different person, so you can like me. Unlike George, I can't suffer fools just because they've got a lot of money and a good position, and are useful to know. What a boring life to live. How can you tolerate someone all night, just because you want something out of them. It's like going out with an ugly bird, isn't it?

Now that I was away from George, I began to think back on our relationship and, you know, I began to wonder whether we'd ever been as close as I'd believed. And the more I thought about it, the more I began to feel that, maybe the love I felt he'd had for me was nothing to do with me at all, but about the money I could earn him. Was all that closeness a con? Had he just been using me all along? What a horrible thought. Don't get me wrong, I'm not whingeing about it in any way at all. The last thing I want, at my time of life, is for people to think: Poor me! I felt betrayed, that's all. And hurt.

One of the things that hurt most was the £10,000 mortgage George made me take out on my lovely house. Why lumber me with a mortgage when there was more than enough money in the company to buy it for me outright? I honestly feel that the one thing I should have got for all the money I earned – let alone all the punishment I took – was a house of my own, paid for out of my boxing career.

But I didn't get it.

✳✳✳

18

The more I'd seen of Jersey, the more I liked it and several times had told Jack I wouldn't mind living there, particularly as the income tax rate for residents was a piddling twenty pence in the pound. But I doubt I would ever have left England had Jack not told me, in the Autumn of 1972, that Jersey was considering changing its residency laws to prevent the island being used as a tax haven. In a couple of years, he said, foreigners wishing to set up home there would have to prove they had a minimum guaranteed annual income of £50,000. If I wanted to live on the island, I'd better apply soon, or I would not get in.

Susan and I talked it through and thought it a good idea: the tax benefits were one attraction, but what convinced us were the estate agent details Jack sent to us. I would lose my purchasing company income when I left but, even after paying off our £10,000 mortgage, we'd still make a big enough profit to buy a similar-size house in Jersey – and have enough to leave money in the bank, earning interest. It seemed too good an opportunity to miss, so we put Dorney on the market for £70,000 and started looking at properties in Jersey. The following year, we found one and sold Gable End to the comedian, Ernie Wise, and his wife for £65,000. In August, Susan and I, the two kids, and our second Labrador, also called Bruno, moved into the most wonderful house with seven bedrooms and four bathrooms, surrounded by fields, in St. Peter's Valley, on the north side of the island. It cost us just £38,000.

I really did believe the move would breathe fresh life into our marriage, both in and out of the bedroom. I was determined to mend my philandering and boozy ways, to value family life, and bring back the happy days Susan and I had shared at the start of our relationship. But in little more than a year, it was clear that we still had problems. Big ones.

Susan's Woking class snobbery drew us into Jersey's rich set and I couldn't bear them. Drawn to ordinary guys, as usual, I was quickly accepted as one of the lads and was chosen to represent the island in a tug-of-war contest in Switzerland. But, typically, most of the people Susan courted as friends were the sons and daughters of wealthy couples who'd settled on the island in the fifties – spoilt children, born with the proverbial silver spoon in their mouths, who'd never achieved anything of any substance in their lives. Susan found them impressive and captivating because they had money and spoke well but, to me, they were shallow, narrow-minded snobs who thought they were better than they were – and certainly better than me. If I'd disliked the people Susan called friends in Maidenhead, I positively loathed the ones she fawned over in Jersey. And it started to widen the rift between us.

Any time I showed interest in making love, Susan would disappear into the bathroom and not come out until she knew I'd fallen asleep. So, it was hardly surprising that when the chance of some fun and games came along I succumbed with little resistance. She was a tall, sexy Scots lass and I took her to dinner at Granite Corner, a restuarant in St. Clements, on the other side of the island. I felt I'd be safe seven miles from home but, as we walked in, two people I didn't know called out: 'Hello, Bill', and I thought: 'Oh, dear'. I was my usual friendly self and bluffed it out, as though I had every reason to be there with a good-looking woman who wasn't my wife. I was lucky that word didn't get back to Susan, but the experience taught me a lesson: Jersey was too small to play around and get away with it. If I wanted to stay married, which I did, I'd have to have my games somewhere else.

Ironically, it was George who provided the perfect opportunity. Since I'd left, he had expanded the business considerably and, to be on hand for breakfast meetings, had bought a flat in the Barbican, in the City of London. I could hardly believe my luck when, during a phone conversation one day, he said I was welcome to use it whenever he wasn't there. It was ideal – a little love-nest for my games. All I had to do was tell Susan I was required in London for something to do with one of George's enterprises, and off I'd go for a couple of days. To make sure she didn't suspect anything, I arranged for George's secretary to ring the house when I wasn't there and tell Susan I was required in London on such and such a date. It was a doddle.

I knew I was doing wrong, but I needed to get my sexual satisfaction somewhere. Anyway, as I've said, what the eye doesn't see, the heart doesn't grieve over. And, for all I knew, I may have been such a drag, Susan was secretly cheering at the thought of being shot of me for a while.

✳ ✳ ✳

Jack Stevens had been generous to me and I was very grateful. But I'd never been able to warm to him: frankly, I thought he was a bit of a phoney. So, when he suggested we all went with him and his wife, and two children, to Portugal on holiday, my first thought was to say no. I just had a sixth sense that all of us, plus a nanny for the kids, in a villa wouldn't work out. And I was right.

I quickly discovered Jack was the type who would have an argument with his wife over something trivial, then saunter off to a different part of the beach to sulk. I'd think: 'Oh, God, how childish.' I've no time for people who sulk. But he obviously liked throwing his weight around with women because, a day or two later, he started having a go at my wife Susan when I wasn't around. I was going to put him in his place when she told me, but she begged me not to, so I bit my tongue.

I did my best to forget it and back in Jersey, a few months later, invited Jack to join me and some mates on our regular Friday nights on the booze. They weren't too keen because they, too, felt Jack was a bit of a plonker, but he clearly fancied a night out with the lads, even though he was much older than us, so I took him along and made him welcome.

One night back at The Bon Air, his guest house in Pontac, however, he said something disrespectful about Susan and the bad holiday memory came back. I told him he'd been lucky to get away with being rude to Susan and I wasn't going to let it pass again. He said something saucy and I grabbed him by the throat with my left hand and pushed him against a wall. I wanted him to throw a punch, so that I could give him a right-hander, but he didn't: he just stood there, rigid as a post,

185

saying over and over: 'Don't be silly, Billy, don't be silly.' He was so frightened he didn't move an eyelid. I was frustrated because I dearly wanted to belt him one, but, in the end, I let him go and settled for telling him what I thought. 'I don't like you, Jack,' I said. 'I've been meaning to tell you, I think you're a prat. And I don't want to be in your company.'

I then walked out and didn't meet him again for twenty years. I made sure I didn't go to places where I'd see him, and he made sure he didn't bump into me. If I did see him, I always made sure I ducked out of sight. He once told his wife Susan that I'd used him. He was right: if someone offers you a free holiday, you'd be a mug to turn it down, wouldn't you? But it wasn't as if he didn't get anything in return. He used me, too. He used my well-known face for his own purposes and even pretended I was his cousin, if it suited him. And, after all, he *did* get a celebrity for a Best Man, didn't he? I didn't feel guilty about Jack – just relief that the idiot was out of my life.

✳✳✳

Suddenly, in 1974, to my horror, inflation went through the roof. And the one thing I thought I'd never have to worry about again became an issue.

Money.

Stupidly, I thought my quarterly wharf income, plus the bank interest on the Dorney profit, would provide enough for the family to live well, and for me to enjoy myself. But, unbelievably, I started to feel the pinch. To add to my problems, the wharf rent was tied into local rates, and the area was in decline, so the property value dropped – and so did my income. The rent did not rise as fast as inflation and was independently reviewed. It was then I realised the lease had been set up really badly and there was nothing I could do to change the fact that I only got half the money I was expecting. It became very clear I had to get a job. That didn't worry me unduly: I knew I'd always earn a living, one way or another. Nor was the prospect of having to work a shock to my system; it was simply something I had to do. What *was* a problem, however, was finding the right job for a retired heavyweight boxer with no professional skills, let alone academic qualifications. I could hardly go down the local JobCentre – or Labour Exchange, as it was then.

I needed a bit of luck and it came in the form of a genial gentleman, I shall call John, who not only represented a UK flooring company in Jersey, but also had the concession for Beardmore Brass, another UK firm, specialising in what its name implied. John was tired of travelling round the island, trying to drum up business; he preferred to stay behind the locked door of his office. He offered me £60 a week to do the job for him, with commission on everything I sold, and I accepted gleefully. I had an office if I needed it but, in the main, I was free to go where I liked, using my name, and friendly easy-going nature, to get business. It suited me down to the ground.

Once I started, I never saw much of John: he'd disappear into his office in the morning and still be there when I reported back in the late afternoon. When I left, I'd call out goodbye, but seldom got an answer. Six months or so later I discovered why, when some men in dark suits, and even darker expressions, arrived from the flooring company's UK head office.

John, I learned, had a drink problem and had got me to do his job so that he could get pissed every day. When his bosses cleaned out the office they found ten empty vodka bottles, but no sign of the money he'd convinced them he was earning the company. John was given his marching orders and, as the only candidate for the job, I was asked to keep the office ticking over until the company wound up the Jersey operation. It was a promotion of sorts and, to my delight, I was given a salary increase. Not that I warranted it: I rarely went into the office, just carried on selling Beardmore Brass products. If anyone rung up, wanting a carpet fitted, a very efficient secretary simply contacted me and I arranged for a fitter to do the job.

A couple of months later, I was thinking what else I could do to make a few quid when a friend, Ted Clucas, brought up the subject of vending machines. He'd sold them in England and knew that ones being sold in Jersey were useless because they kept breaking down and were costing publicans and hotel owners money in repair bills. We had a business opportunity, he said: if we could replace the machines that didn't work with ones that did, we could out-do the company selling them and clean up. We decided to invest a £1,000 each in thirty new machines to test the water. I went to two local breweries and persuaded them to try the new machines in some of their pubs, then started wooing hotel owners. My face was so well known I got a good reaction from every one. 'Hello, Mr Walker,' they'd say. 'What are you having?'

And I'd be there all afternoon – usually with a sale at the end of a convivial session. Mind you, I didn't hang around long if I didn't feel a sale was likely. Much as I like sitting around having a chin-wag over a few jars, business is business.

Within six months Ted and I had installed so many machines our competitors came to us with a proposal to join forces. It was too good an offer to turn down, so we became partners.

✳ ✳ ✳

We'd been in Jersey three years when Susan went to Tenerife with a married girlfriend for some winter sun – and came back a changed woman. She'd met someone else, she said; another man, who had made her question our marriage. She didn't go into details, but my first thought was that she'd been well sorted out by someone with a different sexual technique to mine. I was the only man she'd slept with, after all, and I wasn't dumb enough to think she couldn't be turned on by someone else, given the chance. She never came close to admitting anything happened, just made it clear that whoever it was, and whatever he'd done, had opened her eyes to what a rotten relationship we had.

I went barmy, of course. 'If that's how you feel, bollocks – piss off now,' I said. But I could hardly play the hard done-by Poor Me, could I? Not after cheating on Susan so often. If we hadn't had children, I may have suggested splitting up, because we now both knew we didn't like each other much. But we *did* have two gorgeous kids and I knew that if I kicked Susan out she'd go back to England and take them with her. I couldn't bear that, so I swallowed my pride and suggested we stayed together and tried to make the best of it. I hated Susan's snobbery and prudishness, but I didn't dislike her and certainly didn't want to throw in the marital towel if there was a chance we could battle through. I felt we had a chance: as a Catholic, Susan believed marriage should be forever and would not contemplate divorce lightly; and with the marriages of my parents and brothers still going strong, I didn't want to be the family failure.

As a conciliatory, romantic gesture, I suggested we flew to London in the run-up to New Year, and spoil ourselves: dinner with some friends, a West End show, pampering in an expensive hotel with no expense spared. Susan was all for it. So I booked it and off we went.

Those three days went better than I could have dreamed. Susan was in great form: happy and chatty, and – surprise, surprise – willing to make love every night. Billy boy, for once, you've done the right thing here, I thought. And, flying home on Friday morning, I was in a bubbly, bouyant mood and looking forward to New Year's Eve that night. After all the upset, everything boded well for 1977, I was sure of it.

When we arrived at the house, the postman had been. There was a letter for me. It was from a firm of Jersey solicitors. And it informed me, in the cold, stark manner legal people delight in, that Susan had started proceedings to divorce me.

I could not believe it. I went upstairs to our bedroom. Susan was unpacking.

'What the hell is this?' I yelled, brandishing the letter. 'Why the hell did you come away with me, if this is what you were doing?'

Susan looked at me, then carried on putting things away.

'I don't believe you,' I bellowed. 'How could you let me think you wanted to be with me, when all the time this is what you were doing? Why didn't you say you didn't want to go?'

She looked at me, blankly, then said: 'I didn't want to disappoint you.'

I walked out the bedroom and out of the house. I got in my car. There was not a lot to say to that, was there?

I drove around, my mind in turmoil. *Divorce!* What a dreadful word: it reeked of disappointment and failure. You can't make your relationship work, so chuck the towel in and try again with someone new! I'd never been a quitter in the ring and I wasn't going to start now. When I'd married, I honestly did think it would be forever. And I wasn't going to give up on it without a fight.

When I got home, I went up to Susan. 'This is crazy, bloody crazy,' I said. 'We've got to make this work. We owe it to ourselves. And the children.'

But she didn't want to know. Her mind was made up. She wanted out.

In desperation, I phoned her mother. Being the good Catholic lady she is, she'd be on my side, I was sure of it.

But she was all for it.

'How can you want your daughter to divorce when it's against your religion?' I asked.

'You've been with other women,' she said, coldly. 'That makes a difference.'

'So the Catholic church practises double standards, does it?'

It was not what the woman wanted to hear and I didn't get anywhere.

So, I decided that if divorce was what they all wanted, the sooner we got one, the better for everybody. I was very upset; of course I was. But I had to accept that, back in 1968, I'd been right to worry that Susan might be marrying the image, not the person.

That when the cameras stopped clicking and I became, not the nation's sporting hero but Bill Walker, ordinary bloke, she'd discover that I wasn't really her cup of tea at all.

19

I decided not to contest the divorce. What was the point? Susan wanted out and that was that. The grounds on which she wanted the annulment granted *were* important, however. And we had a problem. Susan wanted to go for physical cruelty, citing – would you believe! – an occasion one New Year's Eve when, she claimed, I made her sleep in a single bed with me and moved around in my sleep so much I caused her to bang her head against the wall!

I said I'd contest physical cruelty, but would agree to mental cruelty, saying I would admit to shouting at her and making her life hell. Her lawyers went along with that and, all that had to be sorted now was the settlement. I knew it was going to cost me, but there was no oddsing that. Susan had never had any money of her own and she had none now. She said she wanted to go back to England with the children, and bring them up in Maidenhead where she'd been happy, so I agreed to sell my interest in the vending machine company to buy her a house there.

Inevitably, the news of the split leaked out, towards the end of January, and I got a call from the *Sun*. I decided to do the honourable thing: 'I blame myself entirely,' I told the reporter. 'I'm the male chauvinist pig to end them all. I'd go out and have too much to drink. I have a foul tongue when I'm drunk and I'd be very cruel to Sue. Finally she could take no more. Deep down, I still love her, but I'm afraid our marriage is finished. We'll be divorced in April.'

And we were.

The three months after that, though, were bizarre. While we looked for a suitable property in the UK Susan and the children lived upstairs, while I lived downstairs. This wasn't much of a problem, because we kept ourselves pretty much to ourselves.

When the divorce was decreed absolute in May 1976 and it was time for Susan and the kids to leave, I knew I would not be able to handle being in the house, so I treated myself to a Morgan sports car and persuaded my mate, Kenny Bailey, to join me for a couple of months in Spain. In the last week of July, we set off for a hotel run by a mutual friend, Russell Martin, in Estartit, near Lloret. It was a rough hotel in a real dump of a resort, but there was loud music and loads of birds to take my mind off what was happening at home.

I'd told Susan she could have anything she wanted from the house. And when I got back, in September, I discovered she'd taken me at my word: the place was virtually empty. I was shocked, but could hardly complain: if I'd been that bothered I would have stayed and supervised what she wanted and what she didn't, wouldn't I?

I immediately went into town and splashed out three grand on new furniture, beds, TV – everything I needed to make the place more or less how it had been. Within two days it was. And I was ready to start enjoying life as a bachelor again.

Ideally, I wanted to sell the house, and buy one of the beautiful apartments overlooking the quay, in St. Helier, and live off the profit from the sale. But, under Jersey law, I was not allowed to buy a property cheaper than the one I was selling. I found it strange living on my own in such a huge house, so when one of my group of pals said he'd had to give up his flat, I suggested he moved in with me. That prompted some of the other guys to ask if I'd rent a room to each of them and, before I knew it, I had all four living there – Kenny Bailey, Kenny Mack, Bobby Floyd, Connie Farmer and, when he returned from Lloret at the end of the season, Russell Martin took over a fifth room.

I was still nipping over to the UK, and it will surprise no one to learn that on one trip, I made contact with Pat Furoborg. Still raw from the acrimony of the divorce, I wanted the company of someone who knew me, understood me, and who could make me feel better about myself. Pat was now married herself, but she was keen to meet with me again, if only for old time's sake, and we spent a couple of afternoons at the White House Hotel, near where I'd had the flat in Ebury Street.

It was wonderful being with Pat again. Not for the first time, I wondered how my life would have panned out if I'd married her, not Susan.

✳✳✳

Now a free agent, I was keen to go where the fun was. And the fun that summer, 1977, was going to be in Corfu, where Russell was now managing a holiday club for 18–30 year-olds. I was left to my own devices – or maybe I should say vices, because, the way he described it, Russell's club was all about laying in the sun all day and laying unattached young women at night.

Russell and I had struck a deal: he stayed at my house in the winter and I'd stay at his holiday club in the summer, acting as an unpaid courier. Wearing a T-shirt with *Russell's Minder* on the front and *Complaints Department* on the back, I'd travel to the airport in a coach and meet the new arrivals off the plane. One girl that summer was nineteen and so strikingly beautiful she looked like a fashion model. To me, she was fresh and innocent, and I felt very protective towards her. All the lads there were rogues, however, and after the girl had shared my straw hut for the third night running, Russell decided it was time I shared her. I was dancing with her in the disco that night when Russell, who was with another girl, said: 'Why don't you bring your bird back to my hut later, Bill. We'll do a swap with mine.'

'Do me a favour, Russ,' I said. 'She's not like that.'

Suddenly, my Miss Innocent broke in: 'What's he saying, Billy?'

'I'm not going to tell you,' I said. 'He's being rude, the rascal. He's terrible, Russell.'

'Come on, tell me,' she said.

She wouldn't let it go, so I said: 'Now, don't be offended, but he wants me to take you back to his hut and have some fun with him and his girlfriend and maybe another mate of ours.'

The girl's face lit up. 'Oh, I'd love that,' she said.

And she did. She was the biggest raver I'd met in my life – quite wild and uninhibited. And totally insatiable. I didn't mind, once I'd got used to the idea but, at first, I was shocked and it dawned on me that, at thirty-eight, I was old fashioned. Young women's attitude to casual sex had clearly changed in the brief time I'd been married.

When we weren't having games, we all drank, of course. Often the boozing went on into the early hours and one morning, around 4 a.m., the drunken talk got around to running. Russell, who loved a bet and knew what I could do, looked at the crowd of young Greek guys, then pointed at me. 'Any of you lot, he'll beat you,' he said, drunkenly. 'A race into town and he'll win.' The crowd stared at me. They'd only seen me in the bar, legless, every night. I must have looked as though I'd have trouble running 300 yards to the beach, never mind twelve miles into Corfu town! One of them laughed and said I wouldn't be able to make it to Ipsos, which was no more than two miles down the road. What neither he, nor his mates, knew was that I'd always kept myself in shape by training. And, even though my fighting days were behind me, I'd kept the habit of going for a run and sweating the booze out of me, no matter how drunk I'd been, now matter how painful the hangover. How were they to know that, when I surfaced in the mornings, I often ran to Ipsos and back to clear my head?

Sensing easy pickings, the young Greeks and others in the bar who thought I didn't have a hope, started putting money on the counter, which Russell said we would cover if anyone beat me. Later that morning, we all gathered outside the bar and lined up, about ten of us. Russell was the starter and, to the cheers of all the young birds who must have thought we were all nuts, he sent us on our way.

Three of the young Greeks went off like gazelles. I plodded on behind at my own pace, more anxious to sweat the booze out of my system than to show off in the early stages. I was fairly sure the leaders wouldn't be able to keep up such a fast pace – and I was right. After three or four miles, I caught the first one, then the second, a couple of miles further on. Some of the girls in a following van kept getting out and ran with me, or ahead, but I took no notice: by now, I was sober and focussed, and determined to catch the leader. I did with four miles still to go, and cruised into town, a winner by at least half an hour. I was knackered, I must admit, but I didn't let on, and when the others in the race finally staggered into town, I made a show of doing some loosening-up exercises and said: 'Right. Let's double the money and run back.'

Thankfully, there were no takers.

I have no idea how much Russell and I won, but it must have come to a few hundred quid, because we put all our winnings behind the bar and seemed to drink free for weeks!

✳✳✳

Now free from a marriage where sex rarely featured, I spent the next year or two revelling in pulling birds who, like me, were not interested in a long-term commitment. This caused something of a problem when Jack Triggett, a promoter pal from Manchester, invited me to a very formal dinner/dance in the city. As it was a Ladies' Night, I was asked to take a female companion but, shame on me, I couldn't think of anyone I knew who was intelligent or worldly enough to mix comfortably with moneyed people she didn't know.

'Don't worry, I'll find someone for you,' my friend chuckled.

Knowing he was a practical joker, I said: 'Now, don't mess about, Jack – I'll have to be with the girl all evening.'

'Relax,' Jack said. 'I'll find someone suitable for you. Someone you'll like.'

I wasn't entirely convinced, but there was nothing I could do. I arrived at Manchester Airport expecting Jack to have my escort with him. But he was alone.

'Where is she, then?' I asked.

'We're meeting her at the hotel,' he said. 'She'll be be waiting outside with Vinnie.'

Vinnie Sciarvo was his pal, who liked a laugh, too.

I sensed a set-up but, again, there was nothing I could do. I was there now.

Outside the hotel, I was introduced to a woman, older than me, who was large, quite large – in fact, very large! Not my ideal date. My heart sank.

'Say hello to Joan,' said Jack. 'She's your lady for the night.'

Being the gentleman I am, I disguised my disappointment and smiled warmly.

'Hello, my love. How nice of you to step into the breach and help me out.'

'Oh, that's no bother, Billy,' she said, in a broad Mancunian accent. 'I'm delighted. I'm sure we'll have a lovely night.'

We stood there, staring at each other, not knowing what to say next, when she suddenly burst out laughing.

'I can't do it,' she said.

'What's going on?' I said. 'Can't do what?'

'They're having you on,' she said. 'I'm not your date. I'm here with my husband.'

I turned to Jack and Vinnie. 'I might have guessed,' I said.

'Now, *here's* your girl,' Jack said, motioning towards a tall, statuesque woman about my age, standing a few yards behind him. She had long blonde hair and was very well endowed – very desirable indeed. 'Monika, meet Billy Walker.'

Monika and I hit it off from the word go and had a fun evening, which continued when she invited me back to her flat afterwards. She was good in the snore, a real bifter, who seemed to have studied every page of the *Karma Sutra*; and what made it even better was that, like me, she wasn't after romance and marriage, only lusty fun. She was bubbly, full of life – one of those birds who were always first on the dance floor, up for any mad-cap experience and who could drink you under the table. She was like one of the chaps, someone you could have a good laugh with, and when I was invited to functions in London I always told George's secretary to book me via Manchester, so that I could spend time with Monika.

We had a highly-charged sexual liaison for about six months and I thought she was enjoying it as much as me. But, one night, she made it clear she wasn't. I was in the bath before taking her out for dinner when she came in, holding a knife.

'You're taking liberties with me, Billy,' she said.

'*What?*'

'You come over, stay here for the night, use me and go off,' she said.

'I'm not *using* you – or your bloody flat,' I said angrily. 'I've got one in London where I can stay any time I want. I come to Manchester and stay with you because I like going out with you. It's fun. I thought you were enjoying it, too.'

She didn't say anything, just stared at me, coldly. I looked at her, then at the knife in her hand. I didn't think she was going to use it, but I was not going to take the chance. I leapt out of the bath, and whipped the knife out of her hand.

'Right, that's it,' I snapped. 'I'm off.'

'Oh, please don't go, Billy,' she said. 'I was only joking.'

Some fucking joke, I thought. I dressed and packed what few other clothes I had into a small bag, in little more than ten minutes. I'd enjoyed Monika's company, but that scary episode ruined everything for me.

Monika may have been sorry the relationship was over, but she didn't show it.

'Okay, if you want to go, fine,' was all she said.

She was fun, but very hard, Monika. As I walked out of her life, she didn't shed a tear!

✳✳✳

Back in Jersey, early in 1979, I was in Thackeray's wine bar when I bumped into Chrissie Price, a bubbly girl about seven years younger than me, who I'd seen in various clubs over the years. When she told me she'd been forced to give up her flat, my heart went out to her.

'I've got some mates living with me, but there's a spare bedroom with its own bathroom,' I said. 'You can stay there for nothing if you keep the house tidy.'

Chrissie couldn't believe her luck. 'That's lovely, Billy,' she said. 'I'll take you up on that, please.'

Chrissie was not fat, but quite buxom with long blonde hair, not what I'd have said was 'my type', and I certainly wasn't hers. But we liked each other and, soon after she moved in we began a very casual sexual relationship. If we found ourselves alone in the house, we'd have a few drinks, then one of us would say, 'Yeah, come on, then,' and we'd have a little game. It was harmless fun which we both enjoyed throughout 1979. Nine times out of ten our games were impromptu and neither of us took precautions. This didn't bother me to begin with, but the more we indulged, the more I began to worry. One day I asked her if she was not concerned about getting pregnant.

'There's no chance of that,' Chrissie said. 'I was told several years ago there's a problem with my womb and I'd never be able to have children.'

✳✳✳

Surprise! Surprise! In the spring of 1979, I received an invitation from George to join him and his family on a yacht he had hired for the Cannes Film Festival, where he was proudly showing his movie, *The Bitch*. It was the sequel to the phenomenally successful *The Stud*, both of which George's company, Brent Walker, had backed financially. I was thrilled to be invited – and delighted when the star of both movies, Joan Collins, turned up as well.

In the days leading up to the showing of the film, I got to know Joan quite well. She was very easy-going, liked a little drink and a giggle, and could be saucy if the mood took her. I got the impression she liked me – a feeling that was endorsed in the early hours, at a party on the yacht following the showing of the film. I was dancing with Joan when she leaned into me and whispered: 'Would you like to come back to my hotel for a drink?'

Like her, I was nowhere near sober, but I knew a good invitation when I heard one. 'I'd love to, Joan,' I said. 'But would you mind holding on a minute? There's something I have to do.'

A couple of days before, I'd embarrassed George by doing something I shouldn't have and he'd made me promise to tell him what I was up to, so that, in his words: 'I can prepare myself.' It was a slap on the wrist and I didn't like it. I felt he had every right to tell his employees what they could, and could not, do, but I was family.

George had gone to bed shortly after midnight and it was now 3 a.m but, buoyed up with bubbly, I couldn't resist getting my own back and having a laugh at his expense. I weaved my way to his cabin and knocked, none too quietly, on the door.

After what seemed an age, George appeared in his dressing gown.

'Yes,' he said, irritably. 'What is it?'

'You know you told me to tell you anything I was doing that might cause problems?'

'Yes,' George replied, even more tersely, fearing the worst.

'Well, Joan has asked me to go back to the hotel with her,' I said. 'Is that all right with you?'

George just glared at me.

'You've woken me up to tell me THAT,' he said. 'Fuck off, you arsehole.' Even George couldn't resist a smile as he slammed the door shut and shouted 'Enjoy yourself!' So I did!

Joan and I went back to her hotel and consumed even more champagne. We chatted for a while and eventually passed out on the bed in an alcohol-fuelled sleep. The next thing I knew it was morning and Joan was nudging me awake, telling me to get up as she had a Press call early that morning.

That night was a crazy, unforgettable experience and I treasure the memory of it. Joan may be a glamorous, larger-than-life showbiz icon, but I found her to also be a nice, fun-loving woman with a cheeky sense of humour. A great lady.

✱✱✱

I went back to Corfu that summer and it was Happy Days again for a couple of months before Russell overstepped the mark and I had to teach him a lesson. As you're aware by now, I'm an easy-going guy, who has always preferred fun to fighting, and I can honestly say I've never – not once – gone looking to fight someone outside the ring. The only time I've resorted to physical violence is when I've been pushed too far and my back is against the wall, with no way out. Unfortunately there have been some blokes who've mistaken my happy-go-lucky, quiet nature for softness and have thought I was a bit of a pushover, someone they could take a liberty with for their own bravado.

Sadly for Russell, he was one of them.

There were a few of us sitting round a table one afternoon, all fairly tanked up, when Russell used the one word I can't abide. I've never liked it being used in front of me, either in a derogatory way about anyone, or even as a joke. And I certainly can't handle it being used to describe me.

The word is cunt. And, that boozy afternoon, Russell called me one.

I don't remember what we were talking about, or what prompted him to use that word. What I do know is that my insides knotted in anger and I glared at him, letting him know he had upset me. Russell wasn't a tall bloke, about three inches shorter than me, but he was very stocky and muscular. He was also a mouthy, bolshie bastard, who believed he was Goliath after a few drinks. Far from cooling it, or even apologising, he continued to mouth off, belittling me in front of the others. I'm sure some guys, if they'd been physically equipped, would have given him one there and then. But that wasn't in my nature. And, as someone who'd slugged it out with the British heavyweight champion, I was on a hiding to nothing: if I knocked him out, I'd be a bully; if he caught me with a lucky punch and hurt me, I'd be humiliated. So, I bit my lip – or wiped my mouth, as we say in the East End. But only for a while.

I waited for Russell to go to the loo, fifty yards or so down the beach, then got up and followed. I bet the others at the table suspected what was going to happen but, to be honest, I didn't give a monkey's: Russell was out of order and he needed to be told.

Alone with him in the loo, I said; 'You took a liberty, Russell. I don't like it.'

Russell's all right, but his mouth often gets him into trouble. He sneered at me: 'So what! What you going to do about it, an old punch-drunk like you?'

If he'd smiled and said: 'You're right, Bill, I was out of order, I'm sorry,' I probably would have given him the benefit of the doubt and swallowed it. But when he compounded the insult, I snapped and gave him a short, but hard, right hand in the ribs. Of course, I could have laid him out with one to the chin, but why would I want to mark his face, or damage my knuckles. By punching to the ribs I hurt him, not myself.

He fell to the floor, winded, then rolled over, got to his feet and ran out the door. I should have left it there because I knew I'd hurt him bad, but I was so steamed up, I ran after him. Russell was such a good, fast runner I'd often joked with him that he should be in the Olympics, but I caught up with him that afternoon and tried to clobber him again. I missed, twice, and Russell took off, even faster, into Ipsos, with me doing my best to keep up. He headed for a club we both used and dived in, past two big lumps on the door. As they moved to bar my way, I said: 'If you get involved, if you're with him, I'll knock the both of you out.'

'It's nothing to do with us, Bill,' one of them said, and they stepped aside to let me in. I had a good look around, but there was no sign of Russell. He'd obviously nipped out the back way, fearing I wanted to do him properly.

The next day, he was all strapped up around his middle.

'What's all that?' I asked, genuinely unaware of the extent of my damage.

'You broke two of my fucking ribs,' he said.

For some reason, it struck me as funny and I started laughing. I don't think he was best pleased but, after a while, he laughed, too, and eventually it became a running joke and he made a point of telling everyone he met. Despite his obvious pain, he seemed to delight in having had two ribs broken by the once-famous Billy Walker!

After apologies from both sides we got our friendship back on track and since that day Russell has never slagged me off in that horrible way. He can still be a bit mouthy, but if he gets saucy I give him the evil eye and say: 'Careful now, Russell, you don't want any more broken ribs,' and he backs off.

✳ ✳ ✳

I hadn't been back in Jersey long when I was invited to London for the premiere of *The Bitch*. If I was nervous about seeing Joan Collins again, I shouldn't have been: she was charm itself and made no mention of our meeting in Cannes.

I was so pleased I made the effort to fly over because I also met up with my old mate, Pat Booth, who was keen to tell me that she had used our relationship for the basis for her latest book, *The Lady and the Champ*, which was due to be published the following spring.

Back in Jersey, I was lounging around the house one Sunday morning, bodies everywhere after a particularly wild party, when I suddenly remembered I'd agreed to be interviewed by one of the BBC's renowned reporters, John Timpson, for a programme about British tax exiles on the island. The film crew arrived and the female researcher had just started asking me questions when, first, one scantily-dressed girl came down the stairs, then another, and another. The rather attractive woman, who was in her early thirties, looked at the girls then looked at me. 'It looks like you all have a lot of fun over here,' she said, with a knowing smile.

'Great fun,' I said. 'Come back when you're finished for the day and we'll have another party.'

'Oh, no, I couldn't possibly,' she said, in her posh BBC accent.

'I'm sure I can persuade you,' I said, with a rascally grin.

I did, of course. And, naturally, we ended up in bed.

I'd continued enjoying casual sex with Chrissie, confident she was unable to have kids, so you can imagine my shock, in February 1980, when she sat me down and said: 'You won't believe this, because I certainly can't, but I'm pregnant.'

'Hold on a sec, Chrissie,' I said. 'This isn't fair. You told me you couldn't have kids.'

'That's right,' she said. 'I didn't think I could. Believe me, I'm as surprised as you.'

Having gone through the anguish of being separated from my two children, the last thing I could face was fathering another child, so I told Chrissie I would pay for her to have an abortion. She shook her head. 'No, Billy. After believing for so long I couldn't have a baby, I'm so pleased I can. And I'm going to have it.' Seeing my concern, she quickly added: 'Don't worry. I'll bring the child up as mine – and mine alone. I won't bother you for anything. Not a penny.'

Around this time, I read that Jersey's housing authorities were keen for big properties to be converted into flats to ease the housing shortage. I applied and was given permission to make my house, Windledale, into a property with a central three-bedroom, two-bathroom accomodation, and two flats on both sides. My mates had to vacate their rooms, naturally, but Chrissie stayed on and lived with me until Kenny Bailey and I bought a lodging house and invited her to move into one of the rooms as manager, collecting rents from tenants.

On 27 September, Chrissie gave birth to a baby boy she named Warren. Despite her assurance that she'd never ask me for money, I did wonder whether she would. But, to her immense credit, she never did; not before the baby was born or afterwards.

20

That November I flew to London for the wedding reception of my uncle Joe's son, Martin. He was marrying Michelle Everett. I didn't really want to go, but mum persuaded me because she wanted as many of the family there as possible. It was a pleasant enough 'do', in her father's pub in Grays Inn Road, in Holborn, but around 8.30 p.m., after I'd been there around four hours, I started saying my goodbyes because I was in a hurry to get to the West End to find a girl to take back to the Barbican.

If I had left that pub a minute – even a few seconds – before, I might not have seen the short, dark-haired young woman stepping from a cab outside. But fate had cast its spell and, most unfortunately, I did. It was, without doubt, the most crucial bit of timing in my life outside the ring – because it brought me into contact with a manipulative, if sexy, lady, who would rob me, not only of my money, but also my confidence and self-esteem.

'Hello,' I said, giving the young lady my widest, most charming, smile.

'How are *you*? Where are *you* off to?'

'In there,' she said, nodding at the pub. 'For a wedding reception. Are you?'

'Yeah,' I replied.

And my goose, as they say, was cooked.

She said she recognised me and her name was Jackie Jones.

I didn't get hold of Jackie that night, as I'd hoped, because she was a friend of the bride's mother and was going on to a private party. But I did get her phone number and, when I rang the next day, she agreed to go out with me. I took her to dinner, then back to George's flat, and after a couple more glasses of champagne, the inevitable happened.

Jackie was sexually adventurous and I found her exciting in bed. I also liked her personality and didn't hesitate inviting her to Jersey. She accepted immediately and, although I could get cheap flights through several travel agents I knew, she insisted on paying her own way. I thought: 'That's nice – that's classy.' She stayed for a few days, went home, then came back, and over the next few months we saw each other fairly regularly in the U.K. when I flew over to see the kids. I'd take them out during the day, then see Jackie in the evenings. We'd go to the cinema or theatre, or just out to dinner at Langan's or Topo Gigio's, with Melvyn or Tommy, or the Everetts.

In the early part of 1981, Jackie started flying to Jersey more and more, bringing various possessions to the house. She'd told me she worked as a movie stunt girl, under the name Tunbridge, so you can imagine my surprise when I discovered her birth certificate in the name of Jones, and her bank account in the name of a bloke, named James, she said she'd gone out with for eight years. I thought having three names a bit odd, but had no reason to question her and quickly forgot about it. I did ask various people about her stunt work, though, and was surprised that no one had heard of her. She told me she did the stunts for *Wonderwoman*, but I never found out if that was true. Jackie was always vague about her work and seemed to live in a fantasy world. In those early days, she'd suddenly say: 'I've got to go to London. I've got a job. Good money.' She'd always come back with money, but never told me where it came from.

Jackie was great fun and, although nowhere near as beautiful as Susan, she had great boobs and a nice arse, and was always up for a party and a good drink. She was a spunky girl, too – which I liked. Once, we were having a drink with some mates outside a pub in Jersey, when the talk got around to sun-bathing. My friend Ronnie Tag said he didn't think Jackie would dare go topless in public. She insisted she would, but Ronnie was adamant she wouldn't. He was very dogmatic, almost daring her, and kept on until Jackie could stand no more and whipped off her bra and T-shirt. Ronnie, who was sitting next to her, was embarrassed and told her to put them back on, but Jackie let him squirm for a few minutes. She wasn't a show-off, by any means, but she didn't like Ronnie's attitude and really did him up. I admired her for that.

She was a bit of a tomboy: she'd lounge about the house in tracksuit bottoms and when she went out, it was always in jeans and a T-shirt, never anything pretty. I'd have a devil of a job getting her to change into a dress to go out to dinner. For all that, I not only fell in love with Jackie, but I liked her, too, so when she cuddled up in bed one night that summer, and said she might be pregnant, I wasn't bothered in the least. Nor was she. And when she took a test the next day and discovered she *was* expecting, both of us were pleased. For me, the thought of getting into a steady, totally faithful relationship and starting all over again with a new family was immensely appealing, and I could see Jackie and I having a good life together. So, after pondering on it for a few days, I said: 'Let's get married.'

Jackie was all for it and on Wednesday, 19 August 1981 we tied the knot at Jersey Register Office. After the shambles of my first wedding, I didn't fancy a big affair, so we invited only Jackie's parents and Joan Bird and her husband, George, and told them to keep it quiet. Joan had been a good friend to me and was one of the few people on the island Jackie was friends with.

Jackie's father, Joe, and mother, Maisie, came to stay before the wedding. I walked in and overheard Joe telling his daughter: 'You must not let this one go, girl.' It unsettled me for a moment. I wondered: Am I being set up here? But my ego pushed the thought away and I convinced myself that he meant I was a great guy and good for Jackie.

When we walked out of the register office, I heard someone shout: 'You crafty bastard,' from the roof of the building opposite. It was Kenny Bailey. So much for our secret wedding! After a great lunch at Victoria's restaurant, the six of us went home and carried on drinking – champagne, of course – in the garden. For me, it was the happiest of Happy Days. I felt good among people I liked and who liked me.

Seven months later, on 16 March, Jackie gave birth to a beautiful baby girl, who we named Kelly. My new family had begun. And I was thrilled.

✳ ✳ ✳

When Kelly was about a year old, Jackie's father and I were wheeling her along a shopping precinct in her pram when I saw Chrissie coming towards us. I hadn't seen her since she'd moved into a council property after Kenny and I sold the lodging house the previous year. Warren was now coming up to three and was holding Chrissie's hand. Oh, God, I thought, what's going to happen here? Introducing Joe, I stressed that he was my 'father-in-law', hoping Chrissie would take the hint and be discreet. But she simply looked at Warren, then at me, and said: 'Warren, this is your father.' The boy stared at me, but the revelation clearly meant nothing and he didn't say anything and, after a few more pleasantries, we went our separate ways. Joe and I had gone only a few yards when he said: 'Do you want to tell me?' I was just about to when I spotted Jackie and her mother. 'I'll tell you later,' I said. And I did. I had nothing to hide, or be ashamed of, and had told Jackie about Warren before we married. She wasn't bothered; I could have told her I had twenty-four kids running around the island and it wouldn't have made any difference. All Jackie was interested in was marrying me.

The following year I was smitten by a large fifteenth-century granite building called The Rectory, which had been extended in the nineteenth century. Not only would it make an idyllic home, but there were several outbuildings in the two-acre grounds, crying out for development. If I could get planning permission to demolish them and build five houses, I was sure I could make a big profit. The only problem was that, without selling Windledale, I did not have the £250,000 asking price. I brought it up in one of my rare conversations with George, and he said he had someone prepared to pay £100,000 for the wharf at Silvertown. I accepted the deal and borrowed the rest of the money from some friends to buy the house, which was beautifully situated a mile from the beach, at St. Ouen, on the west side of the island.

The building was really unusual because of the difference between early Tudor and Victorian architecture. The rooms to the left were the original and the doorways were only about five feet high, whereas the newer rooms to the right had very high ceilings. The house was massive and had wonderful granite fireplaces in every room, which I discovered as I started renovating the place. I restored all the ornate original features and created five bedrooms and bathrooms and a large, light and airy walk-through kitchen, dining and lounge areas. Then I built a triple garage, again in granite, with a flat for guests above. After landscaping the garden and building a swimming pool, we had the dream home.

A month or so after we moved in, the three of us went on holiday to Tenerife to stay with a friend of Jackie's, who had an apartment there overlooking the village of Los Cristianos. We both fell in love with the area and spent £32,000 buying an apartment for ourselves. We were so happy then, Jackie and I, and looked forward to all of us enjoying our little bolt-hole in the sun.

The following Spring, I bumped into a theatrical agent friend, Dick Ray, and when I told him we were spending the summer in Tenerife, he asked if we'd be interested in renting Windledale to the actress, Barbara Windsor. The prospect of the house earning money for us while we were away appealed to the business side of me, and Barbara and her husband, Stephen Hollings, stayed there for four months while she appeared in *The Mating Game*.

Jackie and I had a wonderfully happy time in Tenerife, but were even happier when we returned to find planning permission for the new houses at The Rectory had been granted. I put Windledale on the market and sold it for £340,000 – a profit of £302,000 on what I'd paid for it in 1973. At that time, a property deal I had with George came to fruition and I ended up with another £200,000, which gave me enough to build the houses. My life as a property developer was about to begin – but, over the next few years, my dreams of becoming a millionaire like George would be shattered by a dark, menacing side of Jackie's nature she went to extraordinary lengths to conceal.

✳✳✳

To handle the building development, I formed a company with a friend, already in the construction business. Larry Benison was his name, and he was a sixteen-stone Mancunian, with a huge beer gut and long blonde hair, tied in a ponytail. He liked a good drink, usually rye whisky, by the bottle, and enjoyed a laugh. We were a perfect team.

When we'd finished for the day, we'd go to a pub for a pint or two, and, I'm sorry to say I had to teach one of the regulars a lesson. It was all over that one awful word I can't tolerate.

He was a big Scots guy, named Robbie. I liked him but, after a few drinks, he could get very saucy. For some reason I can't remember, he called me a you-know-what and I told him I didn't like it.

'What are you going to do about it, you old idiot?' he sneered.

'I'm not old,' I said, trying to lighten the mood.

'You've gone,' he said. 'What can you do, you old cunt?'

'If you keep on I am going to have to hit you.'

'Yeah, go on. I'll give you half a chance. Go on.'

So I did. In the stomach. He just folded up on the floor. I looked down at him and said: 'Now, I could kick your head in. But I'm not that type of guy.'

I let him up and said: 'Want any more?'

'No, no,' he said. 'You can punch, I'll give you that. Let's have a drink.'

Robbie was always nice to me after that and we became firm friends. I still see him when I go to Jersey.

I got no pleasure from hitting him. Outside the ring, I'd sought fun, not aggro, and always walked away at the first sign of trouble. What possible satisfaction could it give me to beat up some boozed-up plonker who thought he was Jack the Lad, and fancied his chances? After I retired, I got it a lot. I'd be in a club, drinking with Tommy, or some of my other friends, and hear the drunken stage whisper: 'He wasn't all that . . . he can't fight . . .' and the guy's mates telling him to shut up in case I heard, and the guy, full of bravado, saying: 'I don't effing care if he hears me . . .' All that bollocks. I'd look at Tommy, or whoever, and say: 'Time to drink up.' There was no point in hanging around. If I turned on the guy and he threw a punch, I'd throw one back and knock him out, and the next thing is I'd be nicked. It just wasn't worth the hassle. I'd learned that with the flash Harry sitting on the E-Type. I should have said: 'Keep the petrol cap as a souvenir, mate.' And driven off. So now, I never reacted – unless someone used that word!

✳✳✳

Jackie gave birth to our son, Tom, on 12 August 1985 but, nevertheless was eager to get involved in the development and volunteered to buy the building materials and handle the company's books. Neither Larry, nor I, suspected anything was amiss until three months later when we did our regular check of the accounts and discovered we'd paid for a building material we hadn't ordered. We went through the cheque book, looking at the entries on the stubs, and found we'd paid out for lots of other materials we knew nothing about. We checked with the bank and were dumbfounded to be told that the payments had not gone to any builders' merchants, but into Jackie's personal account.

About £10,000!

I asked Jackie to explain herself. At first, she denied taking anything, but when I told her I had proof she burst into tears, reluctantly admitting she was a compulsive gambler and had taken the money to feed her habit. We had a blazing row and she begged forgiveness, saying she was sorry and would never gamble again. But then she suddenly turned nasty and started screaming obscenities at me, saying it was all my fault. Finally, she ran from the room, saying that she was going to kill herself.

I didn't hear anything for two days, but then got a call from Jackie's Uncle Ted, an ex-Army major, saying she was with him and his wife, Dolly, at their home in Minard, a Scottish village near Lochfyne. The village was so tiny it had only a grocer's and newsagents', and the nearest pub was five miles away. Jackie had turned up, he said, claiming she had run away in fear because I'd hit her. Fortunately, neither Ted, nor Dolly, believed a word of it. I asked Larry and his wife, Julie, to look after Kelly and Tom and flew to Scotland for a showdown.

Jackie spent all night crying, again pleading with me to forgive her. It was a one-off, she sobbed: our relationship was so important, she would rather kill herself than lie to me again; and she swore she'd get help for her addiction. By morning, she had convinced me. I genuinely felt sorry for her; she had touched something inside me that made me want to protect her from herself, and I said I *would* forgive her and put the whole sorry business behind us. I'd repay the money she'd stolen and we'd make a fresh start. To be on the safe side, though, Larry and I would look after the company accounts.

For a while, we *did* get back on an even keel. With lots of money in the bank, we were out most nights revelling in the fun Jersey had to offer. What a naive, trusting fool I was! Far from keeping her promise, Jackie was still gambling behind my back – and rifling through my wallet and pockets to do it! When we went out to dinner, I'd think nothing of it when she volunteered to settle the bill. Being a lazy sod, I'd hand over my wallet and let her go to the desk, not suspecting for a moment that she would help herself to a few quid. Often, she covered her tracks by saying she had left a good tip. I'd check my money the next day, see that I was a bit light, and think: 'Oh, dear, that was a bit heavy last night,' and go to the bank and get some more.

I didn't know all this then, of course, and the marriage carried on, with me blissfully unaware of what Jackie was up to. I always worried she might start gambling again, however, so I was relieved, early in 1987, when she told me she wanted to invest in a scheme, importing Krugerrands from South Africa. She gave me a long-winded explanation of how she'd make ten per cent profit by avoiding paying VAT, buying through Jersey. But I'd just put the houses on the market for £150,000 each then, and I was more concerned about selling them. To be honest, I didn't pay as much attention to Jackie as I should; all that interested me was she seemed to have hit on a good idea that would keep her mind off gambling and get her off my back. She said she needed to invest £20,000 – so I gave it to her.

A few weeks later, I was thrilled when she told me her deal had worked out and had made the expected £2,000 profit. Then, every four weeks or so after that she'd tell me about another deal and say that everything was going well; she was making money. The success seemed to be making her very happy and contented and, often, I'd arrive home to find she'd bought something special for dinner, an expensive bottle of wine she knew I liked – or, occasionally, a present for me. I'd sit in the lounge, well fed and watered, thinking: 'What a lovely wife I have.' At weekends, I'd fall asleep in an armchair after lunch, to find her gone. Not for a moment did I think she'd popped down to the betting shop. And not for a moment did I think to ask to see her bank statement. If I had, I would have seen that, far from making money, Jackie was losing it. Fast.

All her deviousness came home to roost shortly after I'd handed her £5,000 to buy a big shipment of Krugerrands. She'd told me the opportunity was too good to miss, but she didn't have the necessary cash because it was tied up in stock. So, trusting soul that I was, I gave her the money. A couple of days later, George Le Blond, the manager at Barclays, at Quennevais, St. Brelade, who Jackie and I knew well and had often seen socially, phoned the house.

He was perturbed that Jackie's account was seriously overdrawn.

'It can't be,' I said.

'It is, Billy,' he assured me.

'But she's making money, George,' I said. 'She's been telling me for months that this new business of hers is going well.'

'Well, it isn't, Billy,' he said.

I was horrified to learn that the Krugerrand business existed only in Jackie's mind: she had dreamed it up to get money out of me. I put the phone down and demanded that Jackie show me her latest bank statement. She refused, first saying that George was lying, then she said that someone in the bank must have stolen the money. It was all a big mistake, she insisted, and she would prove it to me.

Forcing myself to keep calm, I quietly asked to see the statement. She handed it over, reluctantly. I looked at it, then held it in front of her. 'You lied and spent the money,' I said. 'You've gambled it, haven't you? You've gambled the whole fucking twenty-five grand away, haven't you?'

She started crying and kept saying over and over again how sorry she was, and she wouldn't do it again. But then I lost my temper and started shouting, and she ran out of the room, screaming that she was going to kill herself. I chased her up three flights of stairs to Kelly's room, yelling at her, and she started bellowing back, spittle spraying from her mouth: 'I own half this fucking house. And half your fucking money. You cunt.' I was so angry I was shaking and when she used that word I lost my temper and slapped her twice across the face. She ran from the room and out of the house.

She went to her parents' home in Holborn and didn't come back for a week. I didn't miss her at all. Fortunately, neither did Kelly, nor Tom. They were too young to understand.

Most men, I'm sure, wouldn't have had anything more to do with a wife who'd been so wicked, but I decided to forgive Jackie again. The children were the main reason, of course, but I have to hold my hands up: despite all she'd put us through, I was still in love with her and dreaded the thought of quitting on another marriage after just six years.

That summer, I did have at least some sunshine on the horizon: my mate, Kenny Bailey, was getting married on 16 June, and had asked me to be his Best Man. The reception promised to be something special and I was really looking forward to it but, as it turned out, I ended up going to the City of London Cemetery for a cremation instead – my dad's. He was eighty-two and had been in a lot of pain from a blocked artery, and I'm pretty sure he'd had enough. I missed a good party, but I couldn't have lived with myself if I hadn't said goodbye to my dad – even though we weren't as close as we should have been. Dad was a quiet man, a strong man, and I regretted not having made the effort to get to know him better.

✳✳✳

Jackie and I soldiered on, but this time I monitored the bank accounts and made sure she brought me receipts for everything she spent. Being watched so carefully began to affect her: she became depressed and moped about the house, wearing the same leggings and T-shirt for days on end. At times, I was quite ashamed at how scruffy she was and would joke that her clothes would walk out on their own if she wore them much longer. I was concerned that her mind always seemed to be on other things; that she couldn't be bothered to spend time on herself. But, at least she wasn't throwing money away on the horses. At least we were together, and the children had a mother.

The following year, Jackie told me she was attending Gamblers' Anonymous. I was surprised, because I thought she'd got over the desire to gamble. But I was pleased, too: if she still secretly craved to have a flutter and felt G.A. could help her, then that could only be good news. And the meetings *did* seem to help. She started to take more of an interest in life, and pride in her appearance, and I began to relax, thinking that we'd got through the crisis and I had my Jackie back.

George was back, too. But, as usual, it wasn't for a pleasant chit-chat about old times – he wanted me to open a string of 'Marilyn' bars in various cities, with a Marilyn Monroe lookalike, and would pay me for the pleasure. I'd be met at the airport by one of George's fellow directors, then fly to each location by helicopter, before returning that evening. With money in my pocket, carte blanche to sign for what I wanted in any restaurant I chose, and a bed at the Barbican that night, it was Happy Days and I admit I did hit those wine lists hard. Jean picked me up on it, but George never did. He was not too bad to me then. Maybe he was having some regrets for the way he'd treated me, and for not giving me what I fully deserved from the company.

It was probably just as well he treated my flying visits strictly as business, never once suggesting we go out for dinner, or even a pint. For me, the hand of friendship would have been twenty years too late.

Having sold the five houses at The Rectory, I had £750,000 in the bank and, being generous by nature, started giving Jackie house-keeping again. I was delighted when she came back from the shops with glamorous dresses. She was, it seemed, eager to please me, to make up for all the anguish she'd put us all through. And I was so pleased with *her* that, as a sort of reward, I bought her a new Mercedes sports car. We then went to our apartment in Tenerife and fell in love with a beautiful villa, near another apartment we'd bought the previous year. With Jackie and I back on an even keel, enjoying each other as we used to, I suggested we sold our two apartments and bought the villa. Jackie was all for it.

I was as happy then as I'd ever been: I had a loving wife, who had changed her ways, lovely kids that I adored, two beautiful homes and enough money in the bank to do whatever we liked. That year of 1989 was, indeed, Happy Days. And it was to get better.

I felt we should treat ourselves to a trip to some of the world's most exotic places – with no expense spared. Australia, America, the Far East, Hawaii. 'Let's do the lot,' I said. And hang the cost. So we did. From December to March, we stayed in the best hotels and rented the smartest apartments in Singapore, Melbourne, Sydney, the Gold Coast, California and Hawaii. And loved every thrilling minute of it. Jackie was great company: keen to make me happy and always agreed with everything I wanted to do! Believe it or not, we even went horse-racing at the famous Melbourne track and had a flutter!

Throughout that exciting trip, Jackie and I didn't have a cross word and when we returned to Jersey I felt good about the future. For a guy who wanted nothing more than a peaceful, loving, family life and enough money to have fun, I had it all.

And then Kenny Bailey told me about the Mercedes.

And my bubble burst.

✳ ✳ ✳

It had begun a month or so after we got back in the spring of 1990. The phone didn't ring as often as it had. In the past, people had rung me to arrange to go out, but now I was phoning them, and when I did I found they were cool and distant.

Then, to my horror, I discovered that Jackie was gambling again – and had used the Mercedes to find money to do so. She'd told Kenny Bailey a story about damaging the car and needing £2,500 to repair it before I found out. As a good mate, Kenny lent her the money and agreed not to tell me. And I would probably *never* have found out had Jackie not been greedy and pulled the same stunt on Larry Benison. The two men didn't know each other well but, as luck would have it, they met one day and Kenny mentioned his loan. Larry admitted Jackie had tapped him as well for the same amount and, of course, they felt compelled to tell me.

No one ever mentioned Jackie's gambling to me. A friend, Micky Walker – no relation – who saw her in the bookies putting £1,000 on a horse, assumed the bet was for me. I made some calls and the whole dreadful web Jackie had spun started to unravel. She had clearly never stopped gambling and continued to tell tales to cover it all up.

She owed the bookies £14,000 and, to pay them back, had borrowed from friends, claiming I was desperately ill and going broke and needed money. She played on the fact that people liked me and wouldn't want to see me in trouble. And it worked. Apart from the £2,500, Larry Benison coughed up another £16,500, a farmer who lived nearby handed over £8,000, and over the next few weeks various other victims came out of the woodwork. Suddenly, I understood why people I'd considered our friends had wanted nothing to do with us: they must have presumed we'd conned them out of money and gone on a World trip with it!

When I confronted Jackie, it was the same old story: I called her a liar, she broke down in tears, begging forgiveness, I started shouting, she called me all the names under the sun, then ran off screaming that she was going to kill herself. Of course, she didn't. She came back and, again, I couldn't bring myself to tell her that enough was enough, that I wanted her out of my life. I didn't have the guts because of the effect it would have on the children. And also, deep down, I believed I could cure her of what was obviously a serious sickness.

I decided to sell her Mercedes, not only to recoup some of my losses, but also to punish Jackie in a small way, like taking away a naughty child's toys. I wanted her to suffer some consequence of her actions. But it was me who suffered. I believed I'd bought the car outright, but when I came to sell, I discovered she'd taken out a loan with a finance company so that she'd have £10,000 to gamble. I had to repay the loan, leaving me nothing from the sale.

For the rest of the year, it was like Jackie was under house arrest: I went back to checking everything she did that involved money, even more carefully than I had before, and gave her only enough for what we needed to live on. We muddled along, Jackie acting like a repentant child and, once again, I thought we'd got through the crisis. But then, one morning coming up to Christmas, I got a phone call from the police.

And I knew we had come to the end of the line: I had to do something before she destroyed not only my life, but our children's too.

Jackie had been held for questioning for shoplifting in a super-market. I shot down to the police station and discovered she had been caught, trying to leave without paying for four bottles of champagne and a side of smoked salmon – even though she had more than £100 in her purse. Her ruse was simple: if she came home with champagne and salmon, I was hardly likely to question her about money. And if she was pulled in the supermarket she could claim it was all a mistake by showing that she had the money to pay.

In every parish in Jersey, there is an elected voluntary police force, known as Centeniers, which has more power than the uniformed police. They would decide whether Jackie would be charged. Fortunately, I was well known and liked by our Centenier and talked him round, saying it was a one-off, probably caused by the change of life. I don't think he believed me for a moment, but he agreed not to charge her. If she was caught again, however, he said she would be charged – and this alleged offence taken into consideration.

When we got home, Jackie broke down, sobbing: 'I don't know why I do it, Billy. I feel so ashamed. I'm so sorry. I'll never do it again.'

'You said that the last fucking time!' I yelled.

She quickly turned nasty, spitting out her hatred again. 'It's you,' she shrieked. 'It's you, you horrible fucking bastard – you cunt.'

We bellowed at each other for several minutes and then, as usual, I got the amateur dramatics. 'That's it, I've had enough. Goodbye kids, I'm going to kill myself.'

And off she went.

I'd seen it all before and wasn't fooled. But it terrified the kids.

'Oh, no, daddy,' they cried. 'Mummy's going to kill herself.'

'No, she isn't,' I told them. 'She'll be back in half an hour.'

And she was.

I can count myself lucky that the newspapers didn't hear of Jackie's latest escapade. The headline, 'Ex-boxer's wife accused of theft', would have done me right in. As it was, word that she'd been arrested spread around the island quickly and I was so ashamed and embarrassed I decided we should leave Jersey altogether.

We had our perfect bolt hole in Tenerife; the perfect escape. We'd go there, I decided. We'd go there, start a new life, and try to save ourselves.

21

For a year or so, we were all very happy and content in Tenerife. Kelly and Tom were settled and doing well at school. I was doing everything to be a loving husband and caring father. And, with no betting shops to tempt her, Jackie seemed to be back to the woman I'd fallen in love with. I didn't mention the shop-lifting incident and neither did she. I wanted to put our problems behind us and start afresh. And I hoped she felt the same.

Sadly, our new life didn't last long. The lazy life in the sun began to pall and we missed our friends dreadfully. Finally, shortly after my mother died in January, a year off her ninetieth birthday, we could stand no more and decided to sell up and return to England. Wanting to be near Tommy and Ann, I splashed out £260,000 on Knight House, a six-bedroomed detached property – with a guest wing over the garage – that stood, majestically, on a private estate in Camberley, Surrey.

I had no idea what I was going to do with myself while waiting for the villa to be sold, but David Knott, the guy who'd built Knight House, came up with a proposal that appealed. He needed money to buy old houses and renovate them, he said: was I interested in bank-rolling him and helping with the work? We struck a deal and I started to enjoy getting my hands dirty, especially as it was putting money in our pockets. After what had happened with Larry Benison, alarm bells should have rung when Jackie said she was bored and offered to keep the company's books. But they didn't. I was sure the shock of being arrested had frightened her and believed she wouldn't do anything silly again. And, to give her credit, she was a wizard with figures. So, foolishly perhaps, David and I agreed Jackie should do the accounts.

Much as I did trust her now, I would have kept an eye on the company books, but had to spend three months confined to the house after a back operation called a Discectomy. I was chopping some plaster from the ceiling of a house David and I were renovating and forgot I was fifty-three! I had an accident where I severed my sciatic nerve which robbed me of the use of my left leg.

Jackie was seemingly so concerned about me, and caring, that I didn't feel comfortable asking her about the accounts. And anyway, what worries I might have had about her were dispelled when we received £90,000 for the sale of our villa. On my accountant's advice, the money was transferred into Jackie's account and, every month, she showed me the bank statement, proudly pointing to the amount of interest it had earned. I was delighted: the money was a nice little safety net and I was happy to leave it where it was.

One day, I'd just driven away from the house when the warden who looked after the estate waved me down, looking concerned. He was embarrassed to mention it, he said, but was I aware that Jackie often got in her car and dashed off somewhere whenever I'd left the house? He wouldn't have brought it up, he said, but she always ignored the 10mph speed limit and he felt she was a danger to other residents' children and their pets. When I mentioned it to Jackie, she said the man was 'an arsehole, who was just trying to cause trouble'. I didn't totally believe her, but she was very convincing and, to be honest, I didn't say much, because I was still in pain and wanted a quiet life.

After I recovered from my injury, I threw myself into renovating more houses and, the following summer, was in need of a holiday. I took the family to Majorca and was sleeping by the hotel pool one day when Jackie, who was on a sun-lounger alongside, woke me shouting: 'He's got my bag!' She said a big guy with a moustache had run off with her bag containing her credit cards and cash. I ran in the direction she was pointing, but could find no one fitting her description. When I got back, Jackie was sobbing and saying to a woman, laying nearby: 'You saw him, didn't you? You saw him.' The woman clearly hadn't seen anybody, but Jackie kept on and on at her, insisting she must have, and, out of embarrassment, I'm sure, the woman eventually agreed she might have seen a man. We told the hotel manager what Jackie claimed had happened and he called the police, who took her description of the man. And, naturally, we informed the credit card companies.

A few days later, I was in our room looking for my passport, when I saw the bag Jackie had said was stolen at the back of the wardrobe. Inside was her wallet. And inside that were our credit cards.

I immediately confronted her: 'You told me our cards were stolen.'

'Oh, thank God, you've found them,' Jackie said, quickly. 'I forgot I put them there. What a relief – the guy only took the money.'

Confused, I asked why she'd described the bag to the police when she hadn't taken it to the pool, but she brushed this aside, claiming she must have been mistaken about which bag she'd had. As it was only cash that was missing, I quickly forgot about the incident and carried on enjoying the holiday.

I thought no more about it, but soon after we got back and I was working on the houses again, David Knott came to see me, very worried. He'd been through the company's books, he said, and discovered that £9,000 had been spent on supplies he hadn't ordered. I dreaded the thought of telling him I knew where the money had gone, but had no choice. David was understanding and sympathetic, bless him. But I was beside myself with fury. Suddenly, Jackie's speedy dashes through the estate made sense: no prizes for guessing where she was going when she thought I was safely out of the way!

I pulled Jackie on it and had the customary blazing row, which followed the usual pattern. But, you know, I still couldn't bring myself to kick her out. I'm not sure I loved her any more, but I couldn't face the prospect telling the kids that I was responsible for their mother leaving. So, I made excuses, blaming her sickness on the fact that her mother gambled so heavily, and gave her yet another chance. I clung to the thought that she loved me and the children enough to come to her senses and realise what she seemed hell-bent on destroying.

I was so angry with Jackie that when I was invited to London's Guildhall, to be given the Freedom of the City, I decided not to take her with me: I could not risk her spoiling what would, for me, be a monumental event. Being a staunch Royalist, I felt deeply privileged to be honoured at a ceremony that has survived more than 700 years, and, as I stood there, swearing my allegiance to the Queen, I don't mind admitting I was overcome with the enormity of the occasion.

Not surprisingly, David felt he could not continue in business with me, so we parted company and I hired a builder and continued on my own. Early the following year, I decided to buy a property with vast potential for renovation. I had struck up a good relationship with my bank manager and called to advise him we needed to transfer everything from Jackie's account to the business account, and would confirm in writing later that day.

'I can't do that, Billy,' he said. 'Jackie's account is overdrawn.'

'What!' I said. 'It can't be. There's more than £90,000 there.'

'The account is in the red, Billy,' he said. And, because we knew each other well, he confided that the overdraft was £15,000.

Unable to take it in, I rushed to the bank with statements going back to when the £90,000 from the villa sale was paid in.

The manager looked at them and shook his head. 'They're forgeries, Billy. The motif on our statements is blue. These are black. Someone has photocopied them and filled in different amounts.'

The manager was very understanding and felt sorry for me. But then, a lot of people did. Too late, I realised that by putting the money in her name, it was legally hers, I didn't have a leg to stand on. It was her account, therefore her money, and she spent the bloody lot! What a mug I was, what a first class, prize idiot!

I couldn't afford to withdraw £15,000 from my account without it affecting my business, so I agreed to clear the overdraft in £1,000 monthly instalments. I then went home and did my nut, calling Jackie all the conniving bastards under the sun. She gave me the usual amateur dramatics, wailing that it wasn't her fault, that she was ill and all that.

And then she ran away again – for a month.

I now felt that if I wasn't going to divorce her, I had to help her overcome her problem: if gambling was a sickness that turned her into a wicked, lying, foul-mouthed monster, surely there must be a way to cure it. I decided to seek professional help and went to Gam-On, a group set up to help people suffering the repercussions of someone in their family gambling. I heard stories of people who had lost businesses, who ended up on the dole. But I didn't want sympathy, someone patting me on the head and saying: 'What a poor sod you are.' I *knew* I was being ripped off and just wanted to know *why*. I asked if gamblers ever won and was told that they did, and they then felt great. But the problem was, they always thought they could win more. And more. And more. They are convinced they will make millions and be able to pay back all their debts. But they always lose. They lose because they can't stop. Money burns a hole in their pocket until they gamble it away. I could understand a physical dependency, be it drink or drugs, and I was told this was worse. But it was a disease the same as any other addiction. Like a junkie, the gambling addict will do anything, sell anything, to get that next fix. They don't care who they hurt, mentally or even physically, to get money to bet. I went to only one meeting. I'd heard enough. Jackie wasn't an evil person – she was simply ill. And, for the sake of the children, if not for myself, I felt I had to try to help her.

I wanted her to meet me halfway, though, so I suggested she started Gamblers' Anonymous again. She said she would but, after a few months, I rang the organisation, on the pretext of being worried, and they told me she'd never been there. When I told her, she said: 'I went once and they were all fucking idiots. Some guy was there, rambling on about his sad life story, and they wanted me to get up and tell mine. A load of bollocks, a load of crap. I couldn't handle it.'

I had no answer to that: if she didn't want to go, I couldn't force her. All I could do was watch her carefully and try to be ahead of the game by detecting the signs, as I had been told by Gam-On. I tried; I really did. But then, a couple of days after Christmas, my bank manager rang to tell me there was yet another problem over Jackie's overdraft.

And I knew I couldn't win; would *never* win over her habit.

✳ ✳ ✳

I'd been repaying the overdraft regularly but, amid the hectic build-up to Christmas, I'd forgotten the December instalment. So, the day before the bank closed for the holiday, I handed Jackie a thousand pounds to pay in.

As she left the house, I said: 'I want a receipt, you know, so don't bet it off.'

'I won't, I promise,' she said. 'I'm going there right now.'

When she came back a couple of hours later, she gave me a bank receipt, confirming that £1,000 had been paid in. I thought no more about it but, the day after Boxing Day, the manager rang, telling me the December payment had not been made.

'Yes, it has,' I told him. 'Jackie paid it in last week. I've got the receipt.'

'She paid in only £100,' he said.

'What?'

At first, I couldn't understand it, but when I looked at the receipt, the penny dropped: she'd paid in only £100 and added a nought for my benefit – my own deceit with the butcher's bills, had come back to haunt me. No need to ask where the other nine hundred quid had gone. It beggared belief she thought she could get away with such bare-faced deceit, but that was Jackie: she didn't worry about next week, just lived for what suited her at that moment.

Jackie's parents had come to stay during the lull before New Year, and they were sitting in the lounge with her and the kids. I stormed in and glared at them: 'Do you know what she's done now?' I said. 'I gave her a thousand quid to put in the bank and she's put nine hundred on a bloody horse!' Joe and Maisie looked at the floor, terrified to say anything, because Jackie had been caught, bang to rights, and there was nothing *to* say!

I looked at Jackie. 'I don't believe it,' I said, shaking. 'After all I've forgiven you. I've forgiven you this, I've forgiven you that. I can't believe it. I really *can't* believe it.' I looked back at her parents, still staring at the floor, and all the pent-up feeling about them gushed out in a flood of rage.

'YOU TWO!' I said. 'You've known about her gambling for years. You know she's been ripping me off. Yet you've never marked my card. Not once. All you do is take off me. I've had enough. I can't handle anymore. Now, pack your bags. Don't stay here, 'cos I'm losing my rag. So . . . GO.'

I turned to Jackie. 'And you can fuck off an' all. Go with them.'

Kelly and Tom were crying, begging me to give their mother another chance. But I couldn't. I'd had enough. I'd given her too many chances already. Any more and we'd all end up in the gutter. I took the children upstairs with me and comforted them while Jackie packed her things. She didn't give me the usual histrionics, just left quietly with her parents. She knew she'd pushed me too far.

It's hard to explain, but I'd tried so hard to understand, been so sympathetic and tolerant, that this latest act of treachery killed something inside me. Jackie could have promised me anything – anything in the world that day – and I wouldn't have cared less. I'd given her chance after chance, because all my friends kept telling me 'it's only money'. One of them had said that if she was suffering from cancer and it was going to cost half a million to save her life, I'd find the money, and I agreed with him; of course, I would. But now, I couldn't put up with her and her addiction any more. Once I'd told her to get out, all I felt for her left me and she was now dead in my mind. If I'd had a magic wand that day, I would have made her disappear from our lives forever.

After a few weeks or so, I broke it to the children that I was starting divorce proceedings. They were dreadfully upset, naturally, but I explained that it was for the best and they seemed to come to understand. With Jackie out of the way, I enjoyed spending time with them on my own: I made their breakfast and took them to school before going to work, then picked them up, cooked their dinner and spent the evening together. It was an ordinary family existence. And I loved it.

I had plenty of time to think, and when I thought back to our early life, of course I wondered what Jackie had really been doing on all those trips to London. She'd come back, saying she'd done this and that, and always seemed to have money to show for her trip but, now I knew she lied so much, I had no idea what was true and what wasn't. Certainly I was a 100 per cent prat for believing her, but she was my wife, for God's sake! It didn't occur to me to think: 'Hold on a sec, let's check this out.' Why would I? Why would I think my wife was lying to me?

Come to that, why would I be concerned if I woke from an after-lunch snooze in front of the telly and heard the Hoover running upstairs? Why would I think my wife had left it on deliberately, to convince me she was in the house when she was, in fact, in the betting shop? But that's one of the tricks Jackie's addiction drove her to play, and I'd still be in the dark about it, had her Uncle Ted and Aunt Dolly not told me about it after our break-up.

They had been staying with us for a few days and when Dolly went upstairs for something, she discovered the Hoover on in an empty room, with no sign of Jackie anywhere in the house. When she mentioned it, Jackie simply shrugged and said she'd forgotten to switch it off. Obviously, she thought she'd be out of the house for only twenty minutes or so, and didn't bargain on either Ted or Dolly going upstairs.

For some reason, Jackie wanted people to see me as the villain of the piece; that she was the one having a hard time. A few days after the

Hoover episode, Ted and Dolly heard what they thought was a violent row upstairs: there was a lot of banging of furniture and Jackie crying: 'No, no, don't hit me, don't hit me.' Ted urged Dolly to leave us to it, but the longer the supposed row went on, the more concerned Dolly became. Finally, she was so worried, she crept up the stairs to take a peep. She discovered there was no row – violent or otherwise. All she saw was me, out to the world on the marital bed, sleeping off the effects of another heavy lunch, and Jackie, making all the noise on her own, in another bedroom further along the hallway. When she spotted her aunt, Jackie simply went along to my bedroom, closed the door, and never mentioned the incident.

Just when I thought I couldn't be shocked any more, I got a call from a friend, Lyn Paul, who'd sung with the seventies pop group, The New Seekers, and realised just how low Jackie was prepared to sink to make friends feel sorry for her. Lyn and her husband lived nearby and when she heard Jackie and I had split up, she rang, inviting me out to dinner with them.

They arrived at my house for a drink before going to the restaurant and Lyn seemed a little tense. After explaining the reasons why Jackie and I had broken up, I learned why.

Lyn, who'd hardly said a word, suddenly turned to her husband and said: 'I'm going to tell Bill. He obviously doesn't know.'

'Doesn't know what?' I asked.

'Jackie told us not to tell him,' Lyn's husband said.

'No,' Lyn said, firmly. 'I'm going to.' She took a deep breath. 'Jackie's got cancer,' she said.

I shook my head. 'She hasn't, Lyn.'

'Yes, she has,' Lyn insisted. 'She goes every month for injections.'

'Lyn,' I said. 'Jackie goes every month for HRT injections. It's got nothing to do with cancer. She's never had cancer. And she hasn't now.'

'I tell you, she *has*!' Lyn said, eyes filling with tears.

I kept insisting she wasn't ill and Lyn sobbed as she described how Jackie had asked her and her mother to look after Kelly and Tom when she died, because she felt I wouldn't be able to cope. And they wept in sympathy with her at the suffering they were convinced she was going through. Eventually, I got it through to them it was a load of bollocks and, like the bank manager and everyone else who had fallen prey to her, they said they felt sorry for me. You know, I never thought it could be so humiliating, people feeling sorry for you.

Lyn said Jackie had never asked them for any money – and that disgusted me more than anything. Much as I found her actions sickening, I could excuse them – in a small way – if her motive was money. But to lie so wickedly to win sympathy, and upset people in the process, was unforgivable and showed what depths she'd sunk to. It was just as well Jackie was nowhere in sight that evening because I wouldn't have been able to control myself.

✳✳✳

Once I started divorce proceedings, I arranged for an accountant to go through the books of my four building companies. He went back seven years and discovered unbelievably huge amounts he could not account for. But it didn't end there: I contacted card companies and learned that various accounts in Jackie's aliases had been sent to her aunt's and parents' addresses over the past ten or twelve years. Thousands were owed on each.

I was particularly incensed that Maisie and Joe were party to Jackie's lies. Over the years, I'd always included them in our holidays to America, Spain and the Greek islands and never asked them to contribute anything, because I was pleased to see them enjoying my hospitality while having the opportunity to spend time with their grandchildren. Maisie was a part-time cleaner and always skint, because she gambled. Actually, I felt sorry for her and gave her quite a bit of money over the years. Obviously, looking back, I should have seen that Jackie was her mother's daughter and, in twenty years, would be just like her – a sad, broke and lonely old lady. But I didn't.

I owed it to myself to have it out with Maisie over the credit cards, however, so I went to her council flat in High Holborn. Predictably, she denied knowing that Jackie had given any company her address.

'Maisie, I know you're lying,' I said. 'I've got proof your address was used. You saved the bills until you saw Jackie. Then she paid them with my money.'

After a while, she admitted it. 'I'm sorry, Bill, but what could I do?' she said. 'She's my daughter.'

I also confronted Joe, but he said he knew nothing about it and I believed him. He'd suffered with Maisie's addiction for years, so he knew what deception gambling addicts were capable of.

When I thought I could no longer be surprised – or disgusted – I discovered Jackie had stolen not just from me, but our children, too; how terrible must her addiction have been at that point? I instructed my bank manager to close all the accounts Jackie knew about and he told me that £9,000 in the children's joint account had been cleared out several months before.

I told Maisie to get Jackie to ring me. She did and I asked her why she'd taken the money. 'I don't know, I don't know,' she wailed. 'It's my addiction. I had to do it.' She went on to say she didn't mean it and she was sorry and loved her kids, but then turned nasty: 'What the fuck's it got to do with you anyway,' she screamed. 'I'll pay the fucking money back.'

✳✳✳

Jackie had been gone six weeks when I went to London and bumped into a friend from Jersey, Mickey Holmes, who told me he'd recently met one of my old girlfriends. Resisting the temptation to say that, by now, *all* my ex-girlfriends must be old, I asked who he was referring to.

'Pat Furuborg,' he said.

'Ah, Pat,' I replied, warm memories immediately flowing back. 'She was lovely. How is she?'

'She's okay,' Mickey said. 'Well, I think she is. She's just broken up with a bloke.'

'Have you got her phone number?'

He had. And when I called Pat that evening, she was delighted to hear from me but typically blunt. 'Fancy hearing from you,' she said. 'Are you divorced again?'

We met for lunch at Langan's the next day and I found the years had not changed her: she was still the same argumentative cow – and I loved it. More important, we still liked each other and were comfortable together. With my life in tatters, Pat was everything I needed then and, that night, I went back to her flat in Forest Gate and made love. I felt I was back where I belonged.

✳✳✳

One morning in March 1996, Kelly came running to me, shortly after coming home from school: 'Daddy,' she said, excitedly, 'Mummy's in the guest wing.' It was the most unexpected, and worst, news I could

225

hear, but I hid my anger and went to see Jackie on my own. I told her she had to leave, if only for the children's sakes. They knew we were getting divorced, I said, and had accepted us living separately; we'd settled into a peaceful routine and her coming back would disrupt it. When she refused to leave, I rang my lawyer, who said that, as Jackie owned half the house, I could not force her to go, and I'd have to make the best of it until the divorce was finalised.

'Making the best of it' with a woman I despised was not easy: now that Jackie had got into the house, I suspected she'd try to wheedle her way back into my life, using her womanly wiles to get round me, and I was right. She quickly made excuses to come into the main body of the house to cook for the children. She tried cooking for me, too, but I wouldn't allow it, I knew it was a ploy. Whenever we were alone, she even came on to me, sincerely believing that the fierce sexual attraction I'd had for her would do the trick. So I tried to see as little of her as possible.

With Pat back in my life, I found living in Camberley bizarre, but bearable. I told Jackie we should share the children: I'd spend weekends with them, pick them up from school on Friday, take them to school on Monday, then spend the rest of the time with Pat. This was fine for a while, then Jackie got a job, so we switched: I looked after the children during the week, and spent weekends with Pat. The arrangement worked well: the kids were seeing both of us and, as Jackie and I made arrangements on the phone we did not have to see each other.

When we were both in the house at the same time, however, it was impossible not to have some contact and, inevitably, this led to a bitter confrontation, four months later, that finally tipped me over the edge.

I went for a run every morning and, on one occasion, I came home to find Jackie in the kitchen, in one of her foulest moods. 'I think it's disgusting,' she shouted as soon as I walked in.

'What is?' I said.

'That you carry a photo of your girlfriend. You never carried one of *me*.'

'You cow! You've been down my wallet.'

She looked as though she could have bitten her tongue off, as she realised her mistake.

'You've just shopped yourself,' I said. 'You're still at it, aren't you? Still nicking money from me.'

'No, I'm not,' she screamed. 'I just looked in there.'

'No, you didn't,' I shouted. 'You're a lying bastard.'

We had a blazing row, then she stormed off – back to the guest suite, I assumed. She picked the children up from school but, when she got back she was spoiling for another row over the photo. And this time it went off in front of the kids: how I was a 'fucking cunt', her gambling was all my fucking fault and how she was going to kill herself etc.

Then she stormed off in the car. When I went outside, I saw she'd scrawled unevenly:

I STOLE £150,000 OF KELLY, TOM
AND BILLY WALKER
JACKI WALKER
THE SLAG

in blue paint on the garage door. I couldn't dispute the authenticity of the statement, but why she wrote it, I have no idea. I quickly painted over it, clear in my mind now that this was one blow-up too many and I'd have to leave the house for good. If I didn't, I'd end up physically hurting Jackie, which would be terrible for everyone.

I sat Kelly and Tom down and told them, as gently and honestly as I could, that it was impossible for their mother and I to be under the same roof, even for a short time, and I was leaving. I'd see them often and, if they needed anything, they only had to call. But, I said, I would not be coming to the house again.

If I was devastated when Susan divorced me, I was mortified by Jackie's wickedness and cruel disregard for everything I held dear in our marriage.

That the bitch had been robbing me at all, let alone the colossal sums I uncovered, was hard to stomach but, you know, what was even harder was the realisation that our whole marriage had been a sham. That I'd been so stupid and gullible to believe that I was loved – not merely the sporting hero image Susan had loved, but for myself. I believed Jackie was crazy about Bill Walker, ordinary bloke, I really did. That's why I gave up the ladies, knuckled down to making money, and threw myself into being a considerate and caring family man. I honestly believed I was going to find the happiness I craved, in a loving, contented relationship. When we married, I *did* think it was for keeps. Just like John and George.

Of course, I felt enormous guilt at leaving Kelly and Tom at the mercy of someone I felt cared less about them than placing the next bet. Without Jackie around, the three of us had some really good, close times, and I had this daydream that when Jackie and I were divorced, I'd be given custody and the kids and I would be able to build on our relationship. But it wasn't to be and would have to love them from a distance.

I have no guilt at all about Jackie, however. After what she threw at me, I don't think anyone would have blamed me if I'd thrown in the towel long before I did. Certainly I found it hard, coping with the humiliation and degradation at being pitied by friends who knew what I was going through. But I gave saving the marriage my best shot. Every time Jackie knocked me down, I got up, found excuses to forgive her, then battled on, terrified of the ignominy of another marital failure. In the end, I had to accept that my opponent – her crippling addiction – was far too powerful for me, and I'd never win. There was nothing I could do about it – as, indeed, there was nothing I could do about the thousands I had lost. I had to wipe my mouth and forget it. Actually, I found that easier than coming to terms with the loss of my children and the fabulous lifestyle I'd enjoyed with them.

22

Jackie and I had an arrangement where I travelled from London once or twice a week, picked the children up from school, and took them into Camberley for tea. This worked well for about a month, but something I told my lawyer concerning the divorce, got back to Jackie and she didn't like it. One afternoon, a few days later, I was standing outside Tom's school, Crawley Ridge, with dozens of other parents, when she suddenly appeared.

She launched into a tirade of abuse, calling me all the usual filthy names, then, when I didn't react, tried to hit and scratch me. I knew she was trying to provoke me into hitting her in front of witnesses, so I fended off her blows, then ran away from her, got in my car and drove off. To other parents, the bizarre scene must have looked hysterical, but it was no laughing matter for me: Jackie had clearly heard I was going to fight her over the financial settlement, and wanted to get something on me, to blacken my name.

The divorce hearing at Guildford Crown Court, in October, was nasty, as you can imagine. I was able to prove Jackie had stolen from me and the children, but not that she was a bad mother, so she was awarded custody. I agreed to sell Knight House and buy Jackie a smaller property, but argued against the new house being in her name for fear that she would sell it – or borrow against it – to get money to gamble. The judge agreed and ruled that the house should be in my name, and further ruled that, when Kelly and Tom were old enough to leave home, the house should be sold and the proceeds split equally between Jackie and me.

✱✱✱

The terms of the divorce may have been agreed, but the financial settlement dragged on and on. By the following June, 1997, Knight House had still not been sold and it was getting to Pat and me. Most of the time we kept a lid on our feelings, but it wasn't easy. Once, Pat's frustration got to her and she went into one, calling me all the rotten names she could think of and accused me of messing her about. 'You know,' she said, with a horrible sneer, 'I don't know why I bother with you.'

'If that's how you feel, I'll go,' I said.

'Go ahead.'

'Is that what you want?'

'If that's what *you* want, go,' she said, turning it round on me.

'Right, I'm going,' I said and started packing my bags. Pat waited until the the last one had been packed, then started to cry. 'Don't go, Billy, please don't go.'

'You rotten cow,' I said. 'You waited till I've packed everything. Now, you want me to stay. I've got a good mind to go on bloody principle.'

I didn't think I'd call her bluff; it was seeing me packing the final case that did it. At the same time, she could easily have gone the other way and watched me walk out, even though she didn't want me to. That was Pat. She was a tough bird, who didn't like being taken for granted, and would cut off her nose to spite her face.

✱✱✱

I'd heard that George was doing business in Russia, but hadn't spoken to him for years. So, you can imagine my shock when he phoned me one day, around 7 a.m.

'I had to get you early,' he said. 'What are you doing today?'

'No idea,' I said. 'You've just woken me up.'

'I need you to do something for me,' he said. 'I want you to go to the Russian Embassy. I've got a visa waiting for you there. I want you to go to Azerbaijan.'

'Where?' I asked, sleepily.

'Azerbaijan,' George said. 'It's on the Russian–Mongolian border. You fly to Moscow, then go on up there. I've got an English guy to meet you in Moscow. He speaks the language. Just be there, represent me. I'll give you a nice few quid.'

Silence on the line: I was too dozy to know what to say, but had quickly woken up.

'Will you do that for me?' George asked.

'Bollocks,' I said. 'You're mad.'

And I put the phone down and snuggled up to Pat, thinking, for the umpteenth time, how single-minded and self-centred my brother was. If he had come on, saying he wanted me on the firm for fifty grand a year, but I had to go here, there and everywhere to earn it, I might have said: 'I'll have some of that.' But not just to do some PR for him, for a grand or whatever he had in mind, then be at his beck and call again in six months or so. If he'd started by saying how sorry he was that Jackie had had me over, how he felt for me and the kids, and, by the way, while he was on, could I possibly do him a favour, I also might have reacted differently. Knowing what a silly soft bastard I am, I might just have said: 'All right, then', and got out of my warm bed and gone to Azerbijan, wherever it was.

But George wouldn't have given any of that a thought. He was in his office, having been up at the crack of dawn, thinking: 'I can't make this meeting, but I know someone who can. My brother, Bill. He's a stupid arsehole, he'll go for a few quid!'

So he just picked up the phone and barked at me, thinking I'd jump. Sensitivity and tact had never been George's strongest qualities.

I shouldn't have been surprised by the phone call: George had always been a user of people and he had used me unashamedly over the years, finally dumping me when my usefulness had run out. But I *was* surprised – not that he'd had the gall to call, but that he actually believed I would belt down to the airport and get on a plane to a place I'd never heard of! It seemed to show that George didn't really know me. Not deep down.

Hearing from him after so long set me thinking and an ugly thought that had been playing on my mind for years started to nag at me again. I'd accepted that George and I had never been as close as I'd believed, but I started wondering, yet again, whether he'd used me cynically, in the way he'd used other people? Had he come to that

West Ham gym, all those years ago, and thought: 'Hey, this kid can make us some money?' Seeing the power in my right hand, he'd said: 'We've got something to work on here.' Did he mean: 'I've got a meal ticket here?'

The thought, as always, was painful. And, again, I forced it out of my mind. It's a question I will always ponder and never know the full truth. I've never had it out with George, never asked him if he saw me more as a money machine than a brother. And I probably never will.

Because I might not like the answer.

✳✳✳

In August, the financial settlement with Jackie still hadn't been reached. And Pat was getting the hump.

Finally, one evening I was sitting in the lounge, when she walked in and stood in front of me. 'What's going on?' she said. 'You're living here. Are you going to make it permanent or what?'

'Do you want to get married?' I heard myself say.

'Not really. But, if *you* don't, you can fuck off.'

I took that to mean she did, but wanted a proposal. So I got down on one knee and asked: 'Pat, will you marry me?'

She said yes, and we popped a bottle of champagne. The next day we made arrangements to marry, at Chelsea Register Office, on Wednesday, 3 September.

Tommy and Ann McCarthy were our witnesses and Pat invited her two closest friends – a girl called Cindy and an Italian, named Roberto – she'd known over twenty years. The six of us went to Langan's for lunch, then to The Two Chairmen, a pub now owned by Melvyn's mother, in Trafalgar Square, and drank champagne until nearly midnight.

Neither Pat, nor I, wanted that special day to end. For both of us, the ceremony was confirmation of our intention to be together the rest of our lives. For me, it was an end to all my troubles and a new beginning with a woman I deeply loved.

The next day, the *Daily Express* diary column mentioned the wedding, quoting someone as saying 'the couple are head-over-heels in love and looking forward to spending their twilight years together.' I never found out who said that, or if the paper made it up because Pat and I looked so happy, but it was spot on. We were so comfortable with each other, we did see ourselves growing old together. After the farce of my first marriage, and the crippling duplicity of the second, I was thankful to be with someone I should have been with all along. Even though I was pushing sixty and Pat was no spring chicken, we *were* head over heels in love – probably always had been.

And we *did* see ourselves rubbing along together in our 'twilight years'.

✳✳✳

With Knight House still not sold, Jackie was pushing me for money for herself and took to ringing Pat's flat to try to make me give into her demands. I'd have none of it and remind her that I was paying child maintenance, and that she should do what the judge had said: get a job to support herself. That didn't go down well and, true to form, she resorted to swearing and calling me all the names under the sun. One night, Pat had had enough. She picked up the extension and shouted: 'Listen, you fucking leech. You've nearly skint him – and you're still at it. Phone here again, and I'll come down and sort you out, and you can deal with me.'

Still on the line, I smiled. I'm sure it was the biggest bollocking Jackie had ever had and it was the first time I'd heard her lost for words. She loved an argument, but only with men. Another woman, she couldn't handle. She never had the nerve to ring again.

✳✳✳

I'd been married a couple of months, when I was invited to be guest of honour – along with Henry Cooper – at a black tie boxing dinner in Chelmsford, Essex. It promised to be a good night, so eight of my mates said they would come with me and take a table. When the meal was over, I left the top table to join them for a drink. I'd promised I'd be home at 1 a.m., but was still there at nearly two o'clock, so I thought I'd better ring Pat.

Trying not to slur, I said: 'I'm terribly sorry, darling, but we're still in here. I'll be home as soon as I can.'

I was faithful to Pat, but she could never forget what a rascal I'd been in the sixties. She'd made it clear that if she suspected I was messing around with another woman, she wouldn't stand for it. And, that night, I got the message. Loud and clear.

'Don't you worry about it, William,' she said, coldly. 'Take whatever whore you're with to a hotel and pick your bags up tomorrow.'

That's nice, I thought. What a charming, trusting wife!

Knowing we were going to get tanked up, me and my mates had gone to the dinner in a ten-seater van, driven by one of the gang who wasn't drinking. When we got back to Forest Gate, I asked all of them to stand on the steps down to the flat, so that Pat could see them.

They weren't too bothered, but I insisted because I wanted Pat to know I hadn't been cheating on her. When she opened the door, I pointed to all the big lumps and said proudly: 'There you go – here's who I've been with all night.'

It didn't cut any ice: Pat slammed the door in our faces. Significantly, though, she didn't put the catch on – so I knew I was all right. I was in the doghouse for not ringing earlier, but at least I'd proved she had no reason to doubt me.

Pat wasn't one to hold grudges. Once she'd made her point – entirely justified that night – she quickly forgave me, I apologised, and we got back on an even keel. After the space of Knight House, the tiny flat took some getting used to. But if Pat was happy, so was I. And she was.

They say that if two people are truly in love, they can be happy anywhere and that's how it was with us. We were a couple of newly-weds, all excited about making that modest flat as comfortable as possible. Pat had never had the money to do what she wanted with it, so I tiled the bathroom and kitchen, put in new floors and decorated throughout, then dipped into what savings I had to buy carpets, curtains and furniture for the lounge. Soon, we had it looking the best it possibly could.

The garden, which was split into three – one for us and the rest for the tenants on the ground floor and upstairs – was a mess, so, the following spring I laid a lawn and, between us, Pat and I put in flowing shrubs, rambling roses and many exotic plants and ferns. I replaced the tiny wire fence, separating us from the other gardens, with a six-foot wooden one, to give us privacy, and we were all set to enjoy summer days in our own little cosy haven. It wasn't a big garden by any means, but the foliage grew so high, we were hidden from the grime and general scruffiness of one of London's grubbiest areas. Sitting out there on bright, sunny days, we felt we could be anywhere but Forest Gate.

Having decided she didn't want to get into another relationship after breaking up with her long-term boyfriend, Pat had surrounded herself with homosexual friends, most of whom were well-educated and articulate, and always up for a good discussion. I found them interesting and a lot of fun, and I got a buzz, drinking wine with them in the garden, putting the world to rights. After all the problems with Jackie, I began to feel that life wasn't a mission and, for the first time in years, I felt happy and contented.

In thoughtful and reflective moments, I'd contrast my peace and happiness with how I imagined Jackie might be feeling, as she now faced bankruptcy. I still couldn't understand, probably never would, how the bookies won over the fabulous lifestyle and family love she'd enjoyed but, thank God, it wasn't my problem any more. She and her self-destroying demons were out of my life forever, and for the next couple of years I relaxed, nearly broke, but immensely happy with my soulmate, in our own little Utopia.

And then, one morning in March 2000, I felt a lump in Pat's right breast.

23

Two days after finding the lump, I took Pat to see Barry Jones, a Harley Street surgeon, who confirmed that it was a large cancerous growth in the lymph gland, and Pat's right breast had to be removed as soon as possible. We were devastated, of course, but on the way home, Pat consoled herself that at least she'd be able to have reconstructive surgery when she had recovered.

After the operation, three weeks later, I was relieved when the surgeon told me he believed he'd removed all the cancer, but disappointed when he said Pat would have to have chemotherapy treatment every month at St. Bartholemew's Hospital, in Smithfield, East London, throughout the summer, and radiation treatment after that. I felt she had gone through enough and couldn't bear the thought of her suffering any more.

Pat had begun keeping a diary and when she heard that each chemo injection cost £1,100 and radiation treatment £4,000, she wrote: '*What a sick world. If one hadn't the money, what then?*' Fortunately, we were able to get the treatment on the NHS, but travelling into the City every month for her injection, then feeling sick for two days afterwards, began to get Pat down. The grotty area where we lived did nothing for her depression, but moving to somewhere we liked, and could afford, presented a problem. We had warm memories of south-west London and dearly wanted to live there but, after buying the house for Jackie and the kids, I'd been left with just £150,000, and even two-bedroom flats in Fulham were fetching more than double that. Clearly, we would have to have to stay in Forest Gate or move out of London altogether.

Then, early in August, my accountant invited me to a business meeting at his home in Burnham-on-Crouch, on the south Essex coast. And Pat and I discovered our Shangri-la.

Burnham is a small village with its own harbour, about twenty miles from Chelmsford, and I remembered it from when I water-skied there with my West Ham boxer pal, Terry Spinks, thirty years before. I'd been touched by its quaint, unspoiled beauty then, and I was now. I felt Pat and I could be happy there, so, after leaving my accountant, I called in at some estate agents' to see what was for sale. I was struck by the most delightful detached bungalow and decided to give it a quick once-over. It was beautiful, with much potential, and I drove home, quietly excited.

Coincidentally, Pat knew Burnham, too, because she'd been there with a boyfriend who had a boat and, like me, she thought the village could suit us very nicely. The next day, we went there, and fell in love with the bungalow. The asking price was £150,000, but the owner was prepared to drop it a little because he was emigrating to Australia and needed a quick sale. I couldn't afford to blow all my money, so we agreed a price and I borrowed the shortfall from a dear friend, Fred Lavanni, and a lovely bloke, named Kevin, I'd got to know well in Forest Gate. I was able to pay them back a few months later, after my mate Leslie Squibb – who'd put some PR work my way – arranged a mortgage for me. Thank God for my friends, they all came through when I needed them.

Pat and I moved in on 17 October and, a month later, she started radiation treatment at Chelmsford Hospital, which was nowhere near as painful and harrowing as her chemo. We then attended classes there, learning how to massage away the fluid build-up in Pat's arm that hadn't gone away after her operation. Both of us were pleased to able to do something to speed her recovery.

By Christmas, Pat was feeling much better and on New Year's Eve we sat round our log fire, just the two of us, and toasted the passing of 2000: *'Goodbye. And good riddance.'*

✳✳✳

With Pat now, hopefully, in the clear – and her hair growing again – we revelled in being together, at last, with no one to worry about but ourselves, and all the time in the world to recover from the trauma of the past year, and create another little haven, like the one we'd enjoyed in Forest Gate.

From the outside, the bunglalow was tiny, but behind the honey-suckle and roses on the front door and walls, there was a large lounge, dining room, two bedrooms, spacious kitchen and a study. We were happy to live in one room while we got to work on the others, and once we'd decorated them the way we wanted, we set about adorning each room with all sorts of objets d'art we'd bought at antique exhibitions or boot fairs.

Pat was artistically creative and a dab hand at turning something cheap and ordinary into what, to me, was a minor masterpiece. At boot fairs, she'd send me off to find costume jewellery, telling me not to spend more than a pound on a single item, and go in the opposite direction, looking for bargains of her own. Over the next few days, I'd watch, fascinated, and somewhat amazed, as she carefully arranged the various odds and sods we'd bought to decorate the walls of the bungalow. She was particularly taken with old pictures and paintings, and painstakingly created a stunning collage of memorabilia from the twenties and thirties to cover one entire wall in the lounge. On the facing wall she hung two large, beautiful photographs of my mum and dad, and delighted in putting together a stunning montage of photo-graphs of me with the Queen and Prince Philip, former Prime Minister Harold Wilson, and various celebrities I'd met, such as Ronnie Corbett, Harry Secombe, Hattie Jacques and Diana Rigg. There was even the publicity photo with Oliver Reed when I reminded him that he'd been a naughty boy!

Not that I left all the creativity and hard work to Pat. I bought a couple of dozen wooden roofing planks from a yard in Chelmsford and spent days removing the nails and tar and sanding them until they looked new, then paid someone to lay them in the lounge and dining room. And I took great pride creating a false bookcase on the outside of the study door, using spines of books I'd picked up cheaply at charity shops and book fairs.

The garden was a mess when we moved in, but once we finished the house, we spent hours out there, creating little places of interest, using Buddha statues, a stone head of Maggie Thatcher (whom we both admired) and even an old pair of my running shoes. It wasn't a big garden by any means but, between us, Pat and I made the most of it and, as spring drew near, we were as happy as we could possibly be, and looking forward to enjoying the summer in our haven.

We didn't have much money: I earned a bit from after-dinner speaking and PR work but, in the main, drew on what was left of my savings. We made friends with my accountant and his wife, a local restaurant owner, and our dentist, and went out for meals with them, occasionally. But, to be honest, we were happy just being with each other, and usually drove a mile into the village to one of the quaint restaurants or bars on our own. Pat had always preferred a joint to alcohol, but she would enjoy one or two vodkas as we sat on the quayside, admiring the assortments of yachts and fishing boats. Once, maybe twice a week, we'd go into London for a leisurely lunch, seeking out cheap, but good, places such as The Chelsea Kitchen. Then, more often than not, we'd amble hand in hand, down the King's Road, and I'd indulge myself in all my yesterdays, remembering when I made the heads turn as one of the country's most famous faces. We were so, so happy. We'd been round and round the hectic London nightclub circuit and didn't miss it at all: we were living the simple life, and loving every minute of it.

And then, that June, Pat woke one morning to discover her right arm covered in a rash. She didn't think much about it, but the next day the arm was so swollen and painful she went to bed. I played nurse and was pleased to get a mention in Pat's diary: '*William is a brilliant nurse. Don't know what I'd do without him.*'

Over the next few weeks, the swelling gradually went down but, after what Pat had been through, it was another depressing time for her. And worrying for us both. What fears we may have had that the cancer had come back were allayed in November, however, when a mammogram showed the cancer was in remission, and Pat was in the clear to have the breast reconstruction she desperately wanted, the following February.

Everything seemed fine after the reconstruction, at St. Bart's, but ten weeks later, Pat's arm started swelling again and she noticed what she thought was a suspicious lump underneath it. It was suspicious enough for her to be admitted the next day, to have it removed and to have a series of tests on other parts of her body. While waiting for the results,

Pat was in such a state, she kept having panic attacks and our GP, Dr Latif, put her on a course of anti-depressants.

Four weeks later we went back to the hospital for the results. And the news was the worst I could have imagined.

The doctor didn't tell Pat – he told me. The cancer wasn't just in the lump in the arm, it was in her liver, lungs, bone and skin – every bloody where, it seemed. I couldn't bring myself to tell Pat the truth, but when I told her she needed more chemotherapy, she seemed to know it anyway, and all the bravery she'd shown left her and she broke down and cried. I'll never know whether I was right not telling her the full SP, but the doctor didn't actually say she had only a certain time left: he just said the cancer was back in different places and she should have more chemo, 'because it might work this time'. I knew she'd never get better, but I took the view that having chemo again might make her think she would.

Pat started her chemo on 16 September and within a couple of weeks was suffering more distress: she'd been given a glove and sleeve to compress her swollen arm, but the distention was so bad she could not get them on. Then another lump, near her shoulder blade, appeared. I reassurred Pat, as best I could, and said we'd mention it the next time we went to hospital. I was relieved when she didn't argue. I didn't want to make up a lie. I knew what it was. Another tumour.

Pat and I went to St. Bart's every Wednesday. We made the appointment for 11 a.m. because that meant we could leave Burnham after 9.30 a.m. and buy cheap day-return fares to Liverpool Street. When we arrived, Pat would have a blood test to see what strength of chemo she required. The treatment took only half an hour but, on the first two visits, we had to hang around until 5 p.m., because of the time it took a hospital orderly to take Pat's blood sample for testing. When this dawned on me, I asked a nurse if I could take the blood to the lab myself. She agreed – and, after that, we were on our way home a couple of hours earlier.

Pat found the journey to London and back gruelling and detested every draining moment. It would have been worth it if the chemo was working but, early in October, we were told it wasn't, and she needed a different course of treatment. My poor Pat! When we got home, she'd be terribly depressed, then would be so ill from the effects of the new chemo, she'd spend the next two days in bed. By the time she'd recovered, we were back at the hospital for another dose. This went on until six days before Christmas when Pat went into Bart's for a CT scan – and I was forced the accept the inevitable.

Her good hand was injected with a dye, so that doctors could see what was happening in the brain, but it caused her arm to swell up, and a plastic surgeon had to be called to perform a delicate procedure to remove the poison from the hand. Pat had to stay in hospital overnight, her bandaged arm above her in a sling, and be woken every two hours to have the hand checked.

When I went to the hospital the next day to collect her, the doctor told me that Pat couldn't have any more chemo until her hand had healed. She had only a few months to live, he said.

That New Year's Eve, we went to a party at my mate Leslie Squibb's house in South Weald. And it was then I was certain that Pat, too, knew she didn't have long. I'd never once seen her out of control with booze, but that night she got legless: it was as if, suddenly, she didn't give a monkey's about anything any more. She was quite maudlin about what was happening and I tried to resassure her. 'Come on, love, next year, we'll do . . .'

But she cut me short. 'I won't be here next year, William.'

'Don't be daft. Of course, you will.'

'Do you think I don't *know*,' she said, sharply. 'I *do* know.'

She didn't cry, just poured more vodka down her and started laughing and joking, as though she didn't have a care in the world.

We had checked into a hotel, three or four hundred yards away, down a country lane, and walking back there after the party, Pat and I were larking about and we stumbled into a ditch. We were too drunk to get up, so Pat cuddled into me and we fell asleep.

It had been the most awful, depressing, traumatic and mentally exhausting year. But, at least, we'd seen it out with a laugh.

That New Year's Eve would be the last evening my beloved Pat and I enjoyed together. From then on, I'd see her fade before my eyes.

✳✳✳

On 2 January, I took Pat to Bart's, and a doctor told me she could have another, light, course of chemo: it wouldn't save her, but it might ease the pain and give her a little longer. Fortunately, Pat was able to have the treatment at Chelmsford Hospital, and we were able to drive there, not travel to London. Whenever she said she thought she might be dying, I'd tell her not to be such an arsehole – of course she would get better. I don't know if she believed me, but she seemed to hang on to the fact that I thought she would. Significantly, she wrote in her diary: *'Starting a new chemo – 14 days on, one week off. I'm keeping my fingers crossed. If not, it's goodbye all.'*

The following week, Pat was well enough to go shopping in Chelmsford, in the snow, but the exertion seemed to take it out of her because, the next day, her shoulder and arm were hurting so much she asked Dr Latif for some pain relief, then went to bed. I'm sure she must have felt like staying in bed, but she always made herself get up. And if someone knocked at the door she never let me answer it until she'd put on her wig and make-up. I thought Pat looked good, bald, but she didn't. She had two wigs – one from her first session of chemo in 2000, which she wore around the house; the other one for going out. Often, I'd look at her and think back to our first meeting when I'd been so cruel over her little tuft of hair. How I wished now that her baldness was down to a desire to be blonde, rather than the awful treatment she was enduring.

By the end of January, Pat was on yet another course of chemo tablets, but they, too, didn't seem to help: within days, her right arm started to bleed and the cancer in the lymph nodes stopped the circulation, causing the arm to swell to several times its normal size She wore a bandage to try to reduce the swelling, but it didn't work and, although it's a terrible thing to say, the arm was like a Michelin Man's. Her skin had split in many places where it couldn't take the swelling, and there were supporating sores that needed protecting. So, every day, I changed the lint pads and re-bandaged the arm.

It was another desperate time for Pat but, thankfully, her mind and memory were 100 per cent, because she clearly remembered the time I'd contacted her, then taken her out. I was thrilled to read in her diary: *'8th February, seven years ago, William rang me up. Best thing he ever did. 10th February, the seventh anniversary of our meeting. Isn't life grand!'*

But, quite honestly, that was the only news that brightened her days that month, and early the next. First, she was told that the new chemo tablets weren't working and she would have to take steroids to combat the bleeding in her arm. Five days later, the bridges on her front teeth fell out, rotted by the chemo. Then, as if she didn't have enough on her mind, I had to admit that I was taking bloody pills myself – because all the worrying had given me an ulcer.

Sadly, the steroids didn't ease Pat's pain, and a community nurse who came to the house to dress her arm, alerted the local Macmillan nurses. The following day, the head of the team, a lovely guy named Patrick, introduced a new pain control regime, which at last gave my dear Pat some relief. She was still weak, but refused to give in, and felt well enough to travel to Ascot to see Tommy and Ann, and have a few drinks on the quayside with Jacki's Uncle Ted and Aunt Dolly when they came down for a few days. She was also up for going to a hotel and the theatre, kindly arranged by Fred Lavanni, but, unfortunately, had a relapse and we had to cancel.

To boost Pat's spirits, I took her to the dentist, who suggested she had new bridges made. They would cost £4,500, but how could I tell Pat: 'There's no point – you're dying.'? Instead, I insisted she went ahead; it would make her feel better. And when she did have the new bridges fitted, on 27 March, I genuinely believed she did think she was going to get better.

Pat's arm was so bad, the Macmillan nurses, Jackie and Helen, came every week to dress her wounds. For a while she would be comfortable, but not for long. The spells where she was without pain grew shorter. It got to a point that she was in such agony, the doctor prescribed methadone, a heroin substitute. It was my responsibility to administer this and, thank God, it gave her relief. Obviously, the drug meant Pat was spaced out some of the time but I didn't give damn. If she was away with the fairies, she was not suffering.

Pat and I never talked about death, but in one of her comprehending, lucid, moments I did tell her of my fears. 'What am I going to do without you, Pat?' I said.

'Don't be bloody silly,' she scoffed. 'You'll be all right. You'll have a decent bird on your arm in a few months of me going.'

Terrible, isn't it, feeling sorry for yourself when the other person is the one dying?

✳✳✳

In April, when the end was near, I was told Pat was so ill she could live out her final days in The Farleigh Hospice in Chelmsford. I didn't want that. I wanted her in the home she loved, where we'd been so happy. And when the time came, I wanted to be at her side.

Those wonderful Macmillan nurses came in every day to wash and change her. I honestly didn't think I'd be able to help. I'd never cared for anyone sick before; I feared I'd be clumsy, hamfisted. But I quickly realised I could be gentle. I washed and changed her, too, and did my best to feed her. She didn't feel like eating, but I tried to encourage her by offering to cook anything she fancied. As she got weaker, she found it increasingly hard to swallow, so I cooked casseroles and stews and, in the end, tried children's food. I used a dropper to drip liquid into her poor dry mouth. I was still giving her liquid methadone to combat the pain but, as she became weaker, she couldn't get it down, so the nurses injected the drug in alternate legs every four hours.

Pat's brain was still working, though. She'd never forgiven Jackie for what she'd done to me, and, on 21 April, wrote: *'William's fat loudmouthed wife's birthday again – who cares – dross.'*

That was the last entry in her diary.

Within a couple of weeks, Pat was so weak she could not get out of bed to go to the loo, so the nurses fitted a catheter. One of the few things I could do for her was change the bloody thing. It was a rotten job, but I was happy to do it – even though it made me gag. My poor, poor Pat.

Then the injections stopped being enough to control the pain, so the nurses inserted an automatic timed pump in her arm. Without that drug, Pat would have been screaming her head off, but the downside was that she was compus mentis for only an hour a day, top whack.

I talked to Pat all the time, not caring if she was hearing me, or not. I said everything I wanted to say, leaving her in no doubt how much she meant to me and always had; how happy she'd made me, and how wonderful it felt to be so loved.

When she cried out in pain, I'd think about those euthanasia places in Switzerland. I never mentioned it, but I'm sure that if I'd said: 'Let's go there and have a few drinks and a joint and call it a day,' I'm sure she would have said: 'Let's go.'

Pat had never been a big girl; nine stone was the heaviest she'd been and that was plump for her. But she'd become so thin she was barely recognisable: just a motionless lump of flesh, kept alive only by injections every minute or so from the automated methadone pump. I became very low; I'd lost the person I knew. She had the odd lucid moment when she would wake and ask after her mother, or if any of her friends had rung, but then the drugs would send her to sleep again. I couldn't bear seeing her in pain. And, to be honest, it was a relief, seeing her drift off.

I'd have loved to have gone out for a break, of course I would. But I was a long way from my mates and, anyway, I knew Pat would not want anybody else with her. Some nights, I'd talk quietly on the phone to friends – most regularly, Leslie Squibb's wife, also named Pat – but the rest of the time I spent alone, getting drunk and feeling sorry for her and myself, wondering, over and over again, why the fuck this had happened to us when we'd found each other and were so happy.

Night after night, once I was sure she'd dropped off, I'd walk softly into the lounge and open a bottle of wine. Then I'd put some music on – Queen, Bob Dylan or the Eagles, usually – and sit back, looking at mum and dad on the wall, and wait for the booze to kick in and numb my brain, and all the hurt I felt. How beautiful mum was at twenty-one. How handsome dad, at nineteen. How lucky they'd been to live so long. I hoped their lives had been as happy as mine.

Those long, lonely nights, drinking myself into oblivion, gave me plenty of time to think back on my own life. And, with all that had happened to me over six decades, I had plenty to think about. About my marriages. About George. My triumphs in the ring. My carefree excesses out of it.

For a fish market porter, who never wanted to fight, I'd done okay, hadn't I?

Beautiful girls. Fast cars. Smart pad in town. Money to burn. And my name emblazoned on a building on Piccadilly Circus. One lucky punch on a misty November night had sent it all my way. Gave me all the things I craved as a good-looking, fit young man in the prime of his life. And I enjoyed it all, make no mistake. I had what most young men dream about. And I lived the dream. To the full. And then some.

That makes me sound very shallow, doesn't it? Well, I probably was – then. My head was turned, wasn't it? Hardly surprising. One minute, I'm Mister Nobody, loading fish on to a barrow. The next I'm on TV, the best amateur heavyweight in Britain, knocking over the top man in the States. And then, at twenty-three, I'm as rich and famous as the Prime Minister. Is it any wonder I went a bit mad? I was your ordinary working-class bloke from the East End, for heaven's sake. Until I smacked Mr Perry into oblivion, fame and adulation and wealth were for pop stars, not a drayman's son from Ilford.

But, you know, looking back there *were* times when I did question what I was doing with my life. Not many, I admit. But sometimes, when the party merry-go-round stopped spinning for us all to get our breath back, I'd sit in that Ebury Street flat, on my own, and feel quite depressed that, despite the fun I was having, I was living a shallow existence. That, at the end of the day, my life didn't add up to much. That what I wanted, what would make me really happy and contented, was a stable and loving relationship with someone I truly cared about. And who cared about me. Not just the stardust that came with my celebrity image.

Now, of course, I realised that I should have seen Pat for who and what she was. Someone to be trusted and relied on. Someone who saw me for who *I* was, and who loved me dearly. Someone I was suited to and should have married much earlier, probably when she became pregnant. But my fame was too intoxicating and I didn't see what was in front of me, and those melancholy moments of self-examination and yearning quickly passed and it was on to the next laugh, the next transient young lady, with barely a backward glance.

The deep-seated desire for a strong, long-lasting relationship like my dad and brothers enjoyed with their wives, never left me, though – and undoubtedly led me into marrying Susan Coleopy. What a farce that was! What a shambles! And what a mug I was for not pulling George to one side, before it was too late, and saying: 'Hold up, mate. This isn't right. Not for me. Or for Susan. We're not suited.'

Naturally, in the light of how miserable the marriage was, I deeply regret not standing up for myself over that publicity circus in Clerkenwell. But, you've got to remember that, since he'd come to watch me fight for the first time, George had controlled my life, called all the important shots. He told me how and when to train. He told me who and when I was fighting. He told me when I could go on holiday.

Is it any wonder that he should tell me who I should marry? Or, more to the point, who I should not?

I didn't have the courage to back out of the wedding. And I didn't have the courage to end the marriage when it went wrong. I have to thank Susan for that. She was brave and I wasn't. I couldn't bear the thought of tearing the family apart. I wanted us to stay together for the sake of the children. But that would have been a mistake. And Susan knew it. In retrospect, I think she did me a favour, but, at the time, I was devastated. For, despite my misgivings walking down the aisle, I did feel I was going to be married forever, and, outside the boxing ring, being divorced was my first taste of failure. Since the divorce, I've regretted not staying closer to Daniel and Clare, but Susan married twice after me and, though I've always stayed in touch, you can't stay a close family when you're so far apart and living different lives, can you? For some reason I've never fathomed, Susan found it easier to tell Clare that I wanted the divorce, not her, and, for years, Clare blamed me for their unhappiness. Obviously, I miss the closeness I once had with her and Daniel, but they're grown up now. Clare is a career woman, working in the PR department of a motor racing company, living in London, and Daniel lives in Spain with a family of his own.

Amid the enormous suffering and heartache of my divorce from Jackie, I was determined not to lose touch with Kelly and Tom: I was desperate to show that, despite all the acrimony that was tearing the family apart, I was always going to be there for them. But it was far from easy, not living under the same roof. Happily, we've stayed in touch and I always know what's going on in their lives. More important, we're friends.

I'm pleased to say that I'm still in touch with Warren's mother, Chrissie, too, and feel that she has done a brilliant job bringing him up. Having graduated from university, the young man has travelled the world and we see each other often. I'm proud to be his dad.

Those wild bachelor years after my divorce from Susan might make you think I had a cavalier attitude to women; was hell-bent on resuming my mission to bed as many beauties as possible, with a fond, but fast, farewell after having my wicked way with them. But I don't think I was an arrogant user. Most of my lovers were far from what one might term a 'quickie'. More often than not, I wined and dined them, took them to clubs and functions and nearly always formed a liking, if not a love, that has lasted down the years. Many are still good friends today and we laugh about the old times as only good friends can.

As I sat in the lounge that Pat had made so attractive, I'd think back to those loving reunions we shared in that Ebury Street hotel. Pat was married then, but she didn't seem that happy. What would have happened, I wondered, if I'd asked her to leave her husband and make up for lost time with me. Who knows, she might have said yes, got a divorce, and become my second wife. It was a warm, comforting thought, fuelled, no doubt, by my self-pity and a second bottle of wine. Yeah, if we'd got together, I'd have been with her at that wedding reception in Holborn, not at a loose end and in a hurry to have some fun in the West End. I wouldn't have rushed out that door, then rushed back in with that slim, dark-haired stranger who would destroy my life. As it was, Pat and I just enjoyed each other for the moment in that hotel, neither of us giving a thought to a possible future together. And fate led me to Jackie instead.

Thinking back to the nightmare that woman made me endure, I couldn't believe my luck at finding Pat again, at a desperate time when I needed her most. She was a quiet port in a violent storm, where I could lick my wounds and try to get back my pride and self-esteem that Jackie had stolen, along with my money.

Pat hated her with a vengeance, not only for what her lies and deceit had done to me during the marriage, but also for the pain and anguish she caused both of us after I left. The pressure she put us under was crippling, suffocating, and seemingly never-ending, but, thankfully, Pat and I survived it, and, if anything, it made us stronger and even more loving to each other. Sometimes, when I still had nagging doubts that, maybe, I could have done more to save the marriage, Pat, unselfishly, helped me with much soul-searching, encouraging me to see friends Jackie had hurt, to ask if there was anything else I could have done. That helped me reach the conclusion that there wasn't. That it was time to wipe my mouth, put it all behind me, and move on. Thanks to my darling Pat, I was able to do that.

And now she was in that other room, breathing her last breaths, unrecognisable from the uncompromising firebrand who'd given me such a tough, but fun, time. At those lonely moments, quite drunk and maudlin, I'd have given anything for her to get up and walk into the lounge and snarl and snap at me and call me an arsehole for drinking so much. I missed her terribly – missed the happy evenings, watching old movies, her smoking a joint, me having a glass of wine. Yes, Pat could be difficult with people she didn't like, but those she cared for could not have had a better daughter, sister, aunt or friend. Or wife. It's a cliche, I know, but she had a heart of gold. Pure gold.

Well, that heart was going to stop beating soon, there was no oddsing that. Two months. Maybe just two weeks. After that, what? There would be nothing for Pat: she'd be gone. But what about me? What was I going to do without her? Where would I live?

I'd look around at all Pat's little knick-knacks, admiring the artistry she'd poured into making our little haven complete, and I'd cry at the unfairness of it all. The beautiful home we'd created for ourselves seemed to mock me now and I knew I wouldn't be able to live there without her. I wouldn't leave Burnham, though. I'd buy a small flat on the quayside that Pat and I loved so much, then, in the winter I'd bugger off to Tenerife, to a little flat hidden away in the backstreets. Precisely where I went wouldn't actually matter much, because Pat had been the centre of my life, my touchstone, and I knew I'd find it hard to be truly happy anywhere without her. I'd be overcome with guilt for being selfish, and making plans for myself while Pat was suffering in the next room. But she was no longer a person I recognised, and already I'd started to separate myself from her and grieve. Yes, she was dying. But, in a way, so was I. The life we'd shared would die with her and I'd have to start again.

Often, on those melancholy nights, I'd think of George, too. Despite all that had gone on, I missed him terribly. My other brother, John, a lovely man, would ring, and I appreciated his concern, but George and I had gone through so much together and it was him I needed to hear from. He was long gone, but I still pined for the closeness I'd grown up with. Grief and drink can make one very forgiving and, on those lonely nights, I certainly made allowances for the way George had treated me. I didn't think he set out to hurt me. Let's face it, the business world is tough and when George started making a success, I'm sure he got carried away and forgot where to draw the line between work and his friends and family. He is his own worst enemy: so many people loved and respected him – none more than me – but, somewhere along the line, he found this less important than making money. I still love him, of course I do – he's my brother. And I regret, more than words can say, that we lost the closeness and respect we once had for each other. I feel he has missed out on so much. We have missed out on so much. But, then, to each his own, as some clever bloke once said. My fun-loving outlook on life made me happy and George's uncompromising approach to business made *him* happy. It's just a bloody shame we couldn't have met somewhere in the middle!

The idea that George and I could ever be as close as we once were was wishful thinking, fuelled by too much wine. What I was dealing with now was reality – and that reality was my dear soulmate dying in the next room. There were times when I'd get so drunk, so depressed, that I'd talk out loud to the facing wall, pouring out all my feelings of hurt and injustice to the images of mum and dad. 'It's not fair, it's not fucking fair,' I'd tell them. And it wasn't bloody fair. First there was Susan, who found it hard to like the real me. Then all those horrible years with Jackie. And now I was being cheated out of happiness with the only woman I ever loved.

And then the sound of my own voice would hit me and I'd say, 'Talking to photos of your dead parents, Walke . . . you're fucking losing it.' And I knew then that I'd drunk enough and had better call it a day.

When Pat had begun to hurt so much that even the slightest touch was agony for her, I offered to sleep in another room, but she'd have none of it. 'No, no, darling – I want you next to me,' she'd say. So now, on nights like these, when the booze had helped ease my heartache, I'd make my way as steadily and as quietly as I could, into our room and ease myself into bed, beside her, slowly, carefully, so that I didn't touch her delicate, tender skin and set off the pain.

And then I'd lay there, in a stupor, listening to her troubled breathing, hoping, wishing, praying that, in the morning, it would have stopped and brought her suffering to an end.

✳✳✳

By now, the Macmillan team were with us all the time. Apart from Dr Latif, they were our only company. And they were amazing: so kind, so understanding, so professsional.

One afternoon in June, I had to take some cash to Dagenham, to pay a builder I owed for some work on the bungalow. I went into the bedroom and told Pat I would be no more than a couple of hours. Ten minutes after leaving, my mobile phone rang. It was one of the Macmillan nurses. 'Pat's gone,' she said.

When I got home, Dr Latif was there. He had waited to give me the death certificate. I was stunned when he embraced me, but understood why, when he told me that, the previous year, his wife had died from breast cancer. He was one person who definitely knew how I felt.

Having grieved for Pat for so long, the funeral was just closure to me. She wasn't religious, so I organised a humanist service. I didn't think it appropriate to hold it in London, so I arranged for her to be cremated in Southend, about twenty miles from Burnham. Afterwards, a friend, who owns a restaurant, laid on the most wonderful buffet, and around fifty of our friends and family sat around, talking fondly about the woman we all loved. Afterwards, I took a dozen close friends back to Burnham and we drank and talked some more. It was a sad day, of course; funerals always are, but I did not cry. I felt I had shed all my tears during her last months.

The tragic death of my soulmate was a real punch on the nose, but I like to think Pat would have approved of the send-off we gave her. It's odd to say, but it was the best funeral I'd ever been to.

Without doubt, losing Pat was the most devastating, heartbreaking experience of my life, but it taught me a lot about myself. I'd always had physical strength, but now I knew that, emotionally, I had stamina and was able to put someone else first, to focus on *their* needs. I knew now that when it comes to the crunch, all the money in the world doesn't matter. All that counts is caring for the person you love.

24

Before she died, Pat told me: 'When I go, get on with your life.' It was easier said than done. Everywhere I looked, everything I thought and did, seemed to involve her and the memorable times we'd shared, and I just moped around feeling sorry for myself. Why, after more than twenty years with two women who hadn't made me happy, had I been robbed of those twilight years with the one woman who clearly had? Pat's death didn't make me lose the will to live, but it certainly made me wonder what the hell I was going to do with myself with whatever time I had left. At sixty-four, I was reasonably fit and, in my mind at least, still a young man. But I was a guy who'd always thrived on women's company and I knew myself well enough to know I'd never be happy without a woman in my life. The problem was, now that Pat had gone, would I ever find another woman like her. More to the point, would I ever emerge from the suffocating grief I felt to even try.

And then, late in July, three of my mates – Leslie Squibb, Johnny Simons and Tony Gibbs – decided enough was enough and persuaded me to join them for a few days in Marbella, on Spain's Costa del Sol. The trip worked wonders for me and I'll always be grateful to them. There were no birds around and I honestly don't think I'd have noticed if there were. But there was booze. Lots of it. And the four of us drank ourselves silly into the early hours every night for a week. It was the blow-out I needed and I returned home, still missing my soulmate, of course, but feeling better now that I'd been dragged out of my self-pity to rejoin the land of the living.

The following week, another pal, Fred Lavanni, rang, saying he was going to Jersey to see his accountant and he was taking me with him, he said, to make a long weekend of it. I made some excuse, but Fred was insistent, so we went. Fred did whatever business he had to do and we had a few drinks in the Yacht Club, in St. Aubin, before going on to lunch at the Harbour View, a seafront restaurant owned by Jean Keadell, who I'd first met when I lived in Jersey.

Jean made us very welcome and, over the next couple of hours, served us a never-ending assortment of shellfish to the accompaniment of a jazz band, organised by her partner, Peter Aldridge. Around 4 p.m. Jean joined us and asked if I remembered a woman named Susan Stevens.

'Yes,' I said. 'A tasty-looking bird.'

'Yes,' Jean said. 'Do you remember her husband, Jack?'

'Of course, I do,' I said. 'He used to come to my fights. He got me over here.'

'She's getting a divorce.'

'You're joking,' I said, genuinely shocked, because they'd been together more than thirty years. 'Mind you, it's about time she dumped him. He was always a horrible bastard.'

I was pissed, but I meant it: in all the years I'd known them, I'd never understood why Susan stayed with the man. Jean made some excuse and left the table. Ten minutes or so later she came back, holding a phone. 'Someone wants to speak to you,' she said.

'Who is it?' I asked.

Jean didn't reply, just handed me the phone.

'Hello,' I said. 'Who's that?'

'Susan,' said this quiet, cultured voice.

'Hello,' I said, trying to bring into focus a face I hadn't seen for eight years, when I'd bumped into her and Jack at Goodwood races. 'How are you?'

'Fine,' she said. 'What a surprise to hear from you. The last time we met was at the races. I tried to phone you on Jack's birthday to invite you and Pat to the party but it was the wrong number!'

She was right there. Jack had asked me for my number, but I didn't want him back in my life so I'd given him the first numbers that came into my head. Susan told me she was now living in Vauxhall, in South London and, out of politeness, said I was welcome to pop in for a drink if ever I was in the area.

'That would be lovely,' I said, and took her phone number. Then I poured another glass of wine and promptly forgot all about it. We finally rolled out of the restaurant at 3 a.m. and I was not a pretty sight when Fred and I, and another mate, Brian Bridges, boarded the flight home six hours later. We were on the train from Gatwick to Victoria when Brian noticed we were passing through Battersea.

'That bird you were going on about last night,' he said. 'Where's she live?'

'Near Battersea power station,' I said.

'There's the bloody power station,' he said. 'Why don't you give her a ring?'

'Leave off,' I said. 'Looking like this?' I was in chinos, creased blue shirt and old khaki jacket, unshaven, red-rimmed round the eyes, and looked like something the dog left out.

Brian kept on and on. And I kept telling him, no. Finally he said: 'Give me the phone.' There must have been something in me that wanted to see Susan because I handed him the phone and watched him dial her number. He spoke for a few seconds, then handed me the phone to speak to Susan. I told her we were coming into Victoria and, true to her word, she invited me to pop in for a drink. Ten minutes later, I was in a taxi on my way to her flat, carrying a bottle of champagne. What I wasn't to know was that Susan was excited at the thought of seeing me again after all those years. When she opened the door of her penthouse, I was impressed: she was still slim, with long dark hair, wicked green eyes, and the slightly posh accent I'd always found attractive.

After the usual pleasantries, Susan poured us each a gin and tonic and we went on to the roof terrace, overlooking the Thames, to sit in the warm afternoon sunshine. Susan admitted she never drank much but, over the next hour, she was so relaxed she downed three glasses and was clearly enjoying flirting with me. In the past, I'd never given a thought to getting hold of Susan, but the good-humoured banter, fuelled by the gin and sun, changed all that and, when she went inside to get some champagne glasses, I followed her and decided to try my luck. I said: 'Where shall we go – on the sofa or in the bedroom?'

She was clearly surprised, but said: 'In the bedroom.'

And that's where we ended up. I mean, we weren't kids: we knew what was going to happen.

Afterwards, as we lay chatting, I asked why she had been such a willing bedmate. 'I never saw you like that,' I said.

'Years ago, I'd never have dreamed of doing it,' she said. 'I was a married woman. You weren't an unattractive man but I didn't fancy you. You had a great body, but I thought you were a bit of a tart.'

'A bit of a tart!' I said, shocked. 'What do you mean?'

'That you'd have sex with anything that moved.'

'That's not true,' I laughed. 'It would have to be female! So, what made you change your mind?'

'I hadn't been touched for so long, I just felt like it. And you weren't a stranger. I thought, oh, well – at least I know him – I'm going to go for it.'

It was this basic, earthy desire that prompted a surprising response from Susan when I suggested seeing her again.

'Don't even think about moonlight and roses, love and romance,' she said. 'I don't want another relationship. But I'm happy to have an affair.'

I couldn't believe my ears. A beautiful woman, wanting me only for my body, not my mind? For my prowess between the sheets, not my debonair charm or sophistication? Ha ha! It seemed too good to be true, but Susan was serious. And when it sunk in, I thought: Yippee, yabadabadoo! Lovely, sexy bird, beautiful apartment: I'll shoot round once or twice a week and have some fun, no strings attached. It suited me down to the ground, because I wasn't ready to throw myself into another relationship, either.

I caught the last train to Burnham and immediately I got indoors, I phoned Susan to say how wonderful it had been, how much I was looking forward to seeing her again. My call was unexpected and went down well, and I dropped off to sleep, excited at what lay ahead. The next morning, I phoned again, inviting Susan to join me for dinner at the Sunborne Yacht Hotel, in Docklands, that evening. She said yes but, unknown to me, panicked the moment she put the phone down. Having never been with anyone but Jack in thirty-three years of marriage, she wondered if she'd have the nerve to go through with it. In the end, an aunt convinced her to go but, in the taxi to Docklands, Susan panicked again. And she was about to tell the driver to turn back when I rang her mobile.

'Where are you?' I asked. 'Not going to cancel on me, are you?'

'I'm nearly there,' Susan said, not the slightest trace of panic in that cultured voice.

I greeted her in the hotel foyer and took her to the upstairs bar. We got on really well and, after a few drinks, it seemed natural that we should go to the room I'd booked to make love. Afterwards, we chatted for a couple of hours, had dinner in the hotel restaurant, then went back to the room. I must say it felt great, lying there, chatting to someone I liked and who obviously liked me; someone who was there for just good sex and some fun. But, shortly before 11 p.m. Susan suddenly announced she was going home.

'You must be mad,' I said. 'What on earth for?'

'I just can't stay, William,' she said. 'I just don't feel right. I've enjoyed your company, but I don't want to get into a relationship. I said it would only be an affair, nothing serious, remember.'

I didn't understand; as far as I was concerned, that's what it was. And why should an affair not allow us to be together for the night, then carry on where we'd left off? But Susan was adamant she had to go, stressing that she was worried that Jack would phone the flat and do his nut if she wasn't there.

'But you're divorcing the guy,' I said.

'Yes, but you know what he's like,' she said. 'He can cause me a lot of trouble.'

I couldn't see any point in her staying if she was that worried so I took her downstairs. When I heard myself tell the girl on Reception, 'This lady needs a taxi,' and saw her disparaging look, it was obvious she thought Susan was a hooker. I found it very funny but, being the gentleman I am, I didn't mention it to Susan for fear of embarrassing her and spoiling what had been a wonderful experience. She, bless her, didn't have a clue!

✳✳✳

After that, I phoned Susan every night and found her fun to talk to: she was quick-witted, loved a good banter and seemed to have an opinion on most things. She admitted she hated men, saying that, in her experience, 'whenever you were on the floor they were always around to stick their heel in your neck.' But she would make an exception for me, she said – until I proved her right!

The following week, Susan said it was her turn to choose the venue and booked us a weekend at Cliveden, a stately home in Berkshire. It was a house that for over 300 years had been dedicated to the pursuit of pleasure, power and politics, she said – 'the pleasure bit might suit you!' After a couple of drinks in the downstairs bar, we were escorted to our suite by our personal, very solicitous, butler, who even offered to unpack our bags. We graciously declined, preferring to leave that until after we'd christened the bed! When we did get around to unpacking, I was shocked to discover that, in my excitement of seeing Susan again, I hadn't brought any shirts, so we had to drive into Windsor to buy some. The gardens at Cliveden are spectacular, but neither Susan, nor I, saw much of them: apart from the brief shopping trip, we ate in the hotel, made love and slept in our sumptuous suite, and didn't venture outside the hotel the whole weekend. Wonderful!

We continued to enjoy what was supposed to be a no-strings-attached affair, but Susan and I clearly liked each other outside the bedroom, and it seemed a natural progression for me to invite her to Burnham for a night. And what a night it was! After a lovely meal and lots of wine, I was woken, around 4 a.m., by the sound of glass shattering in the bathroom. I dashed in to find Susan had fainted; she was laying there amid the remains of a bottle of Gaviscon. Apparently, she'd felt unwell and had passed out while taking the medicine. I brought her round, carried her back to bed, then comforted her with a cup of tea and biscuits.

It wasn't the first time a lady companion had had too much to drink, and I thought nothing of it, but Susan was embarrassed and made an excuse to leave soon after she woke. I missed her; I loved her company and was looking forward to spending the day together. I must admit that I was struggling with guilt that Pat had been gone only a few months and here I was falling for someone else. Me! The guy who could love 'em and leave 'em; who didn't want commitment. I was worried I was getting too involved, but kept my feelings to myself; Susan had laid down the ground rules, so I felt it was up to her to change them.

Throughout the autumn, we continued to meet, both of us enjoying the running joke that our no-strings-attached affair was still simply that, with no romance on the agenda. But then, shortly before Christmas, we went to lunch with Tommy and Ann, at Topo Gigio's, in Soho, and it was clear that for Susan things had changed. The four of us were chatting generally when I mentioned I'd been out to dinner with a lady friend a few nights earlier. The look on Susan's face was a picture: I'd never seen her so shocked – or angry.

'What's wrong?' I asked.

'Are you seeing other women, apart from me?'

'Of course, I am,' I said. 'Why not?'

'But you're going out with me.'

'Yeah, but I go out with other girls, too,' I said.

'Do you have sex with them?' Susan said, genuinely shocked. And clearly hurt.

'Yes,' I said.

'Do you think I'm seeing other men, apart from you?'

'I assume you are,' I said.

Her expression left me in doubt she wasn't. She was horrified I'd think her a tart.

'It's not right that you're seeing other women when you're seeing me, William,' she said.

'Of course, it is,' I said. 'That's the arrangement you wanted. No strings attached remember. You said you didn't want a relationship, so I live my other life away from you. What do you think I'm going to do when you're too busy to see me? Sit around, twiddling my thumbs?'

Susan didn't like it. She didn't like it at all.

'We've got to change the rules, William,' she said, tersely. 'I naively thought you'd be having an affair just with me!'

She told me she wanted me to be monogamous and I said I'd try, if I could learn how to say it! In truth, I was delighted, because I now knew I'd fallen in love with her and wanted commitment. Susan was worldly and knowledgeable in business, but she was naive, too, and hadn't been round the block – and I found that attractive. So I knocked the other ladies on the head and started seeing only her. I felt we were ideally suited, and when I was invited to various boxing dinners, or charity functions, it was natural for me to take Susan, too.

Ironically, the last place I'd take her is to a professional boxing match. Gone are the days when people got all dressed up and treated a Big Fight night as a special occasion, respecting not only the boxers, but everyone else around them. Today, that respect has gone out the window and there's often more violence outside the ring than in it. God help the poor fighter who loses: he's likely to have abuse – and even solid objects – thrown at him by so-called fans, who, more than likely, have plonked themselves in the best seats that someone else has paid for! I abhor this unruly, arrogant behaviour as much as I hate the new rules and regulations that, in my view, restrict a boxer's true personality and fighting spirit.

✳ ✳ ✳

Life has a strange way of punching you on the nose when you're at your happiest and, for a while, I was worried that the love I felt for Susan was an illusion, too good to be true, and only happening because I was vulnerable and missing Pat so much. I felt that everything I'd had with Pat I now had with Susan – but would it last? Susan felt the same insecurity and we continued to banter with each other, pushing the parameters of our relationship, looking for flaws. But we could find none. We not only loved each other, but liked each other, too. And, very importantly, we laughed easily together.

Although I still had the house in Burnham, I moved in with Susan. We had lots of commitments – she with the school she ran with her lovely daughter, Jane, me with my role as steward on the British Boxing Board of Control and various after-dinner speaking engagements, as well as renovating a couple of flats in Wandsworth which I'd bought as an investment. But when we had the time we'd spend the weekend in Burnham, strolling along the quayside, holding hands like teenagers and planning our future together over a lunch in one of the pubs. At night, I'd lie in bed, thinking: 'Walker, you're a lucky sod.'

In February, convinced the love I felt was *not* an illusion, I took Susan to Paris to celebrate her birthday, booked a table at a sumptuous restaurant – and proposed. To my delight, Susan said yes, but, deep down, didn't think I was serious. Despite everything that had gone on over the past few months, she remembered the Billy Walker image and my marriage to Susan, and felt she couldn't trust me a hundred per cent. She asked me not to tell anyone until the various financial problems surrounding her divorce were sorted out. Actually, she did tell one person – Jane, who was thrilled to bits. 'Madre, this is your time,' she said. 'You've spent a lifetime working. Now you look more relaxed and happy than I've seen you for years. Grab this time for you.'

Four months later, we went on holiday to the beautiful Greek island of Skiathos. While mooching around one of the tiny, winding streets, we saw a jeweller's, and I told Susan I wanted to buy her a ring to show the world we were committed to each other. She didn't want an engagement ring, so we chose a gorgeous white gold wedding ring, chased around with small diamonds, and, that evening, over a romantic dinner, under a starlit sky, I got down on one knee and proposed properly. Again, Susan said yes. And, after toasting our future happiness with champagne, we spent the next hour on our mobiles, delighted to share the news with various friends in Jersey and Spain. After speaking with Julie, one of her cousins, Susan forgot to switch her phone off and, unknown to us, Julie was party to all our romantic soppiness, telling each other how we were so in love and looking forward to growing old together.

The following May, we went back to Skiathos and, although we weren't yet married, I wanted to wear a wedding ring. So, we went back to our little shop in the tiny, winding street and bought one identical to Susan's. Now, that *is* romantic, isn't it?

✱✱✱

In June, Kelly called to say that she would love me to come to her graduation from Manchester University. In spite of the fact that it was going to be a family occasion, just me, Jackie, Tom and Kelly, I decided to go. Susan is very family orientated and was all for me attending.

I was very proud of Kelly's achievements and it wasn't fair to mar her big day just because I had a problem with her mother. I was relieved to find that I felt absolutely nothing when meeting Jackie again. I had buried that part of my life, let go, and moved on, grateful that she was nothing to do with me any more. In fact, we all had a wonderful day: I took them all to lunch and we attended as proud parents, clapping loudly as Kelly went up to receive her degree in media studies.

Over the next year, the romance blossomed and Susan and I fell even more deeply in love. We knew we'd get married one day, but neither of us got around to doing anything about it. Then, one morning at the end of July, Jane phoned, asking if we were free on Friday, 23 September? Susan checked our diary and confirmed we were – and asked why. 'It's a surprise,' said Jane. Twenty minutes or so later she called back, saying she had booked us in to be married at Chelsea Register Office. Everything was arranged, she said: the cake, the car, all we had to do was book a venue for the reception, invite the guests, and turn up. Susan and I didn't know whether we were thrilled or scared to bits. We were probably both!

We couldn't do better than Topo Gigio's for the reception and, two weeks before the big day, I went there with Susan to work out the table plan for fifty-four guests – the most the restaurant could fit into the downstairs room we wanted. After we'd finished, I ordered a bottle of champagne, and when the waiter brought it to the table, I stood up and took a little black box from one of my pockets. 'I had this made for you,' I told Susan, and handed her a diamond ring I'd designed with a jeweller pal. So, after wearing a wedding ring for so long, Susan now had an engagement ring, and was getting married in two weeks. A bit arse-upwards, but then I've never been a conformist!

On the morning of the twenty-third, I was out of the flat by 9.30 a.m., leaving enough time to get to a pub near the Register Office to drink some pre-wedding champagne with my pals, while Jane helped her mother get ready. I was so pleased that my elder brother, John, and his wife, Irene, were there, but George was conspicuous by his absence. I'd invited him and Jean, but George was working. Seventy-six years old and too busy to attend his brother's wedding! Nothing changes. You really have to hand it to him for stamina; I hope he finds enough time to spend all the dough.

Shortly before 11 a.m., my fifty-four guests and I filed into the reception room, where the marriage took place, and I stood at the front of the seated area, holding court as our friends took their places. Fifteen minutes or so later, there was no sign of Susan and someone called out: 'Susan has lost it and gone home.' No,' I joked, 'she wouldn't be that crazy as to leave someone as wonderful as me.'

The longer Susan took to arrive, the more everyone got fidgety, but I wasn't worried at all: all I could think, looking around the sea of faces, was how lucky I was to have made so many wonderful friends throughout my life. And how lucky I was to be so unbelievably happy with Susan when, little more than two years before, I'd been so distraught.

And then, thankfully, someone said: 'Please be upstanding for the bride,' and there was Susan, embarrassed that her formal interview with the registrar had taken so long, practically running up the middle aisle towards me and the Registrar. Not that I saw her; I was standing at the front with my back to her and she had to tap me on the arm. I turned and looked at her, stunningly beautiful in a cream lace dress and

I was unable to stop the tears filling my eyes. How lucky I am, I thought. How much I love her.

There are moments in life when, if you're lucky, you feel you could not possibly be happier. For me, the wedding reception was one of those moments. So much of my life was there, in that pretty Italian restaurant: my daughter, Kelly, and son, Tom; Susan's daughter, Jane, with her husband Michael, and son, Scott with his wife, Susanne; and many friends, some of whom had been with me when I was on top and were still there when I hit hard times. Looking around at them, as I gave my speech, I felt honoured and humbled.

Susan made a speech, too. She made everyone laugh when she joked that she'd planned to invite all my old girlfriends, but the nursing homes only let them out for two hours in the afternoon – and the restaurant's steep stairs weren't conducive to zimmer frames anyway! Then she became very serious and said something so wonderful I'll never forget it. Looking at me, she said: 'William, I want only one promise from you – a promise that you'll never change. I love you with all of my heart, just as you are.'

How absolutely wonderful, to be loved just for being oneself. The luck is that we have met and fallen in love at an age when we have been through life and all it offered. Our only regret is that we don't have another lifetime to enjoy each other.

Susan always jokes that she was waiting for me to mature but gave up when she realised I'd be eighteen till I die! She's right. The hard knocks I've taken outside the ring have made me grow up but, basically, I still have the sunny, fun-loving outlook I had as a kid. Why spend one moment being stressed or unhappy when you can have fun?

Looking back, maybe I could have done better, gone further, in my career if I'd lived a cleaner life. But I have no regrets – absolutely none. Who knows if the booze did me any harm, stopped me from winning a title? What I do know is that it certainly helped me enjoy life. Without a good drink with good mates, I'd have had a boring time, wouldn't I? As it was, I had fun. I earned money, I lost money; I found love, lost it, then found it again. I lived.

And I became a household name in the process.

I believe that it doesn't matter what you have in life, or where you are – it's who you're with that's important. Susan is my life, my lover and best buddy. She's also my soulmate – and how many are lucky enough to have that twice in a lifetime?

I look back on my life, with all its ups and downs, and think: what a wonderful, exciting time I've had. And I'm not dead yet!

Happy days!

FIGHT RECORD

Amateur Record

1958

16 January	Terry Drudge	W	KO	1	West Ham
17 April	Mick Gannon	L	Pts	3	Bishopsgate
6 November	George Newell	W	RSC	1	West Ham
3 December	Sergio Parkins	W	Pts	3	Kentish Town

1959

15 January	Len Hobbs	L	Pts	3	West Ham
26 February	Albert Roussel		RSC	1	West Ham
20 March	John Bailey	W	RSC	1	Bethnal Green
9 April	Billy Wells	W	RSC	2	Albert Hall
9 April	Dave Thomas	L	Pts	3	Albert Hall
23 October	Ken Potter	W	Pts	3	Morden, Surrey
12 November	Ernie Ball	W	KO	1	West Ham
26 November	Len Hobbs	L	Pts	3	Marylebone
7 December	Hober Helfer	W	KO	1	Bethnal Green
11 December	Ken Potter	W	Pts	3	Bermondsey

1960

14 January	Dave Thomas	L	Pts		West Ham
25 February	Len James	L	RSC	2	West Ham
13 April	Ken Potter	W	KO	1	Albert Hall
13 April	Dave Thomas	L	Pts	3	Albert Hall
29 November	Len Hobbs	W	Pts	3	Marylebone
9 December	Robin Jones	W	Pts	3	Poplar

1961

5 January	Tom Menzies	W	RSC	3	Glasgow
19 January	Manfred Markgraf	W	RSC	2	Albert Hall
18 February	John Bodell	W	RSC	1	Coventry
23 February	Len James	W	RSC	2	West Ham
9 March	Brian Daltry	W	RSC	2	Bethnal Green
10 March	Bill Hamilton	W	RSC	1	Bethnal Green

13 April	Len Hobbs	W	Pts	3	Albert Hall
13 April	Bob Wallace	W	RSC	1	Albert Hall
28 April	Peter James	W	KO	3	Wembley
28 April	Len James	W	RSC	1	Wembley
3 June	Adolf Brandenberger	W	KO	1	Belgrade
3 June	Sigmund Guenter	L	Pts	3	Belgrade
19 October	Klemens Malkiewicz	W	RSC	2	Albert Hall
2 November	Cornelius Perry	W	KO	1	Wembley
9 November	John Spenceley	W	KO	1	West Ham
6 December	Len James	W	RSC	3	Dublin
8 December	Jim Monaghan	W	KO	1	Dublin

1962

11 January	Jackie Fitch	W	KO	1	West Ham
1 February	Emil Svaricek	W	KO	1	Albert Hall

Professional Record

1962

27 March	Jose Peyre	W	RSC	5	Wembley
22 May	Mariano Echevarria	Drew		8	Wembley
14 August	Erwin Hack	W	RSC	1	Blackpool
6 September	Robert Moore	W	KO	2	Liverpool
13 November	Phonse La Saga	W	KO	1	Wembley
20 November	Jose Gonzales	L	Disq.	3	Leicester
26 November	Jose Gonzales	W	Pts	8	Manchester

1963

29 January	Peter Bates	W	KO	2	London
26 March	Joe di Grazio	W	KO	3	Wembley
11 June	Mariano Echevarria	W	Pts	8	London
24 June	Kurt Stroer	W	RSC	2	Carmarthen
10 September	John Prescott	W	RSC	10	Wembley
12 November	John Prescott	L	Pts	10	Wembley

1964

28 January	Joe Bygraves	W	Disq.	6	London
10 March	Bill Nielsen	L	RSC	8	London

12 May	Bill Nielsen	W	KO	2	Wembley
27 October	Joe Erskine	W	Pts	10	Wembley

1965

26 January	Charley Powell	W	KO	2	London
20 March	Brian London	L	Pts	10	London
19 August	Eduardo Corletti	Drew		10	San Remo
19 October	Eduardo Corletti	L	RSC	8	London

1966

31 March	Lars Norling	W	RSC	4	London
2 May	Bowie Adams	W	KO	3	Manchester
20 September	Horst Benedens	W	RSC	1	Wembley
25 October	Jose Menno	W	RSC	10	London
6 December	Ray Patterson	W	RSC	8	London

1967

13 February	Giulio Rinaldi	W	Disq.	I	Manchester
21 March	Karl Mildenberger (European Title)	L	RSC	8	Wembley
7 November	Henry Cooper (British and Empire Titles)	L	RSC	6	Wembley

1968

12 November	Thad Spencer	W	RSC	6	Wembley

1969

25 March	Jack Bodell	L	RSC	8	Wembley

Contests:	**31**
Won:	21
Lost	8
Drew	2